REWORLDING AMERICA

REWORLDING AMERICA

Myth, History, and Narrative

JOHN MUTHYALA

Ohio University Press   Athens

Ohio University Press, Athens, Ohio 45701
www.ohio.edu/oupress
© 2006 by Ohio University Press

Printed in the United States of America

Ohio University Press books are printed on acid-free paper ♾™

14 13 12 11 10 09 08 07 06   5 4 3 2 1

Sections of chapters 1 and 4 have appeared previously in different form.

Chapter 1:
"The Globalization of American Studies," *Cultural Critique* 47 (2001): 91–119. Copyright 2001 Regents of the University of Minnesota.

"Twilight of the Gods: Britain, America, and the Inheritance of Empire," *American Quarterly* 57, no. 4 (2005): 1253–61. Copyright 2005 the Johns Hopkins University Press.

Chapter 4:
"Roberta Fernández's *Intaglio:* Border Crossings and Mestiza Feminism in the Borderlands," *Canadian Review of American Studies* 30, no. 1 (2000): 92–110. © *Canadian Review of American Studies/Revue canadienne d'études américaines,* 2000.

"*Almanac of the Dead:* The Dream of the Fifth World in the Borderlands," *LIT: Literature Interpretation Theory* 14, no. 4 (2003): 357–85. Copyright 2003. Reproduced by permission of Taylor & Francis Group, LLC, http://www.taylorandfrancis.com.

Library of Congress Cataloging-in-Publication Data

Muthyala, John, 1966–
   Reworlding America : myth, history, and narrative / John Muthyala.
      p. cm.
   Includes bibliographical references and index.
   ISBN 0-8214-1675-8 (cloth : alk. paper)
   1. America—Literatures—History and criticism. 2. America—Civilization. I. Title.
PN843.M88 2006
809'.897—dc22

2005032424

To Mom and Nana

CONTENTS

PREFACE

In the first decade of the twenty-first century, we witnessed a spectacular attack on the United States on September 11, 2001, and the rapid disintegration, in the face of U.S.-coordinated offensives, of the Taliban regime in Afghanistan and Saddam Hussein's government in Iraq. At a certain level of generality and without collapsing the crucial difference between Al Qaeda as a decentered association of flexibly structured groups and the United States as a nation-state, we can see how these events involved extensive planning and coordination among peoples situated in different countries and among networks of finance and military resources linking various transnational institutions. Those who planned and carried out the attacks on September 11 were students from, immigrants to, and citizens of several different countries;[1] those who executed military operations in response to September 11 had to develop, through negotiation, a coalition of nations and institutions to facilitate the launching of a war on Iraq; and those who played crucial roles in shaping postinvasion plans for stabilizing Iraq included Iraqi exiles living in numerous countries.[2] In many ways what these events dramatized was not the disintegration of the nation-state in an era of globalization but the fundamental paradoxes generated by globalization—the complex interweaving of national concerns with international events; the dense overlapping of locally shaped micropolities with large-scale collective efforts; the concentration of awesome power in individuals who could launch massive strikes against long-established nation-states; and the centrality of intercontinental migration in effecting profound demographic and cultural shifts in territories over which the nation-state struggles to regain control. At the same time, however, in the run-up to the U.S.-Iraq War of 2003, the large-scale demonstrations against the United States across the world underscored how much a single nation's activities have become a matter of concern to so many peoples and communities. It seems America is on everyone's mind these days, and the more the world thinks about America, the more America is compelled to think about the world.

This sense of the United States entanglement with the world has also become acutely manifest in the realm of economics. Just as U.S. foreign policy was a centerpiece of the 2004 U.S. presidential elections, the phenomenon of "outsourcing"[3]—the flight from America to India and China of white-collar, service-oriented jobs requiring specialized skills in information technology—compelled candidates Bush and Kerry to take public positions on protecting "American" jobs. Both of them were frequently bombarded with the question, how can non-Americans take American jobs and what will you do about it? The question raised the specter of "America" and the politics of belonging in the realm of economics—what makes a certain job an American job and how can we make sure that what "belongs" to us stays with us and what belongs to the world stays with the world?[4]

Another dimension of the world's increasing involvement with the United States is the tremendous increase in immigration to America. The 1965 Immigration Act, which signaled a shift in emphasis from a European-oriented immigration policy to an Asia- and Latin America-friendly policy, has, in the new century, resulted in a demographic shift of seismic proportions. According to the 2000 census report, the Latino or Hispanic population, at 35.3 million, was close to surpassing the African American demographic of 36.4 million. By July 2003 the Latino population had increased to 39.9 million, a growth of 13.0 percent, over four times the 3.3 percent growth of the total population,[5] thus making Latinos the largest minority group in the United States. This is, Nicolás Vaca notes, a "Latino tsunami" that is "sweeping across the nation."[6] What will happen to the black-white divide, as both a model for social analysis and a Manichean binary manifest in social and cultural forms and behaviors, that has dominated America ever since its emergence in 1776 is a question whose import we are only beginning to grasp. But the issue is more complicated than one minority group replacing another. When "Hispanic" as a racial category is further subdivided into "White Hispanic" and "Black Hispanic," the categories "Hispanic," "Black," and "White" as signaling different "races" become redundant.[7] As race and ethnicity become imbricated in complex ways, we are compelled to question what is often presented as a sociological fact, that is, Hispanics overtaking African Americans to become the largest minority group in America. With the idea of race as a reliable sign of social identity becoming leaky, how to define and identify an "American" is turning out to be a vexatious exercise. Even as America extends its military and economic reach in the nethermost parts of the world, the world is settling down inside America's cities, countrysides, barrios, and ethnic enclaves, making it difficult to divide the world into first, second, and third. All these worlds are tending to grate against each other from within and without as they become more intertwined, more implicated in one another's politics, and more hybridized in their forms of social and cultural interaction.

Literature and culture are other spheres of activity in which the meaning of America and the problem of American identity are being thoroughly contested and modified. For instance, consider Azar Nafisi's *Reading Lolita in Tehran: A Memoir in Books*. It was written by a woman who grew up in Iran, studied in America, returned to Iran and taught American literature at the University of Tehran, resigned her professorship in the 1990s, came to America, and at the time of publication of the book was affiliated with the Johns Hopkins University. The memoir narrates the experiences of a few Iranian women who meet in Nafisi's house at considerable personal risk to read, talk, and exchange views about American literature. But it is not just about Iranian women reading American literature. It is also about reading a book written by Vladimir Nabokov, a Russian immigrant to America; about Humbert Humbert and his relationship with a girl-child, Lolita, the object of his perverted fascination; and about that book being read and taught by an Iranian woman who had studied in the United States, has returned to Iran, and teaches *Lolita* to her students there. Profound dislocations are at work here: no longer can we rely on a comparative methodology that takes us back to the United States on the assumption that the "original" novel, Nabokov's *Lolita,* should first be perspectivized in its nationally localized contexts *prior* to its insertion into transnational frames. Nafisi and her female students in Tehran are not reading "our" American text. As "global transit extends, triangulates, and transforms its meaning," and as the memoir becomes a "new semantic template, a new form of the legible, each time it crosses a national border,"[8] we become dispossessed readers and dislocated subjects. We are not asked to use the America of *Lolita* as the first and final measure of the text's ability to translate itself into a foreign register; instead, we are forced to come to terms with "*Lolita* in Tehran, how Lolita gave a different color to Tehran and how *Tehran helped redefine Nabokov's novel, turning it into this Lolita, our Lolita.*"[9] Moreover, what emerges as "America" in the memoir hinges not only on U.S.-Iranian relations and east-west economies but also on the conceptualization and periodization of Iranian modernity, the Islamization of national, patriarchal desire, and the othering of women and America.

Complicating matters further, here I am, a reader of *Lolita* in India and *Reading Lolita in Tehran* in America, born and raised in India, now living in Westbrook, Maine, and teaching American culture and literature for a living at the University of Southern Maine. Nabokov moved from Russia to America, Nafisi shuttled between Iran and America, and I have migrated from India to the United States. Although we are linked in this context by a shared interest in American literature, this shared interest was possible *because* of the global migration of literatures, cultures, and peoples. And when texts migrate, especially across national borders and continental divides, as Edward Said perceptively notes, they move from a point of origin, a "set of initial circumstances in which the idea comes to birth"; they traverse a distance, "a passage through the pressure of various contexts"; they negotiate a new a set of conditions that impinges on them; and as they are read and consumed in different locations, they produce new meanings.[10] What links Nabokov,

Nafisi, me, and you, the reader, located as you may be in Bangalore, Lima, Buenos Aires, Albuquerque, Chicago, Toronto, London, Frankfurt, Hong Kong, Damascus, Dubai, Singapore, Kabul, Tokyo, or Sydney, or in the borderlands of Kashmir, the occupied territories in Palestine, or the U.S. Southwest and northern Mexico, is not our reading and responding to something called American literature that is available to us all in its elemental substance, its core ideas, themes, and myths intact and artfully encoded in textual artifacts. Reading *Reading Lolita in Tehran* in America, reading *Lolita* in Tehran, and reading *Lolita* in India produce very different ideas and meanings about what constitutes American literature because the dynamics of migration—of peoples and cultures—linking America to Iran, Iran to India, India to America are simply not the same. Our responses to it are shaped not only by our individual dispositions towards things artistic but by complex processes of transnational cultural translation set in motion by the migration of texts along global circuits.[11] Migration, border crossing, and the dynamics of cultural translation force American literature to become out of joint with itself, alienated from its long-established myths and cherished points of reference: America as a "city on a hill," a New Jerusalem, a tabula rasa upon which Europe would write a brand new chapter of universal history, the War of Independence, the Civil War, the American Renaissance, turn-of-the-century modernism, World Wars I and II, the civil rights era, post-1960s America, and so on. The narrative threads that bind them together are fraying and fragmenting; these events themselves are being made susceptible to all kinds of odd permutations and new hermeneutic exercises. On what basis something can be called American literature and at what point a text becomes American are not easy questions to answer. Is American literature produced only by Americans? Can literature written in Norwegian or Hindi be called American literature?[12] Indeed, who decides who Americans are, what their color is, what their language is? Can non-Americans write American literature? How does the identity of the reader and the writer determine the "Americanness" of a certain text or work of art? These questions lead us to examine what Charles Bright and Michael Geyer refer to as the "grids of action and interaction that both constituted the United States in a global space and entangled it in the history of globalization," which also prompt them to ask, "Where in the world is America?"[13]

Indeed, where is America, who is an American, what is American literature, and what is American culture? Militarily, economically, socially, politically, and culturally, the more America is becoming caught up in the affairs of peoples and communities outside its national borders, the more its internally generated ideas of cultural identity and historical continuity are being contested. Because "the relation between historical time and national entity has begun to fracture,"[14] the boundaries between outside and inside, America and the world, are becoming harder to delimit, police, and sustain. This is why, as Paul Giles astutely notes, it is imperative to delineate and engage with the "*interference between text and context*, thereby disturbing the tautological assumptions that would seek to explain individual events through metanarratives of American consciousness."[15] We are unable to abstract the politics of American identity (who we are and profess to be) from the politics of worldly location (where we are situated in the world and positioned in society). As we find ourselves at the jagged borders of a new millennium, these questions compel our attention with heightened urgency. One way to respond to these questions, as this book argues, involves reworlding America—a form of discursive contestation that places migration, border crossing, transnational exchange, cultural translation, and colonial modernity at the center of debates and discussions regarding American literature and culture. But what does "reworlding" mean?

Reworlding America

> It [America] developed from a complex, living process
> of exploration and interpretation.
>
> —EDMUNDO O'GORMAN

Why reworld America? First we must understand what it means to world
America. For Gayatri Chakravorty Spivak, worlding is an act of material
and ideological conquest, a form of narrating and inscribing colonial
power that has intimate connections to the very production of history.
"[It] is the reinscription of a cartography that must (re) present itself
as impeccable" on an assumedly "uninscribed earth"; this impeccable reinscription becomes "the condition of the worlding of a world" such
that the colonized consciousness can apprehend itself only in and
through colonial systems and knowledges.[1]

Arif Dirlik offers another dimension of worlding, one that reflects
the ascendancy of the United States as a lone superpower after the collapse of the Soviet Union. The more the United States becomes involved
with the world and recognizes the interdependencies of the current
global condition, the less it is able to sustain its view of itself as a country that is fundamentally different from all other countries and nations,
with a unique history and culture. Even as the United States extends its
reach into remote parts of the world, the massive migration of peoples
to the United States and the growing importance of America as a crucial node in a vast interconnected transnational economy are making
American society increasingly transnational. Dirlik writes: "Both issues
have to do with the 'worlding' of the USA—bringing the USA into the

world as well as bringing the world into the USA."[2] We cannot "pretend that the USA may be studied in isolation from the rest of the world, or that either its achievements or failures may be grasped independently of its activities in the world."[3] For Dirlik, worlding involves locating America within the world by questioning its exceptionalist self-idealization and undermining its status as an entity outside world history, as well as attending to the fluid, oft-changing boundaries—cultural, political, territorial—that the United States sets up, manages, and polices as it negotiates its position in a global world. Reworlding America means not so much returning to the kind of worlding that Dirlik suggests as examining the cultural, political, economic, and social processes that bring the world into America and America into the world.

In a related context, Susan Gillman, Kirsten Silva Greusz, and Rob Wilson conceive of worlding as "an active and vigilant critical and poetic process of bringing nearer the *thinging world* and *worlding world* of plurality and multiplicity, at the same time it entails a process of pushing to the horizon of consciousness and dwelling place those things, forces, instruments, signs, and objects that threaten this building-up and renewing of the regenerative life-world and species being."[4] Worlding the world is a kind of double movement: while it draws the world into the realm of the cognizable by establishing zones of possibility, relation, and encounter within which the world can become "worldly," it relegates to the margins of social existence those elements that seem to threaten this process. Thus, it legitimizes particular ideas of America at the same time that it delimits peoples, cultures, and values that threaten hegemonic ideas of America. The nexus of colonial desire and imperial vision in worlding America makes reworlding America imperative. We must interrogate the maneuvers of language, discourse, history, and cultural signs and symbols that claim to produce an authentic and original national history. We must examine the processes by which particular ideas of America are given hegemonic force in order to affirm only certain ideas as essentially "American." And we must disturb and realign the relations among space, time, and memory that create and sustain official, hegemonic culture by managing and policing those communities, cultures, and histories that threaten their power. Three contemporary examples will demonstrate the power of worlding, the entrenchment of colonial mentality in worlding America in contemporary public discourse, and the urgency of our task.

Peter Jennings and Todd Brewster's *In Search of America* (2002) narrates their discovery of the enduring vitality of particular ideas of "America." As they state in their introduction:

> So here was our experiment: *become reacquainted with the principles of the American founding* and the men who first presented them back in the turbulent days of the eighteenth century; *then go out and look about us for evidence in this America* of the country they so long ago established. If we tell you now that we discovered it—indeed, that the foundations laid back then and built upon in the 225 or so years since, *still form the essence of the American identity*—it should not spoil the experience of this book. In fact, that is the message we hope you will see in every page: that the America of Jefferson and Madison, Hamilton and Franklin, Washington and Adams is as alive now as ever before.[5]

Conceived in the propitious time of "founding" a nation and encoded in the Declaration of Independence and the Constitution are the quintessential meanings of America. Once decoded, they will provide the critical framework not so much to trace an already established American tradition as to traditionalize contemporary America. Hence, Jennings and Brewster's task is to travel the United States north, west, east, and south to discover the essence of America and, in the ephemeral moment of recognition, to historicize and thereby authorize a particular vision of America. For all their liberal sensitivity to issues of slavery, race, immigration, and religion, Jennings and Brewster leave intact the nation and its vision of the United States as the unique embodiment of America. By insisting on the American Revolution as a clean break from every other historical event in the Americas and thus declaring

America's exceptionalism as evidence of its national character, these writers, even in the new millennium, will not dislodge the white, old pantheon of Jefferson and Madison, not because they cannot but because the millstones of their ideology grind exceedingly well. To situate their drama within a hemispheric dynamic would make it well nigh impossible to embark on their secular yet deeply evangelical endeavor: to draw inspiration from the sacred texts of Americanism and find, in today's United States, its manifestations still alive. Indeed, the last chapter, "Homeland," while pointing to the historical debates on immigration and traditionally ambiguous attitudes toward immigrants, ends with the naturalization, or rather Americanization, of immigrants to the United States. Given the tautology built into Jennings and Brewster's "experiment," it is not surprising that they succeed so well in worlding America, particularly in divining its origins in a monolingual, nationalist, ethnocentric past.

The British historian Niall Ferguson takes a similar approach, but instead of beginning at the "founding" moment, he urges America to recognize its English ancestry and, in the name of civilization and modernity, put on the mantle of the British empire. In *Empire: The Rise and Demise of the British World Order and the Lessons for Global Power*, Ferguson offers a rationalization of American empire after the fact: "[America] is an empire, in short, that dare not speak its name. It is an empire in denial."[6] In the sequel, *Colossus: The Price of America's Empire*, Ferguson goes further: to continue to function as an empire, America needs a massive labor force to police and protect empire's interests: "If one adds together the illegal immigrants, the jobless and the convicts, there is surely ample raw material for a larger American army. . . . Revising the draft would not necessarily be unpopular, so long as it was appropriately targeted."[7]

Ferguson goes against the grain of recent studies of imperialism in American studies and colonial discourse analysis, which focus on Western colonialism, its forms of socialization, its Orientalist projections, its epistemes, and its discourses. In order to examine the conflictual dynamics that constituted empire, he audaciously seeks to revise the very terms in which empire can be conceptualized historically. He thus translates empire in the sense that José E. Limón suggests—examining it as the site of "multivalent social and moral meanings and outcomes"[8] and not a homogeneous, all-invasive form of colonial power, both in the colonies and in the home country. A fundamental contradiction of empire is that the very institutions and discourses that were purveyed to justify it also sowed the seeds of national liberation movements. Postindependence societies in several former colonies built national governments by using the ideals and models of administrative governance, representative democracy, and constitutionalism, to name a few.

What Ferguson gains in translating empire, however, he loses in invoking it. The ideology that binds Ferguson's treatise on empire to an ethics of empire is erased from scrutiny in order to emerge rearticulated as a new form of American millennial morality, a secular vision of a just rule whose legitimacy can be obtained only by a renarration of empire as the gift of the white man, the white nation, and the white civilization to the unfortunate peoples of the world. We are asked to applaud as the torch of colonial enlightenment is passed from Britain to America. Lest we misunderstand his intentions, Ferguson prefaces *Empire* with a section from Joseph Conrad's *Heart of Darkness* and ends it with Rudyard Kipling's exhortation to "Take up the White Man's burden." *Colossus*, interestingly but not surprisingly, is prefaced by quotations from Jefferson and from Milton's "Samson Agonistes" and ends with references to the "Terminator," Arnold Schwarzenegger, as the archetype of American empire. Clearly, Ferguson desires to translate and affirm American empire by invoking an imperial ethos and cultivating a hypermasculine sensibility.

As Ferguson, in Spivak's terms, inscribes a colonial cartography on "uninscribed earth"[9] by positing Euro-American modernity as a blessing to the world, he effectively wipes out the cultures, histories, and peoples against which empire defines itself and gives substance to its culture, a soul to its citizens, and a burden to its progeny. Because the subject of history—empire—remains at the level of impersonalized, institutional forces, the agent of empire's history—Europe's hypermasculine subject—can remain uncriticized. But those who bear the real burden of empire are further encouraged to become mute witnesses to their dispossession. The perversity of Ferguson's worlding of America is not that it neglects or marginalizes its subjects; it is that the *historicity* of those it colonizes and controls—non-Europeans as agents of history, as human actors endowed with creative potential—can be given or taken away by imperial edict.

Ferguson, by examining empire in relation to international forces, actors, and events, situates Britain and America in a worldly context, in Dirlik's sense of worlding. However, his worlding of the world according to an Anglo-European paradigm reinforces an important nexus between Britain and America. The claim that a continuity of imperial concerns and national self-conceptions links America to Britain legitimizes a powerful worlding of America. The map of the entire world is drawn according to empire's desires and concerns, and in the very process of imposing a British-American colonial cartography, Americans are urged to imagine themselves as a master race with a divine sanction to lead the peoples of the world into the postmodern Eden of the Pax Americana. But this can be possible only if we are willing to imagine our historical inheritance as entirely Anglo-Saxon. So that we can produce a national subject whose colonial past is inextricably linked to an imperial future, the multiple threads of U.S. history and the long and painful struggle of blacks, Chicanos, Indians, Latinos, Irish, Jews, and numerous others to gain freedom and equality are forcefully twisted into a single-stranded narrative with the unities of time, place, and action impeccably observed. Every other competing claim, every other antagonistic presence and agonistic perspective to such a narration of American nation formation through the workings of empire, is effectively rendered meaningless.

Unlike Ferguson, Samuel P. Huntington, in *Who Are We? Challenges to America's National Identity* (2004), does acknowledge competing perspectives on worlding America, but only to delegitimize them by insisting on a particular worlding of America, the creation of "America" by an Anglo-Saxon Protestant culture. Huntington identifies four factors that have led to the current threat to American identity: the collapse of the Soviet Union, resulting in an absence of an other against which America could define itself; the ascendancy and hegemony of multiculturalism; the post-1965 increase in immigration from Asia and Latin America; and the demands for bilingual education, including the tendency to affirm linguistic plurality in contemporary America.[10] As more and more immigrants and migrants settle down, live, or work in America and, instead of assimilating into mainstream American culture as their predecessors did, celebrate their affiliations to other nations, ethnicities, and languages, America runs the danger of losing "the central elements of American identity, the cultural core and the American Creed."[11] The "American Creed" includes the idea of individual dignity and individualism, emphasis on the rule of law, the valuation of liberty and equality, the notion of popular sovereignty, and the desire for limited government.[12] The culture in which these ideas germinated and eventually flowered in an American demos was, Huntington argues, Protestant and Anglo-Saxon in provenance. Therefore, the process of becoming American necessarily involves accepting *only* Anglo-Saxon Protestant culture as truly American culture. He goes on to observe:

> All societies face recurring threats to their existence, to which they eventually succumb. Yet some societies, even when so threatened, are also capable of postponing their demise by halting and reversing the processes of decline and renewing their vitality and identity. I believe that America can do that and that Americans should recommit themselves to the Anglo-Protestant culture, traditions and values that for three and a half centuries have been *embraced* by Americans of all races, ethnicities, and religions and that have been the *source* of their liberty, unity, power, prosperity, and moral leadership as a *force for good in the world*.[13]

Notice that Huntington does world America in Dirlik's sense—"bringing the USA into the world as well as bringing the world into the USA."[14]

But the project of reworlding America raises other crucial concerns: How and why is the world mapped out as a "world" and the United States as "America"? How are these modes of mapping shaped by the movements of peoples and goods across continents and empires, and how have the narratives of travel and settlement and the discourses of the foreign and strange produced by these movements informed hemispheric social and political interactions, cross-cultural encounters, and transcontinental commerce of commodities and ideas? What kinds of economic and political processes were set in motion to enable the United States to situate itself in the world as an exceptional entity that could transcend history and claim unimpeachable universality? Why is it that Huntington's worlding of America integrates non-America and non-Americans into a vast global network of international relations and systems within which America and Americans can expend their benevolent energies for the benefit of humankind?

It is one thing to argue "for the importance of Anglo-Protestant culture,"[15] but it is another thing altogether to think that the only way to regenerate a nation and culture supposedly on the brink of disintegration is to recover a putatively lost innocence about the violent forces of modernization that influenced the worlding of the United States as the true repository of all things American. What Huntington does not acknowledge is how easily his argument attains the level of self-evident truth; how skillfully the encounters between the Old and New Worlds are given an exclusively racial character; how seamlessly the national becomes the international; and how deceptively the question of empire is erased from the formation of American nationhood, culture, and identity. Why have peoples of many races and ethnicities "embraced" the American creed and Anglo-Saxon Protestant culture? Huntington's answer is simple—because it is only through this creed and culture that non-Americans become Americans and find liberty and justice. What is more, by becoming Americans in this manner, the rest of the world becomes the beneficiary of American benevolence and goodwill.

A thorough process of worlding America and worlding the world American style is evident here: abstract ideas are first posited as having a priori, ahistorical status as *American* ideas; these ideas are then located within the culture of Protestantism that flourished in New England; the dispossession of the Native Indians and the active marginalization of non-Anglo-Saxons as slaves and second-class citizens are reconceived not as an imposition but as an embrace; America as a nation is endowed with the potential to do great and mighty things for humankind; and non-Americans, by becoming Americanized, are urged to position themselves, or rather world themselves, as emissaries for freedom and liberty and their nation as a repository for universal ideas. The next logical step from here is Ferguson's—the establishment and maintenance of American empire. Huntington paves the way, authorizes the policy, and justifies the workings of Ferguson's empire. To become American à la Huntington is inexorably to cultivate an imperial sensibility à la Ferguson. Such is the dangerous consequence of worlding America and worlding the world according to America.

Jennings and Brewster, Ferguson, and Huntington abstract their dramas of empire and nation formation from a much larger, intercontinental New World performance whose scripts and characters, writers and performers have histories more ancient, dissonant, varied, and complex than the histories of Jefferson, Washington, Adams, and Franklin. The genealogy of these worldings of America dates back to the era of "discovery," the coming of the Europeans to the Americas in the late fifteenth and early sixteenth centuries. And while various forms of worlding America emerged in that encounter of Old and New Worlds, a particular narrative of worlding has gained such hegemonic power that today *America* refers not to the hemispheres but to a specific region called the United States. At this point it is worth looking at how these kinds of worldings have also influenced American *literary* studies, one of the central objects of analysis in the reworlding of America.

The notion that the history of America begins with the arrival of the English settlers in New England has been an overarching paradigm in the writing of U.S. history. Speaking specifically of American literary history, Charles F. Richardson wrote in 1887: "The history of American literature is the history of the literature of a part of the English people, under new geographical and political conditions, within the present limits of the United States."[16] Furthermore, Richardson notes that in the early stages of the development of a new American literary tradition, the Amerindians hindered the progress of the settlers. In this early literature there is an abiding concern with the Indian "problem"—how to deal with the primitive peoples and convince them of their need to improve their farming methods and lifestyles, obtain an education, and generally become responsible people and improve their culture. "To this day the Indians, possibly as numerous as in 1607, stand on the *outskirts* of Caucasian civilization in North America, a *problem* and a *menace*, a theme for literature, and a subject for moral and industrial reform."[17] While acknowledging that the Amerindians had a primitive, preliterate cultural tradition, Richardson notes that since their traditions were oral, not written, they were bereft of recorded memory, which was crucial to forming a literary and critical consciousness, and did not significantly affect the formation of American literature. Rather, the literature of the early settlers had strong connections to English and Celtic traditions.

Richardson traces a usable past for American literature, sketching in some detail the strong links from Roman to English to American culture. American literature, seen this way, did not spring up suddenly in an alien environment. To Richardson, the English settlers fashioned for themselves a new culture in a new environment by rearticulating—in a new idiom, in a New World—English and Roman cultural and aesthetic practices. Here is the apotheosis of the American subject: "the individual before his God—such was the Pilgrim or Puritan of Plymouth, Salem, and Boston. The mistakes and triumphs of these brave and self-reliant settlers lie at the very root of intellectual life of New England for two centuries and a half. They made the American nation and American literature possible."[18] Early American literature embodies "an intense and ever-present religious purpose, a grim confidence in the powers of devout Man, and a determination to secure the rights, individual and collective, of the Puritan communities."[19] In short, "the seeds of American literature were most effectively sown in New England."[20]

Earlier, John Seely Hart, in *Manual of American Literature* (1873), had written, "American Literature, strictly speaking, is that part of English literature which has been produced upon American soil," and as such, "American Literature dates from the first settlement of the American Colonies,"[21] meaning the British colonies of New England. Richardson expands upon Hart's observations. In the three-volume *Cambridge History of American Literature* (1917), the essays dealing with the roots of American history follow the same trajectory, affirming New England as central to the origins of American thought and culture. In a related context, when Charles Angoff, in *A Literary History of the American People* (1931), writes that "It is therefore only by politeness that we can speak of literature in the first one hundred and fifty years of the history of the United States. We really had no literature then" and that "the American people before the Revolution produced no literature at all, in the sense of *belles lettres*,"[22] he is evidently calculating backward from 1776, the year in which the United States emerged as a political entity. To Angoff, the nation is the primary category of analysis by which to conceptualize the emergence of American literature in the New World.

Taking a somewhat broader approach, Robert E. Spiller in *The Cycle of American Literature* (1955) proposes the following chronology, which also finds its millennial echo in Geoff Ward's *The Writing of America* (2002): In the late fifteenth and sixteenth centuries we have accounts of the discovery of the New World, such as in Columbus's journals, and in the early seventeenth century we have accounts of its settlement, such as in Bradford's writings. In the eighteenth century we have preachers like Edwards, who was famous for his fiery orations on human spirituality; scientists like Franklin, who pushed the limits of scientific frontiers, and political leaders like Jefferson, who played a significant role in creating the manifesto that laid the foundation for a new republic. In the early nineteenth century we have such writers as Irving, Bryant, Cooper, Emerson, and Thoreau. In the middle of the nineteenth century Poe and Hawthorne emerge, and in the fifties Melville and Whitman gain prominence. In the latter part of the century Howells, Twain, Dickinson, and Henry James continue the literary tradition. In the first half of the twentieth century Dreiser, Pound, Eliot, Frost, Fitzgerald, and Faulkner attain recognition. Like the critics before him, Spiller conceptualizes American literary history solely in terms of a new literary tradition that has its roots in English culture and sensibility and in ways that privilege the experiences of European settlers in the New World. The writers he assigns to a distinct canon for each century are nearly all male and white and write in the English language. More important, the history of the formation of the United States as a nation becomes the governing framework within which to situate the emergence and development of various aesthetic traditions.[23]

The arguments made by Richardson, Seely, Angoff, Spiller, and Ward, among others, constitute what Donald Pease terms the "field-imaginary," the "disciplinary unconscious," or the "fundamental syntax" of American studies—"its tacit assumptions, convictions, primal words, and the charged relations binding them together."[24] As we have seen, the "fundamental syntax" of American studies embodies narratives that begin with the "discovery" of America by Columbus and then with the arrival of the Pilgrim fathers in Massachusetts, the attempts of the British colonies to construct an independent society shorn of all affiliations to the British crown, the growing presence of the English-speaking settlers, and their eventual hegemony in the United States.

But is it historically valid to speak solely about U.S. literature to conceptualize America? What explains the shift from the "United States" to "America"? As early as 1578, several decades before the English settled in New England, the Huguenot voyager Jean de Léry referred to Brazil as "America" in his *History of a Voyage to the Land of Brazil, Otherwise Called America,* and throughout his narrative he used the term "Americans" in speaking about the Tupinambas of Brazil. Furthermore, between 1492 and 1607 (the year in which the first English settlement was founded in Jamestown, Virginia), civilizations like the Aztecs were encountered; numerous Amerindian tribes were subdued; driven further into the land, or simply annihilated; and colonial rule was firmly established in various parts of the Americas by European powers such as France, Portugal, and Spain. By what fiat, then, did "America" come to refer only to a certain region in North America with a history originating in New England?

This worlding of the United States as America, of U.S. history as American history, has gained enormous purchase, and it is the mythic, hegemonic power of this particular narrative, its symbologies, structures of representation, and modes of articulation, that I seek to interrogate in this book. I begin with the premise that we cannot talk about a monolithic America meaning solely the United States. Rather, we must focus on a range of discursive formations and interpretive strategies arising in the collision of European, Amerindian, African, and, later, Asian cultures and societies. My aim in tracing the emergence of diverse literary traditions in the Americas is not to arrive at a new synthesis by creating an overarching framework or critical paradigm that resolves their social and cultural tensions and paradoxes. Instead, by grafting together the contradictory histories and discourses of conquest, displacement, migration, settlement, exile, and border crossings in the Americas, I attempt to develop a critical vocabulary with which to study the Americas in their transborder, hemispheric dimensions. By insisting that all ideas of America are shot through with the woof of "other Americas," I seek to develop different ways of conceiving of historical inheritance that counter the narrowly racialized, excessively territorialized, and deeply gendered ideas of America that have historically gained hegemony.

Rather than offering a clear alternative historical or intellectual tradition with which to reworld America, I have chosen to indulge in a form of disruptive textual play at those discursive sites where the many worldings of America have been and continue to be articulated in the moments of negotiating the incommensurable values and demands of various nations and communities in different parts of the Americas. I reconceptualize America here as "Americas," a plethora of discursive formations whose overlapping, competing modes of narrative address give rise to other ways of articulating the multiple meanings of America. This reconceptualization amounts to a refusal of other worldings that normalize themselves in public imagination and discourse. It is a mode of discursive contestation in developing a critical vocabulary for interrogating and revising the terms in which the literary and cultural history of America has come to be articulated, and for reimagining the Americas in their interhemispheric dimensions.

What, then, is the relevance of the nation to the project of reworlding America? To reworld America, it is not enough to pose the question of the nation. Reworlding America is intimately linked to rethinking the terms in which modernity, and therefore globalization, have historically come to engender and authorize particular meanings of America. It means rethinking modernity as making both visible and invisible a clashing of dissonant modernities in the Americas; it means tracing the lines of continuity and rupture that shape the material and discursive forms of national belonging and sociocultural pollination. In this context the nation and its attendant ideologies are viewed as an intertwined layer of the ideological armature that ensures the continued valence, however transformed and variegated, of different ideas of America. Thus, I eschew mapping an alternative historical narrative that is chronologically patterned and teleologically imbued in order to contest U.S.-centered American literary history. The history of the United States as "America" is part of a complex networking of intercontinental economies linking the Americas not only to Britain but to other European nations, Africa, the Caribbean, and Asia. This is why the historian Ronald Takaki points out that "Americans originated from many shores,"[25] an observation that counters Jennings and Brewster's, Ferguson's, and Huntington's narrow focus on the Anglo-Saxon ancestry of the United States. As Malini Johar Schueller and Edward Watts perceptively point out, America can be neither reduced to the legacy of white settlement in the United States nor envisioned as just another transatlantic extension of Anglo-Saxon culture in the New World, because both these approaches "ignor[e] the complex ways that 'Americanness' as a gendered, raced, and classed phenomenon was constantly negotiated through strategic identification and disidentification with Europeans, on the one hand, and American Indians, African Americans, and other nonwhite populations, on the other hand."[26] Reworlding America involves seeking out the moments when America is "constructed in and through a set of hierarchical relationships with groups, communities, and nations defined somehow as other, alien, or outside."[27] Far from simply extending the spatializing gesture to encompass Northern and Southern Hemispheres, reworlding America reconfigures spatial displacement as marking not just a redrawing of territorial boundaries and a contesting of the sometimes atavistic, sometimes creolized visions that have controlled them, but as making visible the processes by which the dissonances of the sociocultural morphologies of "America" are produced and managed.

Another axis along which the many meanings of America have come to be authorized is language. In paying attention to the dynamic interaction between languages and cross-cultural contact, this book studies eight texts taken from different historical periods, dealing with the commerce of peoples, ideas, and cultures in various parts of the Americas, and written in Spanish, French, English, and Creole. To be sure, even these languages do not quite function as signifiers of distinct linguistic systems. By the time we make our way from the sixteenth-century ethnographer Jean de Léry's learned French, which constantly breaks down in attempting to seek metaphoric correlatives to signify the strangeness of the New World, to Patrick Chamoiseau's effusive late-twentieth-century word scratching in a language born of bastardy and oppression, Creole emerges in the interstices of African languages and French, thus denaturalizing the authority of memory and empire and complicating the nostalgia of the exile's dream of return and the rebel's vision of transcendence. To reworld America is also to acknowledge that there is something more to reading and canonizing non-English texts than unearthing and studying them for their ostensibly transgressive value or potential. Multilingualism does not always provide occasions to contest the ideal of monolingualism, and, in more ways than one, non-English texts may sometimes frustrate the subversive potential of the discourse of multilingualism by subscribing without examination to dominant myths and histories. Texts, like authors, tend to develop lives of their own. Even as they outrun their authors' concerns, they undermine the critics' methodologies. More important, texts, like people, migrate; they may carry with them certain ideas and symbols as useful baggage and abandon them in odd places for inexplicable reasons. If we are to relate the question of language to reworlding America, we should attend to the clashing of linguistic codes and to their uneasy yet fecund cohabitation, as travelers, exiles, refugees, and migrants shuttle among numerous nodal points in a global circuit linking diasporic communities living their anxious lives of survival and chance, compromise and gamble, in their dwelling places in various parts of the Americas. The task, then, is not just to discover what ideas of America, what different dreams of the New World, what kinds of desperate negotiations writers and texts in non-English languages articulate in attempting to give shape and meaning to America. It is also to study how non-English texts can emerge as *American* literary works of art through acts of ideological manipulation that elide their multiple allegiances to conflicting intellectual and aesthetic traditions. We will thus be able to frustrate any attempt to use the logic of supplementation to rectify or add to a particular version of American history or contest and revise the monolingual canon of American literature.

Within these contexts, how can we develop critical vocabularies that will address the complexity of transcontinental patterns of social and cultural interaction and the transborder geopolitical determinations that engender global disjunctions and local sedimentations in the flow of power, capital, commodities, ideas, peoples, and symbols within, between, and across the Americas? In short, how can we effectively contest the nationalist, linguistic, religious, geopolitical, and ethnocentric biases that have historically informed the construction of a Eurocentric America? I suggest that we use three critical models: The first is the dialectical model proposed by José David Saldívar (*The Dialectics of Our America*, 1991),[28] which seeks to map the confluences and divergences of processes of social and cultural exchange between the Americas. This model was adumbrated as early as 1891 by José Martí (*Nuestra América*) and in 1933 by Herbert Bolton (*The Epic of Greater America*), and was later revived and rearticulated by literary critics such as Belle Chevigny and Gari Laguardia (*Reinventing the Americas*, 1986), Gustavo Pérez-Firmat (*Do the Americas Have a Common Literature?* 1990), and Earl E. Fitz (*Rediscovering the New World: Inter-American Literature in a Comparative Context,* 1991). The second model revises, as Paul Jay suggests, the "conception of the emergence of modernity"[29] in the Americas by extending the work of cultural critics like Edmundo O'Gorman (*The Invention of America,* 1961), Paul Gilroy (*The Black Atlantic,* 1993), and Edouard Glissant (*Caribbean Poetics,* 1997). The third model addresses the evolution of a border consciousness in what Ramón Saldívar terms the "social interstices" of Anglo-American and Mexican American traditions (*Chicano Narrative: A Dialectic of Difference,* 1990) and the transborder processes of social and cultural exchange that link the U.S. Southwest to Latin America and the Caribbean as the borderlanders search for what Lois P. Zamora calls a "usable past" (*The Usable Past,* 1997).

Nuestra América and the Other America

Writing in 1891, Martí perspectivizes the development of two Americas—"Neustra América" (our America), meaning Latin America, and the other America, meaning North America—as a process in which the United States slowly begins to emerge as a dominating power.[30] He casts the relationship between the two Americas in a Manichean dichotomy, an idea insightfully addressed much later by Frantz Fanon in an Afro-Caribbean context (*The Wretched of the Earth,* 1963, and *Black Skin/White Masks,* 1967). To use Fanon's terms, the two hemispheres are locked in a "murderous and decisive struggle" for complete economic, social, and political domination.[31] Martí's America resists the expansionist programs of the other America. When he further writes, "Our Greece must take priority over the Greece that is not ours" and "the European university must give way to the American university,"[32] he sounds a clarion call to create an alternative social and cultural center in the Americas.[33]

The publication of *Caliban* and *Nuestra América y Occidente* in the 1970s by the Cuban philosopher Roberto Fernández Retamar marks the fruition of Martí's dream. Retamar recasts the "discovery" of America as the "disaster" of America and employs a new nomenclature to rewrite history from the perspective of the marginalized and dispossessed. In traditional narratives of Old World/New World contact, the first settlers are typically the central figures, whose speech and actions are recorded as official history. Retamar, as a way of bringing the native peoples of the Americas back into the narrative, insists on a reading of Shakespeare's *Tempest* in which Caliban, the wretched half human, half monster, is the central figure. Caliban's famous declaration to Prospero—"You taught me language, and my profit on't / Is, I know how to curse"[34]—provides a model for contextualizing the history of colonialism and resistance in the Americas, particularly Latin America. Just as Caliban uses the very tool (the language taught him by Prospero) that was used to colonize him (or it?), Latin America could use colonial tools to undermine colonial power.[35]

Carolyn Porter's suggestion that we reorganize American studies with reference to places and events offers a productive way of emphasizing alternative centers and marginal spaces. Focusing on Havana, New Orleans, New England, Los Angeles, or Mexico City, or even on events like the Haitian Revolution and the Mexican War, would facilitate an engagement with literary history in which national boundaries would neither disappear nor simply be questioned, but the multiple and nodal points of contact and the varied modes of intellectual and material commerce among cities, regions, and even towns within and between the continents would gain prominence. "Such a framework would necessarily include Africa and the triangular trade route joining its east coast to Europe and the Americas. It would also necessarily multiply vantage points within Latin America, whose cultural and political heterogeneity resists any monolithic overview."[36] The quadruple set of relations that her reconfiguration sets up—between the Americas, between Europe and the Americas, between Africa and the Americas, and between Europe and Africa—would enable us, she contends, to "grasp how the cultural, political, and economic relations between and within the Americas might work to reconstellate the field itself, reinflecting its questions in accord with a large frame. Theoretically speaking, 'America,' both geopolitically and historically would become at once *internally fissured* and *externally relativized*."[37]

For instance, if, in an African studies course or program, we focused on Harlem, we would be able to study not just this local, urban place and its treatment in art, but also its complicated relationship to the history of black migration during the early decades of the twentieth century and to the back-and-forth movement of travel and migration between the South and the North in the United States. We would also be able to highlight, for example, the slow transformation of a southern consciousness, rooted in the memory of slave plantations, into an urban, modern sensibility; address the role and symbolic significance of the city in the black imagination; follow the evolution of gospel and blues inflected with a new modern tone and rhythm; and highlight the interactions between European and black musicians in the formation of a musical tradition like jazz. Moreover, by giving attention to writers like Claude McKay and Marcus Garvey, we can see how the social processes linking Harlem to the South are intertwined with the histories of resistance and opposition to colonial presence in various Caribbean islands. We could also focus on the role of Paris, as a European cultural center, in determining and influencing black aesthetic production during the early decades of the twentieth century, particularly in the works of W. E. B. DuBois and Richard Wright. Here the significance of Harlem and Paris would problematize any Eurocentered ideas about black engagement in the social and cultural milieu of the time.

However, these proposals, while promising, can facilitate only modest reformulations of American literary history; they cannot address the heterogeneous processes of interaction among the Americas, Europe, and Africa. Paul Jay proposes an approach "that confronts the history of the region in terms of a *revised* conception of the emergence of modernity"[38] and suggests paying attention to locations which are not within national boundaries, but which are *"between* or which *transgress* conventional borders—liminal margins or border zones in which individual and national identities migrate, merge, and hybridize."[39] But in what sense can we revise modernity? I suggest that a productive way to begin would be to link Nelly Richard's and Edmundo O'Gorman's crucial conceptual move to *rehistoricize* modernity with Paul Gilroy's notion of the "black Atlantic" and Edouard Glissant's idea of overlapping modernities. Since rehistoricizing modernity would entail reperiodizing modernity, reworlding America's focus on intercontinental migration and cultural translation could go a long way in contesting Eurocentered conceptualizations of modernity.

The Critique of Modernity

Richard's central argument is that the entire project of modernity, in the general sense of European expansion in the Americas, Africa, and Asia, was designed to position Europeans marching towards an ever-unfolding, grand, universal history. As the English, French, Spanish, and other European settlers established themselves as colonial powers in the Americas, native societies and cultures faced the prospect of either complete annihilation or a form of condescending assimilation coupled with native cultural denigration. Speaking of Latin America, Richard writes, "In this Manichean scheme of things, modernity is found guilty of having destroyed the characteristics of a true Latin American identity through a conglomeration of influences which are invariably regarded as threats, falsifications, or travesties of the region's original and authentic nucleus of culture."[40] In other words, modernization in the Americas always meant Europeanization.[41] Richard seems to echo the arguments made by the Mexican philosopher Edmundo O'Gorman in *The Invention of America* (1961), whose thesis is that modernity in the Americas originated not when America was discovered but when it began to be *invented.*

O'Gorman rejects the substantialistic concept of America as a thing-in-itself, already existing in time and space, discourse, and belief, whose discovery would automatically unravel the meaning of America. Rather, O'Gorman argues that America was "produced" in the intersection of Old World cosmographic theories, European political intrigues, religious injunctions and worldviews, and personal idiosyncrasies and dispositions, all of which generated the meaning of America over time.

Coterminous with this production, an incipient humanism that stressed the limitless potential of man to shape his own cosmic destiny began to gain credence.[42] It was in this context that, according to O'Gorman, America "developed from a complex, living process of exploration and interpretation," and its "history will no longer be that which has happened to America, but that which it has been, is, and is in the act of being."[43]

Common to O'Gorman and Richard are the analeptic extension of modernity and the idea of a break or rupture from the past, but while Richard privileges the perspective of the Native Indians and the African slaves, O'Gorman recasts modernity as the undermining of medieval beliefs, beginning with the finding, not the discovery, of a land mass west of Europe. To O'Gorman, it is the very production of America as a narrative strategy that marks the process of modernization, or rather the entry point of modernity, in the Americas. If we follow Richard's and O'Gorman's premise, modernity begins with the era of New World conquest and settlement and the consolidation of colonial power, and then, in the eighteenth century (at least in Europe), coalesces with the project of the Enlightenment, the founding of nations, the establishing of juridical institutions, the development of the army, and the building of roads, bridges, railroads, trains, telephones, hospitals, and so on. It is in this context that we can productively extend Gilroy's idea of the black Atlantic and Glissant's idea of overlapping modernities.

Gilroy argues that it would be parochial to study writers like W. E. B. DuBois, Martin Delaney, Phillis Wheatley, Claude McKay, and Richard Wright strictly within the nationalist framework of the United States, since such a focus would not address these writers' common experience of travel and displacement. Instead, he proposes the black Atlantic "as a single, complex, unit of analysis . . . to produce an explicitly transnational and intercultural perspective" to study the "deterritorialized, multiplex and anti-national basis for the affinity of the identity of passions between divers black populations."[44] It is within the nexus of the black Atlantic, argues Gilroy, that we can see the emergence of a "counter culture of modernity." He uses the metaphor of a ship to

conceptualize the intercontinental engagement of cultures and economies. The ship, perpetually moving, emblematic of the "shifting spaces"
and "half-remembered micro-politics of the slave trade and its relationship to both industrialization and modernization," and shaping the
Atlantic as a "system of cultural exchanges,"[45] dramatizes the dispersal
of migrant cultures, a dispersal that redraws the margins of the nation
by undermining the absolutism of ethnic identity and the provincialism
of nationalism.

It would be useful to link Gilroy's idea of the articulation of a counterculture of modernity with Edouard Glissant's notion of the "irrup-
tion of modernity" in the Americas. Glissant distinguishes between a
"maturing" European modernity and a "living" American modernity.
He argues that literary tradition, and by extension history itself, in the
Americas did not mature and evolve slowly as it did in Europe. Instead,
America experienced a nonmaturing process that Glissant calls "lived
modernity," to connote the sense of immediacy and unpredictability that
necessarily accompanies the writing of history and the quest for identity
in the collision of societies and cultures in the Americas. It is sudden, brutal, and imposed and connotes a "violent departure from tradition, from
literary continuity."[46] Thus, to Glissant, literature in the Americas "is the
product of a system of modernity that is sudden and not sustained or
'evolved.'"[47] But what is crucial in Glissant's formulation of lived modernity is his emphasis that lived modernity "overlaps with the preoccupa-
tions of matured 'modernity' in other zones of culture and thought."[48]
It is here that we can make the link to Gilroy's notions of "syncopated
temporality" and the articulation of black identity as a counterculture of
modernity. The revision of history and the recovery of culture in the
Americas are thus possible only from within the sites of chiasmus—the
inversions, displacements, entanglements—of these modernities.

In the reconfiguration of the very terms in which modernity can be
theorized (Richard and O'Gorman) and delineation of the emergence
of divergent modernities (Gilroy's counterculture in the black Atlantic
and Glissant's overlapping modernities), a crucial question emerges: how
can we, to extend Jay, "complicate how we think about American litera-

ture by *retheorizing the spaces(s) in which it has emerged*"?[49] The impulse, Jay notes, should be not on finding social coherence, political unity, and cultural homogeneity within nations and states, but on "directing critical attention to the liminal margins and permeable border zones out of which the cultures of the Americas have emerged."[50] Jay's emphasis on "spaces," "cultures," and "permeable border zones" has three important implications: first, it enables a theorization of *divergent* responses to modernity in different locations in the Americas; secondly, by insisting on the plurality of cultural formations, it anticipates the "clash" of "values and commitments"[51] in the Americas; and thirdly, it configures the border not simply as something that contains, orders, and restricts whatever emanates from the center, but as a site in which something emerges, is produced, or is given birth to. Approaching this issue by addressing the formation of a border consciousness in the U.S. Southwest not only would be fruitful but would enable us to meditate on the formation of a new border imaginary engendered in the dialectic of global and regional modes of sociality and interaction in the Americas.

Border Crossings

Contemporary theorizations of border experience in North America have focused on the U.S. Southwest, Texas, and those former parts of northern Mexico annexed by the United States with the signing of the Treaty of Guadalupe Hidalgo in 1848: California, New Mexico, Arizona, and parts of Nevada, Colorado, and Utah. But to speak only of these regions is problematic, since the very idea of the borderlands hinges on both the notion of the border and whatever lies on the "other" side of the border. Oscar Martínez helpfully delineates the border as "a line that separates one nation from another or, in the case of internal entities, one province or locality from another. The essential functions of a border are to keep people in their own space and to prevent, control, or regulate interactions among them."[52] In this case the line of separation is the nearly 2,000-mile-long fenced borderline that divides the United States from Mexico. This border is always regulated, patrolled, and controlled. The flow of people and goods across it varies depending on regional political and market demands, U.S. and Mexican foreign policy interests, and, more recently, the pressures of a global market. What gives rise to the borderlands and border experience are the social, political, and cultural policies and activities that necessitate, at different points in time, varied levels of interaction between peoples on both sides of the border.

We can map the diverse forms of social affiliation and cultural articulation in the border regions from the migration of the Aztecs from Aztlán to central Mexico in about 1168 AD and their return to the Southwest as mixed bloods after their defeat by the conquistadors in 1521;[53] through the numerous inland journeys by the Spanish settlers as they moved upward to northern Mexico in the seventeenth and eighteenth centuries; and continuing through the war of 1848, the Mexican Revolution of 1910, World Wars I and II, the Korean War, the bracero program of 1940–50, the establishment of maquiladoras along the Mexican border, the rise of the Chicano movement in the 1960s, the transnational economic policies of the North American Free Trade Agreement (NAFTA) of 1994 ("one of the primary political instruments of globalization in the Americas"),[54] and the postmodern globality of the present, which links the borderlands to larger networks of transnational social and cultural formations. We will then be able to study what Guillermo Gómez-Peña calls the "epistemology of multiplicity and a border semiotics"[55] in which the "phantasmatics of Nuéstra América's borders"[56] are engendered.

We will also, as John Carlos Rowe observes, be able to address the transborder ties between various contact zones within the borderlands to other cities and countries in Central and South America: Southern California's ties to Central America and Asia; Lower Texas's (or "Greater Houston") ties to Mexico and the Caribbean; the Southeast's intimate ties to the cross-continental flows of peoples in the black Atlantic; and Miami's close ties to Cuba, Haiti, and other regions of Latin America.[57] Rowe emphasizes not only the interregional linkages in the borderlands but their Pan-American and intercontinental forms of economic exchange, political economy, and cultural production, which frequently intersect and overlap. The borderlands, in other words, are frayed with multiple, permeable borders and zones of contact. Rowe also suggests that because "America" circulates as a sign, symbol, and "commodity of new cultural imperialism" within and across these multiple chiasmatic sites, we should address the specific manner in which local and regional cultures "'write back' against cultural and even political and economic domination."[58] Such a focus would also involve, to extend Amy Kaplan, the "multiple histories of continental and overseas expansion, conquest, conflict and resistance which have shaped the cultures of the United States and the cultures of those it has dominated within and beyond its geopolitical boundaries."[59] The implications are global in scope as "America's conceptual and geographic boundaries" become "fluid, contested, and historically changing."[60] The implication, as Rowe suggests, is that there can be no monolithic American studies, however much we globalize or internationalize it, that we can "command."[61] Rather, the mapping of "different Americas" can "help foreground the multilingual and multicultural realities of social life and economic opportunity in any of the Americas"[62] as the history of America yields to the histories of the Americas.

These three critical models—the dialectical, hemispheric configuration, the critique of modernity, and border crossings—foreground social and cultural production in the Americas less as monolithic traditions emerging in various geopolitical regions and more as overlapping arenas or zones of competing voices and dissenting histories embodying contradictory articulations of self, identity, and society. The implications for the conceptualization of American social and cultural history and the teaching and writing of American literature can be profound. While contesting the ideological biases and marginalizing tendencies of Eurocentrism in the formulation of a paradigmatic, transcendent, and transhistorical America, these models can help us develop new critical vocabularies and interdisciplinary forms of engagement to examine various forms of artistic and social expression in their inter-American, transborder, and global manifestations and linkages.

The next three chapters take up each of these models respectively in order to demonstrate the promising lines of inquiry they open up and how they may used to reworld America. It is fitting for a project that contests traditional conceptualizations of American history to focus on New World encounters in order to foreground the differential manner in which America "developed from a complex, living process of exploration and interpretation."[63] Therefore, in the second chapter I analyze three sixteenth-century chronicles: one by the Spanish explorer Bernal Díaz del Castillo (*The Conquest of New Spain*), who recounts the fall of the mighty Aztec empire in 1521; one by the French voyager Jean de Léry (*History of a Voyage to the Land of Brazil, Otherwise Called America*), whose account of his journey to Brazil forms one of the most impressive ethnographic narratives of the New World; and one by the Spanish traveler Álvar Núñez Cabeza de Vaca (*Relación*), supposedly the first European to cross the U.S. Southwest from the Atlantic coast to the Pacific coast in Baja California, Mexico, and the first European to see the American buffalo and report it to his fellow Europeans. I argue that by effectively contesting the notion that America was a tabula rasa upon which Europe inscribed its consciousness, these chronicles dramatize the manner in which the "discovery" of America challenged Europe's perception of itself and its relationship to the classical past and its medieval heritage, thus dramatizing Europe's "desperate negotiation" with America's "presence of otherness," which it could "neither securely manipulate nor comfortably embrace."[64]

The third chapter broadens the Euro-American framework of the previous chapter to highlight the patterns of social and cultural exchange among the Americas, Europe, and Africa. My focus on the Caribbean archipelago as a site that registers the warp and woof of these exchanges revises traditional approaches to configuring a Caribbean poetics, which view the region as a cluster of separate island nations and its cultures as extensions of European practices. In my discussion of Patrick Chamoiseau's *Texaco*, I focus on the urbanization of the city of Fort-de-France, Martinique. Emphasizing the ways in which the novel can be situated within a Pan-Caribbean nexus, I argue that the emergence of a black

Martinican feminist consciousness is central to the social efficacy of creolization as a strategy of resistance. I also study Russell Banks's *Book of Jamaica* and *Rule of the Bone*, which highlight the interhemispheric commerce of whiteness in the Americas. I argue that the novels' fetishization of black culture erases the history of slavery and racism and also dramatizes whiteness as an ideological construction that is inextricably linked to the construction of black identity and culture. This imbrication of whiteness and blackness also perpetuates the continuing exploitation of those countries that North America has historically defined as the Third World, in need of progress and modernization.

In the fourth chapter I study United States–Mexico border relations, a more localized arena of migration and displacement in the U.S. Southwest that is engaging a growing body of Chicano/Latino and Native Indian literature. In my study of Roberta Fernández's *Intaglio: A Novel in Six Stories*, I focus on the enduring presence of Mexican and Amerindian religious and cultural practices and icons—*curanderismo, la llorona, la bruja*—and the domestic spaces occupied by border women, in which they often refashion their gendered roles and identities through a process of cultural translation. Departing from established paradigms in border studies, which often neglect the presence of Native Indian tribes in the borderlands, my study of Leslie Marmon Silko's *Almanac of the Dead* makes visible both the novel's weaving of Yaqui history and culture with the tumultuous histories of Euro-American contact and the impact of European colonialism and U.S. and Mexican nationalisms on Native Indian peoples in order to theorize on the formation of transborder subjectivities in the borderlands. Employing a range of critical methodologies drawn from postcolonial discourse, border theory, cultural studies, ethnography, history, and sociology, these chapters take a multidisciplinary approach to the reworlding of America. What follows, then, is a modest argument in response to the question, how shall we enact the labor of reworlding America?

2 Frontier Narratives of the Americas

> The greatest thing after the creation of the world, after
> the incarnation and death of its creator, was the discovery
> of the Indies, and thus, they are called the New World.
>
> —FRANCISCO LÓPEZ DE GÓMARA

Less than three decades after Cristóbal Colón "discovered" America, the New World of myth and fantasy, of fabulous treasures and verdant green, was under siege. No sooner did news of the *other* world reach European shores than adventurers began journeying to America and, upon arriving, began plundering and killing the native inhabitants and laying claim to all they could—gold, treasures, animals, natural resources, artifacts, native women. In the sixteenth century, the Age of Discovery, a vast body of chronicles by French, English, German, Italian, Portuguese, and Spanish explorers relating their experiences of discovery and conquest in the Americas began to appear.

In her study of sixteenth-century Spanish discovery narratives, Beatriz Pastor Bodmer notes that they embody three important impulses, or rather, that they participate in three discourses. The discourse of mythification "shapes a set of representations that distort New World realities and idealize the nature and meaning of the conquest."[1] The discourse of demythification, in acknowledging the myth-making tendencies of the earlier narratives, is infused with a sense of despair and despondency because it is more realistic in acknowledging the harsh realities of the New World and its lack of fantastic cities laden with gold and peopled by exotic creatures. The discourse of rebellion embodies the emergence of a distinct Spanish American consciousness as the settlers

29

and those born in the fourth world begin to question the hegemony of the Spanish crown in New Spain.[2]

Although she speaks specifically about Spanish narratives, Pastor Bodmer's characterization of these discourses also helps frame my study of three travel narratives. In *The Conquest of New Spain* (ca. 1568), Bernal Díaz del Castillo, who had been a foot soldier under Cortés, recounts the Cortés expedition into Tenochtitlán. Jean de Léry, in *History of a Voyage to the Land of Brazil, Otherwise Called America*, an account of his journey to Brazil (1556–57), provides a remarkable ethnography of the New World. And in *Relación* (1542), Álvar Núñez Cabeza de Vaca tells of his experiences as one of the first Europeans to travel, mostly by foot, from the Caribbean/Florida Atlantic into the U.S. Southwest, on to Baja California, Mexico, and eventually to Mexico City. In framing these texts in this manner, my intention is to demonstrate not how neatly and complexly Pastor Bodmer's three discourses, or impulses—to mythify, demythify, and rebel—operate in the narratives, but how they produce various forms of worlding "America" and what it would mean to engage in reworlding them.

In referring to these travel accounts as "frontier narratives," I am conjoining the famous proclamation of the U.S. historian Frederick Jackson Turner with sixteenth-century texts that interfere in the contextual historicity of the proclamation itself. Turner's teleological history celebrating the development of a nation, as it encounters the "frontier," with an organic national character and spirit, is grounded in an analysis of European patterns of settlement in the United States. Inserting Turner's nineteenth-century frontier thesis into a New World configuration to study the travel narratives of Díaz, Léry, and Cabeza de Vaca warrants a rethinking of Turnerian historiography.

The Frontier and Frederick Jackson Turner

In the "meeting point between savagery and civilization," the processes by which European explorers formed settler communities, established farms and ranches, mining fields, and trading relations among the Indians and other Europeans, and eventually created a social and political nation-state grounded in the ideals of democracy, liberty, and justice, is what Turner defines as the frontier experience.[3] The test was Promethean, the significance universal.

Indeed, this hyperbole is not misplaced in Turner's estimation. He quotes the Italian economist Lori: "America has the key to the historical enigma which Europe has sought for centuries in vain, and the land which has no history reveals luminously the course of universal history."[4] The power of Turner's thesis lies in its mythic appeal. It is more than a historical, sociological, or economic account of New World experience. In affirming a gamut of ideologies, social formations, and cultural practices formed and set in motion since the coming of the Europeans into North America, it gives "America" a quality of transcendence and universality.[5]

Turner's thesis has been criticized on the grounds that the entire narrative of settlement is actually a narrative of conquest and colonization of native peoples and that it neglects the influence of industrialization, urbanization, and immigration on the American imagination. The massive influx of immigrants from Eastern Europe, and later from Africa, Asia, and South America, altered the social and cultural makeup of the United States, thus complicating easy affirmations of European ethnocentricity. Patterns of migration within the United States were not simply from east to west but also from west to east and from farms to cities, leading to rapid urbanization. In addition, Turner's frontier "still overlooked women."[6] The frontier was more or less a tale told by men about men in a land called America.

Recognizing such biases that inform frontier narratives, Annette Kolodny suggests letting go "our grand obsessions" and "theories of continuity," which she identifies as linear, chronological, ethnocentric, and nationalistic frameworks, to map the discursive terrain of American literary and social history. Kolodny conceives of the frontier as the "locus of first contact circumscribed by a particular physical terrain in the process of change *because* of the forms that contact takes, all of it inscribed by the collisions and interpenetrations of language."[7]

Like Kolodny, Howard Lamar and Leonard Thompson view the frontier "not as a boundary line, but as a territory or zone of inter-penetration between previously distinct societies."[8] When members of the invasive society penetrate the boundaries of the indigenous society, contact takes place, a process of reciprocal relations is established, and the cultures of both societies begin to change in proportion to the level and nature of various forms of contact established voluntarily or through force.[9] Within such a framework, Kolodny argues, "Geography and chronology must be viewed as fluid and ongoing, or as a cautiously unfolding palimpsest that requires us to include Old Norse, Papago, Nahuatl, Quechua, Spanish, Yaqui, Tewa, Gullah, French, Dutch, Chinese, Japanese, German, Yiddish . . . within our textual canon."[10] The frontier experience embodies, in Kolodny's formulation, more than a coming together of different peoples and cultures; it affords a confrontation with "another's 'otherness,'" which is differentially and to varying degrees accommodated and/or domesticated.[11] Rather than conceiving of a "chronology of successive discoveries and discrete settlements," we can "accommodate a literary history of discontinuous frontiers" since there can be no "paradigmatic" first contact.[12]

Kolodny's frontier paradigm facilitates a transnational Pan-American approach to study the emergence of diverse literary traditions in various parts of the Americas. Rather than certain validated texts, cultural artifacts, and aesthetic movements simply being added to the hegemonic English and Anglo-Saxon tradition, the literary histories of the Americas would be studied in terms of the overlapping of regional and intercontinental patterns of social and cultural commerce. By de-centering traditional accounts of American history that begin with the Puritans in New England, Kolodny's frontier paradigm enables a consideration of histories and narratives written in different languages by peoples of varied races and ethnicities and encoded in hybrid forms of social and artistic expression.

In this context, to denote travel narratives of the sixteenth century as frontier narratives is to perform a catechrestic move—to wrest this idea, intentionally and flagrantly, from Turner's historical frame of reference to create a kind of interference between Turner's text and its context because his worlding of America strenuously attempts to demarcate, precisely and unambiguously, the borders of civilization and barbarism. The Old World's encounter with the frontiers of the New World thus dramatizes Europe's "desperate negotiation" with America's "presence of otherness," which it could "neither securely manipulate nor comfortably embrace."[13]

To Greenblatt, it is Europe's anxious negotiation with America's otherness that is pivotal. But what if Europe's confrontation with America instantiates particular forms of European self-production? What if the discovery and settlement of America authorizes the birth of an othered Europe that Europeans cannot embrace and manipulate? In order to move beyond European struggles to make sense of America, it will be helpful to yoke together Homi Bhabha's idea of the pedagogical and performative dimensions of the nation with Djelal Kadir's notion of the forthgathering and foregathering of New World historiography. By using the conceptual integrity of the pedagogical and the performative, I set up a critical framework that will enable us to examine the cultures of the New World as embodying "the complex or web of certain notions, cultural forms, and conditioning ideas that furnish the enabling requirements and provide the legitimating protocols for a world-transforming enterprise."[14]

The colonial cultures of the New World have two important dimensions: the pedagogical and the performative. The pedagogical dimension seeks to make America the object of knowledge, having a typological history, tradition, and origin. It worlds "America" in history and tradition by bringing it into the realm of the cognizable, into a familiar, recognizable, already inhabited and worlded world—America is located in the world and the world is located in America. More important, worlding America in this pedagogical sense consolidates a European *positioning* towards America both in terms of their relations in an expanding world system and in the colonial gaze that produces ethnographic accounts of the New World. On the other hand, the performative dimension, by "turning the scraps, patches, and rags of daily life,"[15] accumulates, records, names, renames, erases, collects, catalogues, assimilates, diarizes, and produces information and knowledge about the New World insofar as such endeavors and processes justify and consolidate the pedagogical project and affirm the colonial construction of a European self and a non-European other.

What Bhabha identifies as the "continuist, accumulative temporality of the pedagogical and the repetitious, recursive strategy of the performative"[16] profoundly influences what Kadir refers to as the "prophetic enterprise of New World culture."[17] In the drama of Euro-American encounter, history and prophecy cohabit with such promiscuity that they become almost interchangeable—history becomes something to be divined and conjectured; prophecy becomes something to be recorded and discovered. History, Kadir observes, "as constellations of prefigurations, comprises the study of typology"; and prophecy, "as precognition of the inevitable," a "viewpoint of eschatology," affirms the "*forthgathering* of typological promise and the *foregathering* of eschatology's last things."[18] The forthgathering of "scraps, patches, and rags" of the New World— Renaissance inquiries and Indian orature, diaries of captains and foot soldiers and songs of captives and runaways, medieval rationalities and Aztec cosmologies, slave ships and haciendas, Protestant reformations and Andean pictographs, Greek philosophies and Tupi cannibalism, plantations and Creole vernaculars, Old Testament dispensations and Mayan calendars, the *encomienda* and European anthropophagi, mestizo affiliations and mixed-blood progenies—these and many more are all turned into the "ideological scaffoldings"[19] of New World cultures. From such accumulative forthgathering a pedagogy comes to be authorized—the European burden of modernizing America. Europe's prophetic tradition can thus render Europe's refashioning of America as the final culmination of world history, whose future was already encoded in the archives of a classical Greco-Roman-Christian past.

The move from discovery to conquest involves the forthgathering of history and the foregathering of eschatology—to discover and conquer America was not just to fulfill an ancient prophecy; but also to construct a certain version of history to validate a narrative of cosmic time in which Europe would emerge as the pivotal player on the world stage and America would ratify Europe's global centrality. The cultures of the New World bear witness to the transmutation of history and prophecy as Europe worlds America: what emerges as "America" determines not just how Europe will interact with America but how Europe will begin to relate itself to its own past, to its own memories and histories. For Europe to shore up its colonial ventures in the New World, history needs to be scoured and divined in such a way as to enable Europe to advance upon the New World, occupy it, possess it, claim it, Christianize its populace, and bring civilization into its wild frontiers. It is in this sense that the "New World" can be conceptualized as a hodgepodge collection of desperate beliefs, fanciful longings, prophetic visions, grotesque dreams, political intrigues, personal vendettas, historical archives, and religious discourses that in particular ideological constellations, formed within historically specific conjunctures, give birth to and authorize multiple ideas and meanings of "America."

By building upon Kolodny's reformulation of frontier experience and using Bhabha's and Kadir's ideas to configure New World cultures, I argue that (a) in Díaz's chronicle, the social and topographical implications of how the naming and renaming of the frontier, the rugged terrain of Mesoamerica, become a form of worlding America in which the conflictual economy of colonial desire—to mythify, demythify, or rebel—is negotiated by turning writing into a form of history making with Europe as the historian; (b) in Léry's ethnography, worlding involves a European subject struggling to comprehend the incomprehensibility of the self that America discloses as Europe's unmanageable otherness; and (c) in Cabeza de Vaca's narrative, worlding embodies an inversion of colonial codes in order to affirm a "soft" cultural and religious colonialism as it turns cultural hybridity not into a sign of transgressing colonial culture but into a valuable register in which another self can be produced in order to justify the claim to conquer and obtain rewards for doing so.

Bernal Díaz del Castillo and the Frontier of Mesoamerica

The conquest of Tenochtitlán, or Mexico, by a band of Spanish explorers lead by Hernán Cortés in 1521 "provided [Europeans] their first great paradigm for European encounters with an organized native state" in the Americas.[20] It thus dramatically influenced the course of much future contact between European explorers and native peoples. Consider the case of the chronicler Fray Bernardino de Sahagún, who, although he lacked Díaz's experiential authority, devotes the twelfth and last volume of his *General History of the Things of New Spain* (also called the *Florentine Codex*) to the conquest of the Aztecs. The manuscript contains three drafts on each page: a draft in Nahuatl, written in 1569; a revised draft of the first; and a Spanish translation, completed in 1579, of the second draft. Sahagún constructs his narrative by culling accounts from numerous Indian sources, or rather informants, who witnessed the tumultuous events of 1519–21. Interestingly, in 1585 Sahagún issued a revised version of the twelfth volume. This version, referred to as the 1585 revision, contains a prologue that was absent in the first manuscript; as S. L. Cline notes, it "is essentially Sahagún's own interpretation of the conquest."[21] The revision seeks to undermine the first version's predominantly Indian point of view of the conquest, as if Sahagún is now at pains to avoid any ambiguity in justifying the Spanish siege of Tenochtitlán. The 1585 revision is "more elegant and literary,"[22] but the "perspective is completely changed"[23] as Sahagún "injects the Spanish viewpoint in the chronicle, profoundly altering the earlier account and clearly expressing his own opinion and judgement."[24] Cortés, referred to as "the most valiant captain,"[25] is recast as a man divinely ordained to spread the Christian faith in the New World, and the entire program of conquest is affirmed as fully justified given the barbarous pagan practices of the natives.[26] The history of the writing and revising of Sahagún's chronicle amply demonstrates the importance of the Spanish confrontation with the Aztecs in the historiography of New Spain.

Written about forty years after the siege of Tenochtitlán in 1521, Bernal Díaz del Castillo's *Conquest of New Spain* narrates the progress of a Spanish expedition led by Hernán Cortés, beginning with explorations in Yucatan and ending with the defeat of the Aztecs and the conquest of Mexico. These travelers do not encounter a frontier of rock-hewn terrain and unpopulated landscapes marked by pockets of Indian settlements. Rather, from the time of their arrival in Yucatan to their meeting with the Aztecs in central Mexico, the soon-to-be conquistadors confront highly developed societies of Indians, of whom the Aztecs are singularly impressive. So marvelous are the sights and sounds of this city that Díaz compares it to famous cities of exotic legend: "[They] seemed like an enchanted vision from the tale of Amadís" (Díaz, 214).[27] Tenochtitlán, like the cities of Palenque, Tikal, Tula, and Monte Albán, was a modern city bustling with urban activity.[28]

The purpose of the narrative seems simple enough: Díaz, the chronicler, wants to testify as an "honest eyewitness without twisting the facts in any way" the "adventures that befell [the Spaniards] and the heroic deeds [they] performed during the conquest of New Spain" (Díaz, 14). Díaz believes that other chroniclers, including Bartolomé de Las Casas, Gonzalo de Illescas, and particularly Francisco López de Gómara, had not related the tumultuous events in Mesoamerica[29] with an eye toward historical accuracy. It is thus his moral imperative to broaden their narrow perspectives and provide an account of what *really* happened in the New World. Gómara, in the dedication to his biography of Cortés, presents the conquistador as solely responsible for the conquest: "Long live, then, the name and memory of him who conquered so vast a land, converted such a multitude of men, cast down so many idols, and put an end to so much sacrifice and the eating of human flesh."[30] Gómara begins his narrative with Cortés's birth and ends with his death; the man, not the conquest, is his most important focus, leading Lesley Byrd Simpson to conclude that Gómara is "consciously writing a prose epic and that virtually everything in the book [is] designed with this end in view."[31] Gómara thus mythifies Cortés, and in so doing neglects, according to Díaz, the significant roles played by several other soldiers, including himself, in executing Spain's imperial mission. The fact that Cortés "never did anything without first inquiring our opinion" amply proves how much he relied on chiefs and lieutenants like himself, notes Díaz (Díaz, 204). Thus, in his prologue the singular yields to the plural as he notes that he intends to "extol the adventures that befell *us*, and the heroic deeds *we* performed during the conquest of New Spain and its provinces *in the company* of that valiant and enterprising captain, Don Hernando Cortés" (Díaz, 14; emphasis added). But despite an important focus of Díaz's impulse, as an "honest eyewitness," being on demythifying Gómara's Cortés, this shift from the singular to the plural also signals, as Rolena Adorno perceptively notes, the "intersection between written history, law, and eyewitness testimony."[32]

Díaz wrote his chronicle in order to justify Spanish colonization of the Americas and, quite specifically, to claim the rewards due to him for his deep involvement in extending the empire from the Iberian peninsula to Mesoamerica. His account began as a *probanza*, a legal document submitted by petitioners to stake a claim, in this case his right to an encomienda, a grant of land and Indian labor in the Americas. As he becomes increasingly embroiled in producing his probanza, he is compelled to account for his narrative exposition of the conquest not only as a writer but as a historian—he has to produce before the court eyewitnesses who can testify to the probanza. As the probanza soon extends into a long narrative about the conquest, Díaz changes the singular to the plural, something which the document he was working on in Guatemala (referred to as the Guatemala manuscript) nicely demonstrates, observes Adorno.[33] Díaz's demythification of Gómara's Cortés is thus not a clear-cut instance of a desire to give voice to marginalized players in the conquest.[34]

In addition, there is a tension in the narrative between Díaz's desire to report as accurately as possible, without exaggeration and rhetorical embellishment, the realities of the New World and the manner in which this desire is constantly undermined by his propensity to make sense of what he experiences through the dominant ideologies of his time. But while contesting Gómara's representation of Cortés, Díaz's text also participates in what Pastor Bodmer calls the "discourse of mythification." It is precisely this tension between an avowed desire for historical accuracy and rhetorical indulgence, between demythification and the nagging propensity to engage in mythification, that I want to underscore as the worlding of the New World.

Worlding, to quote Spivak's definition again, "is the reinscription of a cartography that must (re) present itself as impeccable" on an assumedly "uninscribed earth," which "is the condition of the worlding of a world."[35] The worlding of America that we find in Díaz's account (and in Léry's and Cabeza de Vaca's narratives, which I shall soon discuss) is not so much an attempt at a direct, straightforward exercise of colonial power as it is an elliptical, contradictorily inflected negotiation with the conflictual economy of colonial desire. To put it another way, these writers set up for themselves a few agendas in their narratives. But at several places these agendas clash and threaten to undermine the subversive potential of another critical agenda. How they deal with such impasses is at the heart of my argument: they begin to world the New World by *managing the contradictions* of their narratives. What they gain is a certain kind of centrality—the centrality of their narratives, their histories, Christian Spain, and, more generally, European thought and culture.

Whether they are successful in consolidating this centrality is a different question, though an important one. To be sure, Tzvetan Todorov, in a related context, contends that Cortés did demonstrate an "art of adaptation and improvisation" that enabled him to manage and control the codes of communication with the Aztecs successfully and consequently subdue them;[36] however, that they would even attempt to engage in improvisation points to those "ideological discourses of modernity that attempt to give a hegemonic 'normality' to the uneven and the differential."[37] To world the New World is to produce an impeccable discourse of Euro-American encounters, a discourse that normalizes the differential and thus brings into the realm of prophecy and historical truth that which threatens to disclose the incoherent, recidivistic character of Europe's transoceanic missions. To Enrique Dussel, such strategies of management bespeak large-scale endeavors in the sixteenth century to create a world system with a center-periphery dynamic that implicitly and explicitly positions Europe at the center.[38] Much is at stake for Díaz, Léry, and Cabeza de Vaca; much is at stake, indeed, for modernity in the Americas.

Let me elaborate, with reference to Díaz, a particular instance of worlding: the naming and renaming of the frontier to authorize a colonial cartography. Several times in the narrative we find Díaz describing in detail skirmishes with Indians; discoveries of other Spaniards who had come before them (including the shipwrecked Jerónimo de Aguilar, who eventually becomes Cortés's translator) and were rumored to have been marooned on unknown islands; and sickness, death, or fortuitous happenings. On Francisco Hernández de Córdoba's earlier expedition to Yucatan, in which Díaz participated, the explorers are met by hospitable Indians who give them food and shelter and invite them to their houses. The Spaniards decide to call the place Cape Catoche, after an Indian word for "invitation" (Díaz, 18). After sailing for fifteen days from Cape Catoche, they anchor their ships and go ashore on St. Lazarus's Sunday. For this reason they name the place Lázaro, although "the proper Indian name for it is Campeche" (Díaz, 20). When the Indian warriors at Champoton attack them and inflict heavy losses, they rename the place La Costa de Mala Pelea (the Coast of the Evil Battle) (24). When they discover that what they had thought to be a river is really a harbor, they name the place Boca de Términos (Boundary Bay) (Díaz, 30). Later, on an expedition with Juan de Grijalva, when they come to the Tabasco River, named after the Indian chief of Tabasco, the Spaniards rename the place Río de Grijalva because Juan de Grijalva was the "discoverer" (Díaz, 31). When they see female idols in Indian places of worship, they call the place Punta de las Mujeres (Cape of the Women) (Díaz, 66). These and many other examples in the text demonstrate the manner in which the Spaniards name (when they do not know the name of a place, or it does not have one) and rename (when they do know the name but choose to give a new one). At several points in the narrative, immediately after mentioning a new name that has been given, Díaz makes observations such as "and it is so marked on the charts" (Díaz, 37) and "so it is still named on the charts" (Díaz, 18). It does not take a leap of faith to assume that these charts are the maps and topographic notations created and used by the Spaniards, not the ones made by the natives. This practice of naming gains added significance given that the Aztecs had their own ways of charting and mapping Mesoamerica. At least twice in the narrative we see Moctezuma, to clarify the Spaniards' questions regarding specific locations of Indian tribes, mountain ranges, and rivers, asking for a cloth or tapestry on which local topography is inscribed.

To observe, as Díaz does, forty years after the conquest, that "it is so marked on the charts" points to the possessive, appropriative nature of the practice of naming and the manner in which his narrative gains official status as an authoritative historical "document." Far from being a mere substitution of one map for another, the practice of naming participates in the mythification of the frontier, the strange world of Mesoamerica, insofar as it redraws the topography of the New World in ways that privilege European experiences and perspectives while effacing and delegitimizing Indian presence and history. Several things are happening here: the frontier is becoming less an inhospitable terrain and more a familiar entity, i.e., domesticated; the maps and charts drawn by the Spaniards are gaining official status as historical records and authoritative sources of New World history; and Indian presence and worldviews are either losing their validity or simply being erased from "official" history.

Naming, renaming, writing, and historicizing—these are the axial principles of Díaz's worlding of Mesoamerica; it is in and through the process of naming that writing and history emerge as discursive acts of power. Writing can emerge as a "will to power," Michel de Certeau emphasizes, because it generates an archive that, in its accumulative and citational register, which is also a form of repetition, can produce history. "With writing," de Certeau notes, "the Westerner has a sword in his hand which will extend its gesture but *never* modify its subject. . . . *It is tautological, immunized against both any alterity that might transform it and whatever dares to resist it.*"[39] How does this relate to Díaz's worlding of America?

We have already noted that naming domesticates the frontier, consolidates a Eurocentric worldview, effaces native presence, and embeds the chronicle in the realm of history. Texts—Díaz's own writing and numerous other charts and maps that embody naming and renaming—while seeking to record the past, end up as historicized objects, that is, historical documents. Notice that Díaz is writing his chronicle more than forty years after the fall of Tenochtitlán. While he may possess a fantastic memory, what is important is that his recourse to memory and his attempt to record it in writing involve the production of a narrative—the ordering, selecting, and sifting of things, events, peoples, and ideas and the frequent reading and citation of numerous other documents, maps, and letters, all having to do with the act of writing history. When he notes that what he and his fellow explorers did forty years earlier is "still on the charts," the writer becomes a historian: he consults texts, which he himself and others like him have written, in order to engage in a process of historical verification and, thus, truth telling. What emerges, then, is the practice of writing as the practice of history making; it is writing as the production of history, America's history, with Europe as the historian.

The impeccability of such a worlding is the deliberate attempt to normalize any kind of alterity that can "transform" and "resist it"—the other's names, the other's languages, the other's worldviews, the other's histories, the other's historical presence. This is why writing in the New World becomes a force of violence. As José Rabasa perceptively notes, "The concept of writing violence comprises both the representation of massacres, tortures, rapes, and other forms of material terror, as well as categories and concepts informing the *representation of territories for conquest*, the definition of Indian cultures as inferior, and the *constitution of colonized subjectivities*.[40] In Díaz we have an artful spinning of discourses and names in which the role of the European subject as recorder, as truth maker, as producer of history is, in the larger scheme of New World enterprise and culture, discursively consolidated in the very act of rendering the New World cartographically. To represent the fourth world is to generate a knowledge that is already riven with a colonial desire to contain the strangeness of Mesoamerica within a logic of calculation that enables Spain to advance upon the New World by rendering it a tabula rasa—a land without history, a people without writing. That will to power and mastery, that anxious desire to resist transformation by managing alterity, is what makes Díaz's chronicle, in its gestures of naming and renaming, emerge as an impeccable worlding of New World frontiers.

I am not arguing that the entire text, the chronicle in all its textual modalities, instantiates this kind of worlding. As Inga Clendinnen pointedly observes in disagreeing with Tzvetan Todorov's argument that the Spaniards improvised and masterfully controlled communication between themselves and the natives, by the time the Aztec empire falls, the siege and final destruction of Tenochtitlán demonstrate the opposite— "a terrifying, terminal demonstration of 'otherness,' and of its practical and cognitive *unmanageability.*"[41] In destroying what it so ardently desires, the conquest yet again confronts what it has sought to codify and contain, suppress, and efface—alterity, the presence of the other. Thus, what I have argued about the impeccability of naming and renaming should be read in relation to those other instances where, as Clendinnen points out, the management of alterity becomes unmanageable. Because they mark the forked articulation of modernity's dreams, the syntactical dislocation in the New World's dissonant imaginary, these moments of impeccability and unmanageability should be viewed as "the half-hidden stress points in the official structures, the tensions, ideological negotiations and rifts" in the discourses of colonialism.[42]

In such a conceptualization of New World frontiers, we perceive a shift in the idea of the frontier, from a geographical entity lying outside the boundaries of civilization to an overlapping of "contact zones," which Mary Louise Pratt describes as "social spaces where disparate cultures meet, clash, and grapple with each other, often in highly asymmetrical relations of domination and subordination—like colonialism, slavery, or their aftermaths as they are lived out across the globe today."[43] The frontier becomes a "zone of interpenetration"[44] and interpretation where the realities of the New World are not recorded in a transparent system of representation so much as its landscapes are charted and mapped in ways that privilege European experiences and languages.

These zones of interpenetration become discursive sites for interpreting the other and the unfamiliar in asymmetrical moments of contact. The writings produced in these zones by chroniclers like Díaz are not just exhaustive descriptions of Mesoamerican life but descriptions whose processes of ordering and selecting people and events to be described are inextricably linked to the overall purpose of the imperial expedition and the chronicle: to "conquer and convert,"[45] which was, comments Francis Jennings, a "propaganda" that "took standard form as ideology with conventional assumptions and semantics."[46] This is the overarching framework within which Díaz wants his readers to situate his chronicle.

Unlike his Spanish counterpart's travelogue, which attempts a systematic and impeccable worlding of the New World, Jean de Léry's *History of a Voyage to the Land of Brazil, Otherwise Called America* (1578) falls short of mastering America. This is not because he or his French compatriots are a kinder, gentler people than the Spaniards, but because the system of resemblances that Léry constructs, the ethnographic discourses that he generates to make intelligible the otherness of the Tupi, or Tupinambas, are not able to render impeccable the fundamental ambivalence that structures frontier experiences.

Léry's chronicle questions the assumption that in the drama of Old World–New World contact, America is the psychosocial, material terrain upon which Europe inscribes its consciousness. Instead of asking only, What happened to America when Europeans landed on its shores? Léry raises another set of questions: What impact did America have on European consciousness? How did the discovery of America alter and challenge European conceptions of the world? How did Europe assimilate America, and with what results for both Europe and America?[47]

These questions open up a discursive terrain that necessitates an intercontinental approach to study Euro-American contact. My analysis of Léry's text is somewhat Janus-faced because I situate the chronicle in the nexus of the shaping forces of Calvinism, the St. Bartholomew's Day Massacre, and the "many-stranded spiral of discourse the discovery of America engendered, and which profoundly transformed both

America and Europe in the sixteenth century."[48] I take up two specific aspects of Léry's worlding of America: sociocultural transplantation and comparative relativism.

In using European categories of thought, in frequently juxtaposing French manners and customs with Tupi culture, and in using a language of metaphor and synecdoche to bring, for his European audience, the otherness of the Amerindians into the realm of the cognizable, Léry begins to "invent" an America, not simply represent it. As he moves systematically from chapter to chapter with an ethnographer's eye for observation and with "zoological precision,"[49] Léry details the first impressions of the Tupi on the French explorers and ends with their return to France after a stay of about eighteen months in Brazil. Such is the power of Léry's observant eye that, to Frank Lestringant, this French adventurer is "able to create an illusion of reality without equal among Renaissance voyagers."[50] Léry begins by sketching out in some detail the physical appearance of the Tupi, their colorful feathered regalia, tonsured heads, pierced chins, and bracelets, and their indifference to nakedness. Léry also comments on the manner in which the Tupi prepare their food and cook and eat it, and on their ingenious ways of using a variety of plants and shrubs for making oils and fermented drinks (Léry, 69–77).[51] In addition, he describes the shape and texture of the flowers, seeds, fruits, and leaves of various trees and plants and discusses the appearance of several animals, birds, and "other monstrous beasts," including lizards, snakes, bats, gnats, bees, and parrots (Léry, 78).

One of the most fascinating descriptions in Léry's text is the chapter on war and cannibalism, an issue I address later. Other chapters focus on marriage, child rearing, property management, laws, civic responsibility, illness, death, and burial. Léry also includes a colloquy between himself and some Tupi in which their dialogues on European and Tupi society are rendered in the native language of the Tupi accompanied by translations in French (Léry, 178–95). Like a grammarian, Léry identifies certain Tupi words and phrases and studies them in a comparative context to give readers some understanding of Tupi grammar and syntax. He renders his notes on singular, plural, and case forms and on adverbs, verbs, imperatives, and participles in the native tongue more accessible for his readers by providing examples for his descriptions of word formations and language use among the Tupi (Léry, 178–95). Léry then recounts the privations suffered by the explorers on their return to France and their acclimatization to the French weather and environment, and ends his chronicle by emphasizing the omnipotence of God, his graciousness in rescuing them from death, and his faithfulness in restoring them to their families.[52]

In the strategies of representation that Léry uses to render a strange, other New World in familiar terms, we begin to see the process of worlding America. Often, as Léry describes the plants and herbs that are grown and eaten by the Tupi, he draws attention to the plants grown in France and stresses that the land of Brazil is fertile because the vines "that we transplanted took very well and put forth fine very fine stalks and leaves, *clearly showing the bounty and fertility of the country*" (Léry, 72; emphasis added). In describing the vessels that the Tupi use to store their beverages, Léry compares them to the vats used for laundry in Bourbonnais (Léry, 73). The natives, writes Léry, concoct *caouin*, a "cloudy and thick beverage," and "they have it in both red and white, *just as we do our wine*" (Léry, 74; emphasis added). Regarding animals, Léry comments that there is absolutely nothing in Brazil that "is in all respects exactly like any of ours" (Léry, 78). The *touous* (lizards) are like the lizards in France except that they are gray and not green as they are in France; further, "all these animals are strangely *defective with respect to those of Europe*" (Léry, 85; emphasis added).

The New World's fertility is evidently construed in terms of the effects of transplanting European flora and fauna onto an unfamiliar terrain. As these examples demonstrate, to describe something from the New World, Léry will often compare it to and contrast it with a term, thing, or person familiar to his European readers. In the New World frontier, Léry begins to construct structures of similitudes and dissimilitudes to fashion a vocabulary of juxtapositions—of similes, memories, artifacts, myths, and metaphors. As Peter Mason comments, by Léry's using a "system of resemblances," an "exegetic apparatus is imposed on the New World to assimilate it to the *closed circle* of words and things."[53] What we have here is a fortification of European centrality to codify America's use value—making the New World a garden by transplanting European practices. Such is his desire to authorize an impeccable world-ing of America that in chapter after chapter Léry refuses to move beyond the "closed circle" of the familiar and the known. In so doing he is able to "deny to America its own historicity" and "reduce its alterity to a familiar form that is accessible to the self."[54] What happens, however, when Léry's strategies of juxtaposition lose their representational authority? In his straining to describe America, what if Europe no longer affords a stable ontology to fashion a New World episteme? How does Léry deal with those moments of cognitive dissonance when his circle of juxtapositions threatens to implode as its whorls begin to spin not circularly but elliptically, disjointedly? When this happens, the consequences for this ethnographer and his episteme are deeply unsettling.

At one point in his narrative, Léry flusters: "But their gestures and expressions are so *completely different from ours,* that it is difficult, I confess, to represent them well *by writing or by pictures*" (Léry, 67; emphasis added). Discussing the way in which the Tupi women chew certain roots and millet, spit the chewed matter into their palms, collect it, and cook it to brew their special concoction, caouin, Léry informs readers that they may find the practice disgusting. Immediately, however, he warns those who experience revulsion on reading this passage that in France the winemakers tread and crush grapes in large tubs with their feet, adding, "on this point one custom is as good as another" (Léry, 77). The impulse here is to call into question the parameters by which his European audience may judge the Tupi as primitive or modern peoples. Ostensibly relativistic arguments of this kind are also made when discussing the childbearing practices of the Tupi. Upon giving birth, the women of Brazil, unlike the "dainty ladies" of France, resume their daily domestic chores both inside and outside the house within days (Léry, 154–55). Léry also notes that although the Tupi, unlike the French, do not swaddle newborn infants to avoid deformity or bowleggedness,

Tupi children do not develop any kind of deformity. Without seeming to make an issue of such French practices, Léry pokes fun at his readers' lack of critical acumen (Léry, 155).

However, in his discussion of cannibalism the anchoring of the New World discourse in a Eurocentric episteme begins to come unhinged as that earlier sense of mastery, of impeccability, evident in his exegetic worlding of America turns out to be a mere rhetorical ploy; the chronicle has only been masquerading as an ethnographic treatise. When Léry, like Díaz, notices that "side by side with manifestations of undeniable moral greatness are signs of extreme barbarity" that point to the "disconcerting ambiguity" of New World cultures, how does Léry's negotiation with this "deep contradiction"[55] differ from Díaz's rationalization of the contradiction as yet another instance of Amerindian primitivism? Indeed, the more this ethnographer ponders an anthropophagous America, the more he is compelled to acknowledge European cannibalistic proclivities even as he reckons with Europe as an invention, a form of textual affiliation to culture, identity, place, gender, religion, ideology, and memory.

Cannibalism among the Tupi, observes Léry, cannot be interpreted as a definite sign that they are less human and more animal-like than they first appear to be, especially in light of his account of their cultural and religious practices. In a surprising move of self-reflection, he points to the practice of cruelty and cannibalism in medieval Europe and asks his readers whether they, as Europeans and products of a medieval past, have the right, observing the practice among the Tupi, to judge them to be inhuman (Léry, 132). Instances such as these may lead us to consider Léry a social reformer like Bartolomé de Las Casas, intent on resisting the savagery and unchecked greed of the explorers and striving to establish a system of accountability. But what are we to make of his arguments regarding religious and cultural relativism? What relation do these arguments have to my earlier comment about Léry's growing sense of Europe as an imagined community, a form of social and textual affiliation? The chronicle's treatment of cannibalism marks Léry's growing inability to sustain a European cosmogony so as to impeccably world a different, other America. That system of resemblances that he had relied on for so long threatens to implode as his ethnographic production of "America" unravels a long history of Europe's self-invention and material and epistemologically violent self-fortification.

When Léry warns his readers not to conclude that the Tupi are more despicable than Europeans by reminding them that "one need not go beyond one's own country, nor as far as America, to see such monstrous and prodigious things" (Léry, 133), his immediate reference is to the long series of religious wars that erupted in France in the middle of the sixteenth century as the Catholics sought to contain the growing influence of the Huguenots, French Protestants, who, under the tutelage of John Calvin in Geneva, Switzerland, began to embark on a program of evangelization. In 1572 two events in quick succession started a chain reaction of bloody reprisals and massacres between Catholics and Protestants. On August 18 , King Charles IX's sister, Marguerite de Valois, and Henri de Navarre, a Protestant, were married; and on August 24, St. Bartholomew's Day (St. Bartholomew was the patron saint of butchers), Gaspard de Coligny, admiral of France and a popular Protestant leader, was murdered and his body was dismembered and displayed publicly. A murderous rampage followed, with Catholics murdering Protestants by the thousands and plundering their houses and businesses.[56] These killings, generally referred to as the St. Bartholomew's Day Massacre, are to Léry as incomprehensible and despicable as the cannibalism of the Tupi.

Generally, discussions of cannibalism refer to accounts by noncannibalistic people describing the acts of those who practice cannibalism. More often than not it is a European who witnesses or hears about this practice among non-Europeans, thus leading him or her to assume that cannibalism was a non-European affair, revolting to the European reporter.[57] Hans Askenasy, however, observes that cannibalism was reported to have occurred during famines dating back to the eleventh century in Europe, Asia, Africa, and America.[58] While not denying that certain peoples actually did practice cannibalism, William Arens argues that the entire gamut of eyewitness accounts, travel reportage, anthropological writings, and treatises on cannibalism for the last few hundred years, and the meanings we attribute to cannibalism today, are "boundless displays of interpretive fancy" in which the figure of the naked savage hovers eerily "on the horizon of the Western world."[59] This much-needed caveat draws our attention to the exaggerations (both subtle and overt), ideological agendas, and fanciful ideas that embody eyewitness accounts and reports of cannibalism, and to the myth-making tendencies of various interpreters and readers. The crucial point is that cannibalism is not an exclusively non-European affair. The issue of cannibalism, comments Peter Hulme, is central "to the whole question of Western attitudes towards [an] understanding of non-Western cultures."[60] However, the cannibalism of the Aztecs, Incas, Tupi, and Iroquois of the Americas operated on a systematic level, incorporating a wide spectrum of attitudes towards worship, gods, death, dead bodies, and fertility. It was not gastronomic cannibalism, the consumption of human flesh as a delicacy, a special food. It was not survival cannibalism, the reliance on the flesh of dead bodies for sustenance when, due to a sudden and unforeseen event, all normal food resources had been depleted. Rather, as practiced by certain Indian tribes in the Americas, it was ritual cannibalism, in which the entire community participated. Cannibalism was common enough to be part of the quotidian reality of these tribes; it provided a meaningful structure for understanding the world at large and their role in it.[61]

Far from affirming Tupi cannibalism as legitimate and therefore condonable, Léry emphasizes, writes Janet Whatley, that "cannibalism is first and foremost ritual—a socially interpretable act," which "if not redeemable" is "at least tolerable to contemplate."[62] And in comparing the Tupi ritual to instances of mutilation during the Massacre, Léry is not affirming a hermeneutic practice in which all moral judgments are deemed illegitimate and rendered superfluous. Recognizing that his fellow Europeans are capable of atrocious treatment of flesh, which he witnessed firsthand as a Calvinist in France, Léry does seem reluctant to dismiss the Tupi as pagan brutes. In his essay "Of Cannibals," Michel Eyquem de Montaigne, Léry's contemporary, makes a strong case for viewing the cannibals of America as inhabitants of a golden age "still very close to their original simplicity" and living in a "state of purity" with "so little artifice and solder."[63] Speaking specifically about their practice of eating human flesh, Montaigne warns his readers to refrain from passing harsh judgment lest "whilst rightly judging their errors, we should be so blind to our own."[64] Evidently, like Léry, Montaigne refers to the Massacre and finds the killing and mutilation of people, dead and alive, "under the cloak of piety and religion"[65] as reprehensible as the Tupi's more organized and systematic man-eating rituals.

Three important issues emerge from Léry's and Montaigne's discussion of Tupi cannibalism: the inability to make absolute judgments regarding the other while using ethnocentric frames of reference; the Tupi's close affinity with Nature and their tremendous intuitive capabilities, an idea that Montaigne validates by appealing to the myth of the Golden Age; and the demystifying of cannibalism by questioning its singular association with non-European peoples and seeking to ground the practice in more generalized phenomena of war or famine. In chapter 22, "Of the Extreme Famine, Tempests, and Other Dangers from Which God Delivered Us as We Were Returning to France," in describing their near-shipwreck due to a leak and their starvation due to water and food shortage, Léry seems most concerned with thanking God from saving them from the pangs of hunger, "which can truly be called a kind of madness" that can lead to cannibalism (Léry, 213). The focus here, as Léry acknowledges his fellow Europeans' susceptibility to resorting to cannibalism when there is no other food, seems to offset chapter 15's singular focus on Tupi cannibalism.

But here is another possibility: Maybe we have misunderstood the central purpose of this ethnographer's fascinating experience; maybe his transoceanic journey has little to do with discovering and conquering a New World; maybe his perplexing concern is to reaffirm particular beliefs and practices of the Old World, to accomplish which he had to travel the oceans, cast his epistemological anchors in distant seas, and cultivate a double gaze. It is worth considering how and why these maybes may be related to the semantic incoherence created by the syntactical dislocations in his New World episteme.

Let me stretch this line of thinking a little: in Léry's transcontinental drama of belief and heresy, commitment and betrayal, revolving around historians, admirals, ethnographers, and theologians, the anthropophagous Tupi are characters who have their entrances and exits. This is to say not that the focus on Tupi cannibalism is of incidental concern to the chronicler, but that cannibalism becomes the central problem for French overseas expansion and Christian theology because in the ethnographic mirror that Léry constructs to represent the other, what becomes reflected is a double gaze—the gaze of the other and the gaze of the self in the other. America is not just the flip side of Europe, or Europe in a different guise. To comprehend the "kind of gaze and conscience that emerge in the face of the other,"[66] Léry cannot have recourse to European philosophies or Old Testament theology. Indeed, even Calvinism becomes a set of beliefs that individuals can profess to affirm and deny in ways that Léry finds hypocritical. In chapter 16, as theological differences sharpen in New France between Villegagnon and Léry regarding the Eucharist, the chronicler notes:

> For although they rejected the transubstantiation of the Roman Church, as an opinion which they openly said was stupid and absurd, and although they did not approve of consubstantiation either . . . they remained obstinate; to the point that, without knowing how it might be done, nevertheless they wanted not only to eat the flesh of Jesus Christ grossly rather than spiritually, but what was worse, like the savages named *Ouetaca*, of whom I have already spoken, they wanted to chew and swallow it raw. (Léry, 40–41; emphasis in original)

Given Léry's awareness of European instances of extreme mutilation, noted above, what is the significance of this passage? Léry can no longer rely on Christianity, in particular Calvinism, to position the peoples of the fourth world in a cosmic order, a universal history. These are not just Europeans who are wont to engage in cannibalism; these are Calvinists who have become papists—therein, for this ethnographer, lies the rub, the most disconcerting rub of all. When he confidently proclaims in the dedication that the narrative was written "for the express purpose of establishing the pure service of God, *both among the French who had retreated there, and among the savages*[67] *living in that land*" (Léry, xli; emphasis added), it becomes clear that right from the beginning of the voyage to its end, Christian recidivism and Tupi paganism are inextricably linked. How to make the connection between the propensity of members of the reformed religion to backslide and partake in Catholic Holy Communion and the unstable position of the Tupi in a Christian and classical idea of world history despite their anthropophagous nature becomes his *History's* central concern. The crucial link between the sinners and the pagans is not that they both engage in cannibalism but that they engage in cannibalism *as a ritual*—this marks the fundamental moment of dissonance in Léry's treatise because it presents an "inferior and distorting mirror of the chief sacrament of the Christian religion."[68]

Survival cannibalism was something that Léry and his crewmates came close to engaging in; ritual cannibalism was the one defining feature that positioned the other outside God's fold. Ritual is the pattern by which life's exigencies and discontinuities become intelligible. It binds together the earthly and the divine, the phenomenal and the experiential. If to the Tupi cannibalism was a ritualized form of socialization, to the reformed Christians in New France the blood and body of Christ signaled an aporia—transubstantiation or consubstantiation, Protestant reform or Catholic dogma.[69] But, and this is the crux of the issue, they did it "without knowing how it might be done." No longer, then, are we left with a European subject struggling to comprehend the otherness of the other. It is the incomprehensibility of the self that America discloses as Europe's unmanageable otherness, which returns as the gaze of the other.

Whether it was in understanding the nature of the world, in mapping its geographical contours, in apprehending the rich natural world of plant and animal life, in making a taxonomy of it, or in bringing the savage Indian into the realm of the human, America distorted and re-framed

Europe's relationship to antiquity and to the Judeo-Christian tradition, even as its meaning and significance began to emerge in the very intersection of the rediscovery of these traditions and the discovery of a fourth world.[70] Hugh Honour goes further when he notes that Europe began to "project [its] own aspirations and fears, [its] self-confidence and sometimes [its] guilty despair" onto America.[71] The point is not that America is entirely a figment of the European imagination; rather, it is that a study of America reveals less a thing-in-itself and more a gamut of overlapping and mutually influencing narratives and discourses embodying the working out of the tensions and contradictions of Europe's angles of vision toward the classical past and the Christian tradition.

In pointing to the Renaissance, Calvinism, and the St. Bartholomew's Day Massacre as the matrix that shapes the chronicle's narrative exposition of New World encounters, I am not arguing that Léry's text, in a brilliant deconstructive move, undercuts it own worlding of America. To argue as I have done here that his chronicle cannot sustain an impeccable worlding of frontier experience is to understand why the heterology of his New World episteme pulses with heterotopic desire and demand, estrangement and fantasy. To be sure, Léry finds Tupi beliefs and practices very strange, but he is more interested in what makes them strange to a European like him. However, this does not mean that we can view Léry's *History* as primarily concerned with demythifying the New World. Rather, Léry's narrative traverses an uneven, ever-shifting interpretive terrain. It does not so much affirm the humanity of the other as it dramatizes the tenuousness of the critical parameters by which notions of humanity and community, America and Europe, self and other are constructed. To Léry, negotiating the otherness of America means being estranged from the norms and values of the familiar. There is a certain paradox in this estrangement: Europe loses its normative hegemony even as the strange world of America becomes increasingly and uncannily familiar. It is this sense of estrangement in travel, of a partial and momentary loss of mastery, of implosive anxiety that turns the chronicle's worlding of America into a polymerous locution of New

World experience. However, Álvar Núñez Cabeza de Vaca's *Relación* moves even further: it subverts the codes of colonialism in the Americas. What such an inverted subversion entails in terms of worlding America is the question I take up next.

The Model Conqueror of New Spain

Relación is an uncommon discovery narrative. Where Díaz displays the arrogance of the conquistador and shows no modesty in boasting of the heroism of the Spaniards in their siege of Tenochtitlán, and where Léry demonstrates a self-reflective disposition interested less in pillaging the New World and more in pondering the philosophical implications of cross-cultural contact, Cabeza de Vaca[72] chronicles the experience of a group of Spaniards who set out to conquer the fourth world in the name of God and king, and fail.[73]

The chronicle tells how, in 1528, nearly six hundred explorers, led by Pánfilo de Narváez,[74] set sail to explore Florida. After a series of miscalculations and shipwrecks, they end up as castaways in south Texas, where the land is dry, water is scarce, and, much to their chagrin, there is no gold. In 1536 the four who are left—Cabeza de Vaca, Andrés Dorantes, Alonso del Castillo Maldonado, and an Arab, Estevanico—arrive in Tenochtitlán, from which they later journey back to Spain. In their eight years as castaways, the men had traversed the coastal areas of Texas, traveled into its southwestern regions, and, after walking the trail leading into northern Mexico, finally reached the Spanish garrisons in the capital of the former Aztec empire.[75] They had made the journey, a "pedestrian tour" of about three thousand miles, observes Cleve Hallenbeck, by following Indian trails and pathways, and sometimes by charting their own routes.[76] *Relación* revived the interest of explorers, including Fray Marcos de Niza and Francisco Vásquez de Coronado, who traveled into Arizona and New Mexico, and Francisco de Ibarra, who traveled into the northern regions of Chihuahua.[77] It was also, for its humane portrayal of the Amerindians and for the pacifist attitude of Cabeza de Vaca, often cited approvingly by writers like Bartolomé de las

Casas and El Inca Garcilaso de la Vega, who initiated reformist campaigns to contain the growing atrocities perpetrated on the Amerindians by the Spaniards. Such was the impact of the four Spaniards' deeds and activities that they even became part of Amerindian lore and legend.[78] The most puzzling issue in the chronicle is the change in the attitudes of the would-be conquistadors, who begin their expedition with the sole intention of conquering the Amerindians and end up defending them against Spanish colonizers. *Relación* narrates "not the seamless, triumphant story of Castilian expedition and conquest but rather a tale of both mundane and momentous expeditionary challenges."[79] These aspects "have made it symbolize the benevolent and paradigmatic encounter of two worlds," thus making it the "prototype of expeditions" called "acts of pacification."[80] What explains this change in attitude? How can we put into perspective Cabeza de Vaca's tendency, in relating his experiences to the king, to refer to the vast stretches of dry land he encountered as "visions of wealth"? How can we explain this about-face, which Rolena Adorno calls an "interpretive gap"?[81] What is the nature of such a worlding of America, in which there is a fundamental inversion of imperial Spain's colonial codes?

The *razonamiento* (reasoning) Adorno offers is to situate these tendencies in the context of the "process of cultural adaptation" into which these explorers are compelled to immerse themselves so as to avoid the risk of being killed by their Amerindian hosts. Positioned in between Indians and Europeans, these mediators become "keys or catalysts to intertribal exchange,"[82] thus endangering the mission to conquer and colonize. As they perform the roles of servants, slaves, traders, and shamans in and between different warring native tribes, Cabeza de Vaca and his three companions become mediators and interpreters of European and Amerindian social mores and beliefs to the natives, on the one hand, and to the encroaching conquistadors, on the other. As professional traders, Cabeza de Vaca and his companions move from one group of Indians to another selling and exchanging their wares—seashells, cockles, shell beads, hides, and red ochre. Soon, at the insistence of the Indians, they are asked to pray for a sick man, who, much to their astonishment, becomes well. Forced to play the roles of medicine men or shamans, the explorers develop reputations as miracle-working "children of the sun" (Cabeza de Vaca, 165)[83] and end up using native credulity to their own advantage. Observing that shamans are often deferred to, provided with food and shelter, and given the respect due chiefs and leaders, Cabeza de Vaca soon perfects his role and begins to enjoy the material and psychological comforts of being a shaman: "[I]n boldness and daring to perform any cure I was the most notable among them" (Cabeza de Vaca, 165). Here, native credulity and superstitiousness are implicitly regarded as definitive signs of Amerindian primitiveness and therefore backwardness; unlike the natives, the Spaniards are viewed as humans possessed of a higher intellect. This assumption, though, is soon undermined when Cabeza de Vaca realizes that the natives embellish the mystical powers of the European shamans as a way of dealing with intertribal antagonisms and threats of war and robbery: "[All] these Indians are very fond of tales and very deceitful, *particularly when they are pursuing some gain*" (Cabeza de Vaca, 205; emphasis added). As a mediator, Cabeza de Vaca is unable to maintain clear divisions between colonizer and colonized, manipulator and manipulated. It is one thing to realize that his reputation as a healer is partly a result of naive gossip and rumor; it is another thing to acknowledge that such gossiping and rumormongering are a deliberate attempt by the natives to negotiate tribal rivalry by using the Spaniards to deflect and redirect ancient animosities. There is a pivotal lesson here that does not go unlearned by this "benign" conquistador—the heterology of native resistance and agency. This conquistador's problem is not that he has lost his European civilization and is now in the company of barbarians. It is something more vexatious—he is unable to sustain the very notions of civilization and barbarity that had propelled him to undertake the mission to explore and claim the fourth world for the crown. The exercise of colonial power, as Bhabha has astutely emphasized, can sometimes be fundamentally ambivalent because its authority is constantly disrupted by the native subject, who both fulfills and undercuts the desire of the colonizer. The relationships between colonizer and colonized are not oriented entirely in a way that will benefit the colonizer, for colonial power is not easily and predictably directed at the native in order to obtain complete subjugation. What links the colonizer and the colonized is an odd, disjunctive circulation of affective force and desire that often threatens to undermine the logic of rule and conquest, the impulse to civilize and domesticate.[84]

As he becomes the most notable of shamans, Cabeza de Vaca finds himself not so much transforming into a shaman as playing a role in a cultural game that the natives ostensibly believe in as a religious ritual. Thus, his Christian beliefs remain firmly intact even as he goes native, so to speak. But what undermines his role-playing is not an awareness of his incapability so much as it is the "look of surveillance" that "returns as the displacing gaze of the disciplined."[85] Notice that it is not until Cabeza de Vaca can play the game that he can rest assured in his secret knowledge that being a shaman is a sham. This secret knowledge makes him a more enlightened person than the natives, who believe that the shaman is divinely inspired and has true healing powers. What separates him from the natives is his unbelief in shamanism and his firm conviction that the natives are capable only of otherworldly ignorance. This is why he can study them, observe their behaviors and practices, and produce an ethnography about them from the privileged standpoint of civilization mixed with pacifist benevolence. The stability of this look of surveillance, however, is disturbed by the eruption of a different knowledge that his worlding has so far sought to deny or disavow—the natives' knowledge that shamanism is a cultural and social performance and not just an orthodox religious belief. When Cabeza de Vaca realizes that the natives are also playing a game, in which he can play the game of being a shaman, a fundamental disruption occurs in his colonial look of surveillance and a dislocation is effected in his relations with the natives: First, his secret knowledge is no longer secret, and he, the conquistador, stands exposed as the naive subject who had believed, quite orthodoxically, in the natives' ignorance. Secondly, the natives' knowledge of the role he was playing was designed to prop up the game of shamanism itself so that the natives could use his performance to their own ends—the natives sham the shaman! In other words, the ethnographer is the one who is being observed, and despite all his supposed understanding of Spanish-Amerindian encounters, he is firmly located as a character in a game over whose social and political ends the "notable" shaman has little control, having become a dispensable social instrument to the natives. Whereas colonial surveillance positioned the natives as passive, mindless, exotic subjects in a cultural economy designed to civilize the barbarians, native agency is now manifest. Returning the look of surveillance by subjecting the conquistador to an ethnographic gaze, against his intended desire, amounts to displacing his position of enlightened superiority. It is Cabeza de Vaca who is being watched; it is the conquistador who is being played with; it is the skillful rhetorician who is now simply a prop in a cultural performance he cannot fully control. No wonder this conquistador cannot produce an impeccable worlding of the New World. The unseen, unpredictable ways in which submission to colonial power turns into a form of accommodating "foreign" presence; the deflective maneuvers of hospitality and friendly gestures; the secret deliberations among the natives to sham the shaman—these form the cross-cultural morphologies that emerge in the meeting of Old and New worlds.

Moreover, in stark contrast to Díaz's and Léry's chronicles, Cabeza de Vaca's narrative intriguingly lacks the one defining feature of Amerindian behavior that positions them, without any doubt to the Europeans, outside the realm of humanity—native cannibalism. To Díaz and Léry, cannibalism fundamentally undermines any easy identification of the natives as human beings on the same evolutionary continuum as the Europeans. Both chroniclers devote considerable space to detailing the intricate symbolism of the rituals relating to human sacrifice and cannibalism. Cabeza de Vaca does mention cannibalism, but it has to do with the horrifying spectacle of four dead bodies strewn around the solitary figure of a fellow Spaniard. During their stay with the Capoques and the Hans, five Spaniards, experiencing extreme hunger and thirst, "ate one another until one remained, who because he was alone, had no one to eat him" (Cabeza de Vaca, 107). In another incident, two

Spaniards, Pantoja and Sotomayor, who died after inflicting fatal wounds on each other, are eaten by others (Cabeza de Vaca, 135).[86] What is remarkable is the stark difference between the responses of the Indians and of Cabeza de Vaca to these acts. The Indians, he observes, "became very upset because of this and it produced such a great *scandal* among them that without a doubt, if at the start they had seen it, they would have killed them, and all of us would have been in great danger" (Cabeza de Vaca, 107; emphasis added). As José Rabasa has observed, "In their abhorrence of Spanish cannibalism, the Indians embody European values, for Cabeza de Vaca imagines them as inflicting death as punishment."[87] Morris Bishop notes that cannibalism among this group of Indians, the Attácapas, was reported during the eighteenth century but not earlier, suggesting that they may have developed the practice later on.[88] Whether the Attácapas were in some way influenced by the Spaniards is a topic worthy of critical consideration. In narrating the second instance of cannibalism among the Spaniards, Cabeza de Vaca offers no explanation, gloss, or comment whatsoever. His matter-of-fact tone in recording these events gives rise to several important questions: Would he have evinced similar indifference had he and his companions encountered Amerindian acts of cannibalism? Was survival cannibalism—the consumption of human flesh to survive in the event of famine or starvation—a practice that he was familiar with? Is there any gradation, such as we find in Díaz's and Léry's chronicles, in his views toward different kinds of cannibalism—is he more sympathetic to survival cannibalism and antipathetic toward religiously sanctioned cannibalism? What role does cannibalism play in Cabeza de Vaca's worlding of New Spain?

Because they subscribe to the idea that it is "America," the New World, that is the object of the chronicle's pedagogy, such questions are legitimate, but I think they are a little misplaced in this context. Unlike Léry, this nomadic shaman does not dwell much on the historical and philosophic problems thrown up by anthropophagy, whether European or American. Indeed, it is plausible that the central object of the chronicle's pedagogy is Cabeza de Vaca himself, not the New World. What emerges

as an impeccable worlding of America is not the conquistador's management of the incommensurable demands and obligations of intercultural
exchanges, but the role—of mediator, cultural translator, power broker—
that he fashions for himself in a language of pacifism. What is important
in this context is that Cabeza de Vaca infuses into his narrative a sense
of the worldliness, not of the New World, but of the conquistador-
turned-shaman—himself—and his role and his destiny as a "model conqueror" in New Spain. By inquiring into the reasons why Cabeza de Vaca
undertook to write his chronicle and what he hoped to achieve from
it, we can better appreciate this notion of worlding as a form of self-
fashioning in which he affirms himself "as an exceptional subject" and
"law-abiding faithful servant" of King Charles V.[89]

As the first few sentences of the narrative demonstrate, his primary
audience is the king of Spain, who authorized him and his companions
to "conquer and govern the provinces that are found from the Río de
las Palmas to the cape of Florida" (Cabeza de Vaca, 23). The chronicle,
then, must demonstrate that after all the privations and near-death experiences they suffered, the entire enterprise was not in vain but to the
glory of God, king, and Spain. Soon after his return to Spain, Cabeza
de Vaca petitioned the king to be appointed governor of Florida. Hernando de Soto had already been granted this position, so in 1540
Cabeza de Vaca was given the title of *adelantado* (an enormously powerful appointment made by the crown) and made governor of the regions
of Río de la Plata in South America.[90] Prior to the publication of
Relación in 1542, part of the manuscript appeared in a letter submitted to
the king by Cabeza de Vaca and the others who survived the journey.
The historian Gonzalo Fernández de Oviedo y Valdés, in his *Historia
general y natural de las Indias,* published the letter in full with his own com-
mentary on it.[91] *Relación* was first published in 1542 in Zamora, Spain,
and republished in 1555 in Valladolid. As Adorno and Pautz pointedly
comment, the 1542 edition, "unlike the 1555 edition, designed to be read
at leisure and at intervals suggested by its chapter divisions and titles,"
was clearly published so that the "emperor would read with favor and
respond to by bestowing a new royal commission on its author."[92] All

this underscores the importance of appealing to the king in as appropriate a manner as possible to gain courtly favor and a measure of political power.

Like his contemporary Bartolomé de Las Casas, who had already begun writing about Spanish atrocities in the Americas, hoping to persuade the king and the Council of the Indies to implement a structure of accountability, Cabeza de Vaca was concerned with convincing the king and his European audience that other, nonviolent ways of negotiating with the natives were more promising than those that were being used. He writes, "[T]hese peoples, to be drawn to become Christians and to obedience to the Imperial Majesty, must be given good treatment, and that *this is the path most certain and no other*" (Cabeza de Vaca, 241; emphasis added). Thus, Cabeza de Vaca sets himself up as the model conqueror, a pacifist, and an ardent believer in reforming Spain's colonial programs.

In describing the barbarous act of cannibalism committed by his fellow Spaniards, Cabeza de Vaca could have dismissed it, in disgust, as human nature gone awry in the face of extreme privation. But the Indians' anger provides him with an opportunity to invert the "codes of conquest"[93] and affirm the ideological position that he and others like Las Casas were attempting to articulate: the common humanity of the Indian. This was in opposition to the dominant Christian worldview, which relegated all nonbelievers to the fringes of civilized society and made them deserving of severe punishment inflicted by God, through man (in this case the Spanish), if they continued to transgress the laws of God. By positioning the Indians in the role of Spaniards, Cabeza de Vaca effectively subverts the powerful myth of the European civilized subject and disturbs settled assumptions about Europe's others.

This said, we need to remember that such a repositioning and subversion does not imply that the chronicler moved in a linear fashion from justifying conquest to apologizing for it. Hovering ambivalently between these poles of ideological justification, Cabeza de Vaca struggles not to reconcile but to sustain the "paradoxical coexistence of an imperial and an empathetic perspective."[94] Oddly enough, where Díaz and

Léry struggle to resolve contradictions in order to produce an impeccable discourse, Cabeza de Vaca deliberately sustains the paradox of sympathy and colonial desire, refusing a resolution. But to view this refusal as an instance of epistemic rupture and a subversion of colonial authority would be going too far. The uses to which this paradox is put betray such a reading—educating and civilizing the natives are not the issue so much as *how* education and civilization may be imparted. This insight complicates any tendency to view this conquistador-unlike-a-conquistador as a unique product of the Renaissance, embodying its pacifistic, democratic ideals.

Indeed, José Rabasa goes so far as to argue that Cabeza de Vaca shapes his narrative around one of the most important reformative aspects of the ordenanzas of 1526, which spelled out the Council of the Indies' policies towards Spanish-Indian relations. The ordenanzas had mandated the restricted use of military force to conquer the New World, and this is exactly what *Relación* strains to affirm as the most effective way to pacify the Indians.[95] To Cabeza de Vaca, culture is the most potent weapon of colonialism. As Rabasa comments, "the Ordenanzas of 1526 advocate a peaceful conquest, and Cabeza de Vaca's ideal imperial policies and legitimation of his procedures *follow these laws to the letter.*"[96] In this context, the impeccability that we find in Cabeza de Vaca's worlding of his own role as a mediator caught between two cultures is of a kind that adroitly harmonizes juridical oversight and legal discourse with his own peculiar experience as a Spaniard who, without the comfort of European civilization in the Americas, can yet find, in inverting the codes of conquest, another powerful justification for conquest. I point this out because the dimensions of worlding that this chapter has examined in Díaz's, Léry's, and Cabeza de Vaca's frontier narratives should not be viewed as overwhelmingly dominant impulses that masterfully subvert any lapse or dissonance in worlding the New World. On the contrary, worlding occurs elliptically and disjointedly. Our task is to pay attention to the historical, material, and rhetorical conjunctures specific to these texts and to how they are enmeshed in the authors' personal desires and intentions. We can thus see how particular worldings of the New World emerge despite the textual maneuvers that these chronicles perform in order to gloss over these moments of double bind and ellipsis so as to produce an impeccable worlding.

In concluding this discussion, I want to draw attention to a novella from 1936 by Haniel Long that rewrites *Relación*. In *Interlinear to Cabeza de Vaca*, an imaginative reconstruction of the Spaniard's peregrinations in the fourth world, Long gives narrative voice to the profundity of Cabeza de Vaca's existential experience. To Long, Cabeza de Vaca's "lackadaisical way of telling" his story, while in sharp contrast to the extreme nature of his experience of starvation, slavery, and wandering, points to the dialectical relationship between the expectation of his audience and the purpose of his chronicle. *Interlinear* signifies upon Cabeza's chronicle to tease out the implications of the narrative's moments of indifference, silence, and ambivalence; Long places emphasis on Cabeza de Vaca's reaffirmation of the religious injunction to "conquer by gentleness."[97] The impulse here is to provide a corrective to the Christianizing program gone awry in the hands of self-promoting men with voracious physical and nonspiritual appetites. Deprived of water, food, clothing, and, for a considerable time, the companionship of his fellow travelers, stripped of all those things that remind him of home, Cabeza de Vaca is faced with the prospect of starvation or murder by the strange Amerindians whom he serves as a slave. The "European world of which [he] had been a part" becomes "fantastic" (Long, 23). He is alienated not only in the physical sense, but also in the social and cultural sense. What disturbs Cabeza de Vaca is the manner in which he is compelled to part "little by little with the thoughts that clothe the soul of a European and most of all the idea that a man attains strength through dirk and dagger, and serving in your Majesty's guard" (Long, 14). It is significant that Cabeza de Vaca's epiphany is intimately related to the nature of his encounters with Spanish Europe's others, the primitive and unreasonable Amerindians. When Long writes, "The moment one accosts a stranger or is accosted by him is above all in this life the moment of drama" (24) and that such encounters with strangers would engender "steady currents of adaptation and of sympathy" (25), he comes close to affirming the modernist idea of a common human nature: man's humanity as having a fundamental, existential essence, with everything else—culture, language, religion, etc.—being like outer layers of skin and nerves, tissue and bone. Long's valuable recognition of the constructedness of culture and society leads him to affirm, though in rather simplistic ways, a core humanity, an essential human nature, recognition of which can render the other the same. Such a view neglects what I earlier referred to as Cabeza de Vaca's worlding of America as a form of self-fortification.

In a similar vein, Kun Jong Lee, arguing that Cabeza de Vaca "uses Saint Paul as his biblical prototype consistently and profoundly throughout this narrative," draws parallels between Cabeza de Vaca's experiences and Paul's: Paul had been shipwrecked on his journey to Rome, had been stranded on an island inhabited by strange people, and had eventually obtained fame by performing miracles among the inhabitants of the island.[98] Just as Paul, protesting the rigid hierarchy between Jews and gentiles, had ministered to the gentiles, thereby incorporating them into God's divine plan for man's redemption, the peace-loving conquistador "represents himself as the Spanish Paul among the American Gentiles"[99] and becomes a shaman not to cast aspersions on Catholicism but to prove to his European audience that the Christian God was equally concerned about the pagans. That God, through Cabeza de Vaca, performed wondrous deeds in terra incognita for the benefit of the non-Christians affirms the idea that these heathens were part of the human race. Commenting on the unique mediating role played by Cabeza de Vaca, Lee notes that unlike Cortés's Indian mistress Doña Marina (La Malinche) and Gonzalo Guerrero, who immersed themselves in the other's society and culture, this benign conquistador's assimilation into native culture is superficial at best since he "sloughs off only his outward appearance leaving his European and Christian core intact during his stay with the Indians."[100]

Interestingly, where Long sees a common humanity, Lee sees a core European and Christian ethos and identity. But there is a crucial difference in their notions of essentialism. To Long, human nature in its naked existential sense, bereft of cultural clothing, is essentially the same. To Lee, the notion of a core emerges in the border zones of New World frontiers: it is in the perplexing encounters of radically different cultures and societies that the struggle to negotiate difference and otherness is so central in maintaining a semblance of historical continuity or racial commonality and, in the context of Lee's analysis of Cabeza de Vaca as St. Paul, ideological certainty. The demythification of *Relación* is a complex process of revising accepted codes of conquest, questioning traditional European conceptions of the world and the different "races" of people who inhabit it, and exploring the potentialities of cross-cultural encounters in ways that undermine monolithic configurations of colonial experience by particularizing Europe's colonial enterprises in the Americas.

Pan-Caribbean
Hemispheric Poetics

The Caribbean, the *Other* America.

—EDOUARD GLISSANT

Beginning in the fifteenth century, the Greater Antilles—Puerto Rico, Cuba, Jamaica, and Hispaniola—and the Lesser Antilles—the string of small islands that stretches in an arc from the Virgin Islands to Trinidad and Tobago—have formed a pivotal locus for Euro-American contact and exchange, with profound consequences for the rest of the Americas. But how can we theorize about this archipelago that forms a "line of steppingstones . . . spanning the distance between the Americas, North and South"?[1]

Generally, the tendency has been to "fragment the Caribbean into zones of linguistic influence of ideologically determined categories"[2] and view "Antillean writing as an expansion of the literatures of European colonial powers"[3] or the Antilles as "imperfect replicas of European countries."[4] The islands, as Silvio Torres-Saillant observes, have been either regarded as offshoots of European nations or measured primarily in terms of their "past, present, or future connection with Western societies." The assumption that the peoples of this region were not "makers of history and producers of culture" led to a systematic neglect of autochthonous traditions as the Caribbean was reduced to an artifact viewed through a European lens.[5] In addition, the critical impulse has been to seek patterns of order and evenness in order to view the region as a cohesive unit embodying stable social, cultural, and national communities and traditions. Richard Burton identifies three models in debates concerning the emergence of cultural formations in the Caribbean: the Eurogenetic, the Afrogenetic, and creativity or creolization. In the Eurogenetic view, Native Indian and African cultures did not survive the onslaught of colonialism, and the large-scale spread and dominance of European culture resulted. The Afrogenetic view, in direct contrast, emphasizes the absorption, with varying degrees of assimilation, of European culture by the natives and African slaves. Finally, the creolization view rejects both these tendencies and sees the intermixing of European, Native Indian, and African elements as a dominant process in the Caribbean.[6]

But how valid is it, historically and conceptually, to speak of cultural distinctiveness, national unity, linguistic commonality, and political and economic uniformity in the Caribbean? Rather than privileging either the Eurogenetic or the Afrogenetic tendency over the Creole tendency, it is important to distinguish among various forms of European colonialisms, their modes of operation in the different societies the settlers came into contact with, and the diverse and contradictory effects of such imperial programs. What marks the Caribbean as an especially complex geopolitical and discursive terrain is its location as a nexus of several European empires and nations, each competing with the others over hundreds of years for control of the Caribbean's peoples and resources.

Because the manner in which different peoples "came together in the context of shock, contraction, painful negation and explosive forces," the history of the Caribbean, contends Edouard Glissant, is fragmented. Here, instead of having history unfolding according to a recognizable, coherent principle, we have a "dislocation" of history, resulting in the "inability of the collective consciousness to *absorb it all.*"[7] Glissant calls this dislocation "non-history," that is, histories of fragmentation and disruption, of tenuous connections to shards of other memories and histories. In such a context, Torres-Saillant suggests that to theorize a Caribbean poetics would be to "devise an *amalgamated image, a composite metaphor that points to the contemporaneous coexistence of multiple signs*" and to "conceive of a space of *inbetweenness,* where things enjoy a sort of elasticity that permits them *to be neither this nor that.*"[8]

Like Torres-Saillant, J. Michael Dash argues that "a hemispheric identity is an *essential mediating context* for understanding the Caribbean as a whole" and proposes viewing the Caribbean in both a regional and a global framework. On the one hand, all these islands have a "shared heritage, parallel sensibilities, and commonality of interests that link them across the region, beyond nation, race, and language";[9] on the other hand, the Caribbean is another geopolitical node in a vast network of transnational economic and social relations. The focus, to Dash, should be on the dialectic of local and global forces at work in the Caribbean. "Dismantling those notions of nation, ground, authenticity, and history on which more conventional surveys have been based and exploring concepts of cultural diversity, syncretism, and instability that character-ize the island cultures of the Caribbean" would have significant impli-cations for any critical practice dealing with the Caribbean.[10]

So how can we configure a Caribbean poetics while attending to Torres-Saillant's amalgamated image and Dash's global-local dialectic? I propose conjoining Antonio Benítez-Rojo's ideas of chaos and repeti-tion (*The Repeating Island*, 1992) with Edouard Glissant's idea of the "prac-tice of diversion" and rhizomatic thought in the Caribbean (*Caribbean Discourse*, 1989; *Poetics of Relation*, 1997). This will provide valuable models for reimagining the Caribbean and, while bearing directly on my analy-ses of the literary texts in this chapter, enable us to rehistoricize this "other America" and thus configure a Caribbean-inflected poetics of the Americas.[11]

Repetition and Chaos in the Caribbean

Because it defies our attempts to cohere its fragmented topography and history into a metanarrative, the Caribbean, observes Benítez-Rojo, is "a field of observation quite in tune with the objectives of Chaos." Drawing on chaos theory, he points to specific features that repeat themselves, "unfolding and bifurcating until [they reach] all the seas and lands of the earth, while at the same time [they] inspire multidis-ciplinary maps of unexpected designs." Repetition does not mean the reoccurrence of an event exactly as it first occurred: "every repetition is a practice that necessarily entails a difference."[12] The plantation, comments Benítez-Rojo, is one such repetition: it has repeated itself endlessly, as a machine, a "self-perpetuating entity," in the Caribbean and in the rest of the Americas.[13]

Benítez-Rojo notes that the "machine" that Columbus started had to be connected to other machines—"a naval machine, a military machine, a bureaucratic machine, a commercial machine, an extractive machine, a political machine, a legal machine, a religious machine." The plantation also emerged as a machine, with its own patterns of regulation and function. The Europeans controlled the "construction, maintenance, technology, and proliferation of the plantation machines, especially those that produced sugar."[14] The machine, thus configured, underscores the mechanistic, repetitive, exploitative, nonhumanistic character of the plantations, the institutionalization of slavery, and the structural, systemic nature of European colonialism in the Americas

To Benítez-Rojo, the intermingling of peoples of diverse cultures and races in the Caribbean dramatizes the syncretic nature of its cultural productions, which are polyrhythmic—"rhythms cut through by other rhythms, which are cut by still other rhythms."[15] Caribbean art forms "communicate their own turbulence," and "the literature of the Caribbean can be read as a *mestizo* text [emphasis in original], but also as a stream of texts *in flight*, in intense differentiation among themselves and within whose complex coexistence there are vague irregularities, usually paradoxical."[16] As is evident, instead of trying to explain away the region's immense heterogeneity by using linguistic, religious, or racial categories exclusively, Benítez-Rojo devises critical models that will take into account features of the Caribbean that defy systematized, holistic explanations.

However, in trying to configure the Caribbean as a region with its own distinct and disjunctive cultural morphology, Benítez-Rojo, argues Keith Alan Sprouse, ends up configuring it as a separate complex system operating by and large with its own internal mechanisms. Because Benítez-Rojo, writes Sprouse, does not "account for the non-Caribbean influences in the region," he is "unable to theorize how Caribbean peoples might make productive connections with other peoples, many of whom share similar postcolonial concerns."[17] Sprouse's criticism is not convincing: far from creating a tightly enclosed, self-referential region, Benítez-Rojo teases out the self-governing mechanisms, like the plantation, that emerge in the Caribbean even as they shape and are in turn influenced by interhemispheric and transcontinental processes of social and economic exchange. Thus, there are fundamental paradoxes—highly differentiated, multiply encoded—in the complex system that is the Caribbean. Glissant's focus on the immense heterogeneity of social practices and cultural forms in the archipelago, particularly his idea of a Pan-Caribbean rhizomatic dialectic, adds a promising dimension to Benítez-Rojo's reconfiguring of the Caribbean.

Diversion and Rhizomatic Thought in the Americas

Noting that to trace the Caribbean's diverse historical trajectories, we cannot adhere to the "totalitarian drive of a single, unique root," Glissant argues that rhizomatic growth (a horizontal rootlike formation) provides a model for theorizing the multiple fusions of the archipelago's immensely variegated cultural and social processes, in which the roots of identity overlap and merge with other roots, thus undermining the notion of single roots growing vertically and in isolation.[18] Moreover, such a rethinking of rootedness, I want to argue, also undermines the vantage obtained in being positioned vertically. If the tendency with verticality is to "look down" from "up above," rhizomatic development foregrounds the dependencies of roots on other roots and their embeddedness within other root formations. Connectivity, instead of hierarchy, becomes central to the rhizomatic process as patterns of growth connect and interconnect, only to break and make still more new connections. This is why, notes Glissant, rhizomatic thought can "overturn the order of the world"[19] conceived in rigid binaries and orthodoxies.

Glissant locates, embedded in the Caribbean's rhizomatic growth patterns, what he calls the "practice of diversion," an idea he elaborates in *Caribbean Discourse.* When a people are brutally oppressed and cannot go back to their original homes and conditions of living, the impulse is "that of reversion," which is an "obsession with a single origin: one must not alter the absolute state of being."[20] Reversion neglects change and contact; it valorizes "permanence." But as the memory of the Old World fades, this impulse loses its urgency. Sometimes, as in Martinique, notes Glissant, where the "community has tried to exorcise the impossibility of return," they resort to "the practice of diversion," a deliberate act of linguistic and social mockery and disruption.[21] Creole, a language derived from French and remnants of African dialects in the New World, becomes the "first area of diversion" as it is employed by the oppressed peoples as a "trickster strategy."[22] The language performs important strategic functions: it creates bonds of solidarity between the speakers; it marks as outsiders those who do not speak it; and more important, for Glissant, it embodies the act of mimicking the master language while refusing to modify and correct its mongrel, borrowed nature.

Benítez-Rojo's focus on the plantation as a machine and on repetition as a differentiating and self-perpetuating form of recurrence, and Glissant's stress on diversion as a strategy of resistance and on rhizomatic socialization, provide useful models for my study of Patrick Chamoiseau's *Texaco* and Russell Banks's *The Book of Jamaica* and *Rule of the Bone.* Although *Texaco*'s focus is circumscribed by Martinican geography and history, I argue that in creolizing Caribbean intellectual and cultural traditions through a gendered representation of Martinique's transition from a plantation-based economy to an urban economy, the novel allows itself to be situated within a pan-Caribbean nexus in which France's programs of modernization in the Caribbean are, in their chaotic modes of repetition, intimately connected to the larger European project of modernizing the New World. In Banks's novels, by contrast, Jamaica and the United States, the locales of both novels, function as nodules or hubs linked to larger transnational socioeconomic processes that both consolidate the United States's historical domination of the Caribbean and manage what I refer to as the "flow of whiteness" in the

Americas. How, I ask, did whiteness repeat itself in the Americas? How did it function, as did the plantation, like a machine? How did it proliferate endlessly? How did it manage itself, through what institutions, and in what discourses? What was and is its social and cultural symbology? But first I will begin with Chamoiseau's Creole novel *Texaco.*[23]

The City and Modernity

"One of the defining marks of modernity," write James Holston and Arjun Appadurai, "has been the use of two linked concepts of association—citizenship and nationality—to establish the full meaning of membership in society."[24] Beginning in the eighteenth century, citizenship and nationality, by displacing cultship, subjectship, and kinship, emerged as central apparatuses in the categorization of peoples and the organization of social life; it is the city that stands as a material and figurative embodiment of the democratic ideas embedded in discourses of the nation-state. But, as Holston and Appadurai note, this significant change "has been both revolutionary and democratic, even as it has also been conservative and exclusionary."[25] More important, the coexistence of these opposing tendencies has made cities the sites of constant disruption, upheaval, and change, and, as Holston and Appadurai comment, "with their concentrations of the local, the strange, the mixed, and the public, cities engage most palpably the *tumult of citizenship.*"[26] Because the city signals the transition from the rural world of the plantations and the countryside to the urban spaces of the city, to Dash, "it is in the city that the Caribbean's encounter with modernity is most obvious."[27] The occasion in *Texaco* for the narrator Marie-Sophie Laborieux's imaginative retelling of Martinican history is Fort-de-France's urban initiative to "destroy poor quarters to civilize them into stacks of projects" (Chamoiseau, 10) by sending the Christ, the urban planner, to make initial inquiries and submit a report on the city's squatter towns. Appealing to the squatters' "ancient custom of survival" (Chamoiseau, 25), Marie-Sophie, hoping to change his mind, tells the planner the history of their "conquest of City." Her "oral history of epic proportions,"[28] as Juris Silenieks calls it, begins in the 1800s. It narrates the birth of her father, Esternome, on a plantation in Martinique; the tumultuous events of 1848, when slavery was abolished in the French colonies; the arrival of East Indians, Chinese, and Syrian workers and merchants following Abolition; Mount Pelée's eruption in 1902, which completely destroyed the city of Saint-Pierre; Marie-Sophie's birth; the effects of World War I on the social and political culture of the Caribbean; the deaths of Idoménée, Marie-Sophie's mother, and Esternome; the establishment of oil refineries by Texaco; World War II; the election of Aimé Césaire as mayor of Fort-de-France in 1945; Marie-Sophie's founding of Texaco, a squatter district; and the arrival of the urban planner in Texaco, the event with which the novel begins.

Born in the Quarters of Fort-de-France, her umbilical cord "buried at the entrance of the hutch," Marie-Sophie is neither a runaway seeking refuge in the forest or the countryside nor, like her father, a product of the plantation (Chamoiseau, 189). Shaped by the "force of urban space," she is an "urban maroon."[29] Because Saint-Pierre is "very much a product of plantation Martinique" while Fort-de-France "represents a rupture with a rigid, hierarchical past,"[30] Marie-Sophie's experience as an urban maroon and her founding of a squatter district in the city can be juxtaposed with Esternome's experience in Saint-Pierre. Why Abolition, urbanization, democracy, and citizenship, as powerful markers of modernity, authorize other forms of oppression in the name of modernization is a question that links two pivotal movements in *Texaco*— the transition from the plantation to the city and the transformation of the city by the inhabitants of its squatter towns.

Esternome's "descent into the City" (Chamoiseau, 58) is dramatized as a narrative of "discovery" as the son of the plantations confronts the demands of the city. It is useful to keep in mind the linking of the city with modernity and modernization as theorized by Holston and Appadurai and the distinction between Esternome's and his daughter's city experiences. To Esternome, born and brought up in the fields, Saint-Pierre, with its rigid social structures, its harsh conditions, its animosities between masters and slaves and between land slaves and house slaves, and its culture of survival, is quite unlike the plantation. "Open to the winds of the world" (Chamoiseau, 66), the city was a metaphor for freedom itself. However, because of its close links to France, the imperial center, the city, for all its promise of freedom and upward social mobility, continued to secure the power of the landowning classes even as it incorporated the squatters, the free slaves, and the poor into its social hierarchy.

Mariam Slater notes that social life in Martinique can be analyzed historically according to the following dimensions of "color": phenotypic (based on appearance), genotypic (based on lineage and genealogy), associational, cultural or behavioral, and structural. The *békés*, descendants of the early white settlers, are in appearance and in genealogy closely related to the Caucasoid group. Also called *blancs*, that is, "people set apart from all people with Negroid ancestry whatever,"[31] they are not "pure whites" like the "France-whites," recent immigrants of European descent from France (Chamoiseau, 399). Since mixed marriages almost automatically meant expulsion from the béké group, the number of cross-racial relationships (but without marriage) was relatively high, and children from such intimacies were referred to as *chabins/es*, depending on the lightness of their pigmentation. Although they made up only about 1 percent of Martinique's population, the békés were powerful families who owned 75 percent of land and controlled 85 percent of sugar and rum exports, according to figures from 1938.[32] The *noirs*, or black slaves and their progeny, who made up 70 percent of the population, formed the lowest class, and between these groups existed a very large group of mulattoes, people of mixed ancestry. Although not purely white, they nevertheless had a "white bias,"[33] which meant that the more Caucasian the features of a mulatto/a were, the more likely he or she would be to attain respect and prestige in society. With their penchant for all things French, the mulattoes tended to view the noirs with disdain. Although they formed an intermediary race between the békés and the noirs, factors such as wealth, property, and education also contributed to a blurring of these social divisions. For instance, a wealthy noir would be "structurally white," which Michael Smith defines as "an abstract analytic category reflecting distributions and types of power, authority, knowledge, and wealth, which together constitute the social framework."[34] One could be a noir or a mulatto and yet be structurally white or have access to most of the privileges enjoyed by the békés and the France-whites, due to what Michel Giraud refers to as the "whitening effect" (Chamoiseau, 79).[35]

Esternome soon realizes that although the city offers greater mobility and economic opportunity than the plantation does, it is "the province of the store-békés and boat-owning france-békés" (Chamoiseau, 77). The noirs and the affranchis (freed slaves) are relegated to the lowest rung of the social hierarchy, with the France-whites and the békés occupying the highest positions and controlling government offices and the mulattoes "liv[ing] in their shadow" (Chamoiseau, 69). As an affranchi, Esternome perceives the growing alienation between people like himself and the land slaves who often come to the city on Sundays, who are, he thinks, too preoccupied with imitating the békés and the France-whites. They would "write lines in pretty-pretty French" and "venerated the books brought back from France by schooners" (Chamoiseau, 70). Thus influenced by the mulattoes, even the blacks "dreamt of whitening themselves," which does not stop them living as if "they had insuperable zombies to civilize under their resplendent rags and descendants to *humanize with a ray of whiteness*" (Chamoiseau, 70; emphasis added). The city is, in this sense, structurally white and has a whitening effect on its inhabitants. But there is a peculiar ambivalence to the desire and dream for whiteness: "That didn't stop them, all the same, in the depths of their being, from *hating that white skin*, the mulattoes' bearing, that tongue, that City, and the rest of all these wonders" (Chamoiseau, 70; emphasis added). It is this ambivalence that creates a colonized consciousness, in which the colonized subject perpetually vacillates between appreciation and denigration of both his native culture and the master's society. It is this pathology of colonialism that Esternome perceives in the noirs and the affranchis as they struggle to negotiate the perverse demands and obligations of their systematic marginalization by the békés and mulattoes in the city of Saint-Pierre.

When slavery was abolished in the French colonies in 1848, the noirs looked forward to a new Martinique where their rights would be officially recognized and they would be given full membership in the new republic. In the post-Abolition period, the noirs were promised parcels of land, the same land they had toiled on for more than two hundred years as plantation slaves. But this feverish anticipation was short-lived. What accounts for the continued dominance of this white minority, the békés, in Martinique?

After 1848, the black majority should theoretically have come to power. But as Constant notes, through all the periods of social unrest and change in the island colony—the Emancipation of 1848; the "gradual application of republican laws such as universal adult suffrage" (Constant, 172) beginning in 1848 and renewed in 1870; the *départmentalisation* of the French colonies in 1946; the reform of *décentralisation* in 1982, which stressed the distribution of power and not its consolidation at the center; and the Single European Act of 1993, which emphasized the creation of a Pan-European economic bloc—the békés have been able to sustain their social and political clout in Martinique and Guadeloupe (Constant, 178). The békés played the role of mediators between France, the central governing power, and the new island republic; since this gave them access to monetary aid, they were able to "convert French national public funds into private profits" (Constant, 173), which helped them retain control of the land. When the blanc creoles felt threatened by France, they resorted to the ideology of "rights to roots," which stresses local autonomy and independence; and to shore up their own power bases in the island and impede democratic processes, they "base[d] their lobbying on the acknowledgement of their French citizenship and universal rights and values applicable to all French citizens" (Constant, 175). The blanc creoles used the new discursive apparatus—the judiciary and the law—to regain property rights over the plantation fields, thus effectively maintaining their power to buy labor and control the allotment of land. Because "a citizen's first duty is to respect the laws of the Republic," every time the noirs organized themselves and demonstrate in front of the government offices, they were asked to behave like citizens whose sole interest should be the welfare of the city—"The word of interest was citizen. How are you, citizen? . . . Well, hello, citizen . . . Excuse me, citizen . . . Hey, citizen . . . citizen in all flavors" (Chamoiseau, 110–11). In short, it was slavery all over again because "Citizen Béké despite his citizenship came by at the same time on the same horse, gauged the work with the same eyes" (Chamoiseau, 113).

Thus, the modernization of Fort-de-France, couched in the discourse of democracy with its ideals of citizenship, equal rights, protection of personal property, and the obligations of citizens to submit to the greater good of the republic, became a marginalizing force in Saint-Pierre. It is in this context that Holston and Appadurai's linking of modernity with the social meanings of the city and the obligations of citizenship embedded in the discourse of the nation-state gains significance. The institutional structures that existed prior to Abolition become reified, resulting in a new discrimination against the slaves and the poor mulattoes. In short, if we regard the transition from a plantation order to an urban economy as marking the entry point of modernity, it also became the bane of modernization in Martinique because this new order continued to perpetuate the institutional oppression of and domination over the noirs.

However, Saint-Pierre's programs of modernization came to an abrupt end when Mount Pelée erupted in 1902 and completely destroyed the city, resulting in a massive exodus of people to another city, Fort-de-France. Soon squatter districts sprang up all around Fort-de-France, inhabited by those whom the city would not assimilate into its social hierarchy: noirs, affranchis and the sons and daughters of affranchis, and lower-class mulattoes, the Chinese, and East Indians. The quarters became the new arrivals' introduction to the ways of the city: "The Quarter was the port of registry" (Chamoiseau, 172). After Esternome's death, when Marie-Sophie builds her own hutch around Texaco, an oil refinery, it serves as an "anchor in City" because she "was entering [herself] directly into *that very old struggle*" (Chamoiseau, 296; emphasis added), that is, the more than hundred-year fight by the noirs for recognition and legitimation as citizens in post-Abolition Martinique. To Marie-

Sophie, the city is unable to absorb the people from the plantations because it was designed for and by the landowning békés, the wealthy France-whites, and the large mulatto middle class:

> [The city] had been structured by military necessity, shaped by the import-export business, leaving it to the plantations to house the thousands of hands used in agricultural production. When these hands piled up in the city, an unproductive trading post city, they could be channeled neither into jobs nor into housing. They had to *force themselves into the interstices*. (Chamoiseau, 234; emphasis added)

It is precisely this idea of forcing themselves into the cracks and folds of the city's laws of social organization by transgressing its racialized political imaginary, in which the noirs are effectively relegated to the fringes of the city, that *Texaco* dramatizes, not simply as the "conquering" of a city or a revolutionary drama of subaltern resistance, but as a tumultuous staging of social and cultural antagonism embodied in processes of creolization. It means recognizing the city as a Creole space, one facilitating all kinds of crossings over and mixtures of languages, cultures, and classes, while, in Esternome's words, "not being forgetful of [one's] chained roots" (Chamoiseau, 81).

The recognition of the city as Creole space does not mean the celebration of mestizaje or hybridization per se. *Texaco*, I want to emphasize, avoids what Shalini Puri notes are the dominant tendencies in contemporary discourses on hybridity: its use as a "way of advancing culturalist notions of difference as inclusion or nonconflictual diversity," couched in the rhetoric of assimilation; the manner in which it "provides an enabling discourse for the aggressive economic expansion of capital" and its potential to critique Enlightenment philosophy, where hybridity "is treated as a *formal* principle of interruption of pure origins and destabilization of centers."[36] Arguing for a discrimination "between the diverse modalities of hybridity, for example, forced assimilation, internalized self-rejection, political co-optation, social conformism, cultural mimicry, and creative transcendence,"[37] Puri cautions against displacing the politics of hybridity with the poetics of hybridity. What is needed is a fundamental disruption of hegemonic struggle "at the level of political economy."[38] Avoiding these pitfalls, *Texaco* instead dramatizes creolization as a discourse of difference grounded in materialist configurations of contesting social, cultural, and political hegemony—whether it is the city's lackadaisical attitude toward the plight of the squatters or the uneven relations of power between France, the center, and Martinique, the periphery. This is not the grand revolution of the orthodox Marxist or the utopian vision of the committed revolutionary. As a Creole tale, the novel "reveals that overt force guarantees eventual defeat and punishment, and that through cunning, patience, nerve, and resourcefulness (which is never a sin), the weak may vanquish the strong or seize power by the scruff of the neck."[39]

A Creole Uprising

The dream of conquering the city through what I am arguing is a process of creolization involves rejecting dominant European paradigms in Martinique. How else can we understand Marie-Sophie's insistence on having city officials recognize the squatter districts, with their cultural ambience, as legitimate and native to Fort-de-France and not simply as shantytowns to be modernized? She is demanding that the squatter districts be incorporated into the city without necessarily being assimilated into the city's spatialized program of social organization. Planned and organized in a linear, predictable fashion, the city stands as the embodiment of the Enlightenment ideals of the triumph of reason—the categorization of phenomena, the valuation of stability, predictability, and repeatability:

> In the center, an occidental urban logic, all lined up ordered,
> strong like the French language. On the other side, Creole's
> open profusion according to Texaco's logic. Mingling these
> two tongues, dreaming of all tongues, the Creole city speaks

a new language in secret and no longer fears Babel. Here
the well-learned, domineering, geometrical grid of an urban
grammar, over there the crown of a mosaic culture, crate
wood, asbestos. The Creole city returns to the urban planner, who would like to ignore it, the roots of a new identity:
multilingual, multiracial, multihistorical, open, sensible to the
world's diversity. Everything has changed. (Chamoiseau, 220)

To intervene in the materialist exercise of socioeconomic and political power is the central impulse of *Texaco*'s creolization of urban space.
The city is not a place of stability but "a place of transition" (Chamoiseau, 226) because "the Quarter[s] ceaselessly crashed onto City—the
way the sea undermines a disdainful cliff" (Chamoiseau, 172). For the
city to grant official status to the squatter districts would mean yield-
ing to the influence of the squatters, their impure dialects, their cross-
racial intimacies, their mongrel cultures, their nonlinear patterns of
organizing urban space. As Edward Soja points out, to "recompose the
territory of the historical imagination through a critical spatialization"
involves "a transformative re-theorization of the relations between history, geography, and modernity."[40] Reinscribing into public discourse
the history of the squatters and the dispossessed of Martinique is un-
doubtedly an important concern of this Creole epic. If I can extend the
implications of Soja's observation, the task of historicizing alterity necessitates a subversion of the spatial dimensions of metropolitan power,
a power that actively seeks to reproduce the matrix of social relations
and economic practices that historically shaped its emergence. Marie-
Sophie's Creole confrontation with the city marks an intervention in
the "production of space as a social process rooted in the same problematic as the making of history."[41] In suturing together Caribbean history, Martinican geography, and American modernity, Marie-Sophie's
Creole tale begins to spatialize, in a politicized historiographic register,
the discordant politics of the Caribbean archipelago.

Other axes along which creolization engages with modernity's management of the social world in Martinique are language and gender. As

Richard Burton notes, Creole is a language "neither 'African' nor 'European,' but a dynamic synthesis of both . . . exist[ing] in a state of tension," and the relationship of "parallelism rather than of conflict" between the two languages engenders all kinds of borrowings and transformations in both languages in unpredictable, irregular ways.[42] As Glissant observes, "What is most apparent in the dynamics of Creole is the *continuous process of undermining its innate capacity for transcending its French origins.*"[43] These ideas of mockery, subversion, and a rejection of transcendence, which Glissant calls a practice of diversion, are crucial toward understanding the function of Creole in the Caribbean and, in the context of my discussion, the significance of Creole in *Texaco* and the language politics of its writer, Patrick Chamoiseau.

Burton's stress on parallelism and Glissant's practice of diversion raise a pertinent question—what kind of resistance to or subversion of French hegemony does Creole signify? The creolization that writers like Chamoiseau, Confiant, and Bernabé and critics like Benítez-Rojo and Glissant affirm as paradigmatic of a Caribbean poetics and politics can be viewed as a revisionary intervention in the Caribbean intellectual tradition, which has long been, as Paget Henry argues, "a series of extended dialogues that arose out of European projects of building colonial societies around plantation economies" but also involved a devaluation of African and indigenous thought patterns and categories.[44] To Henry, critics like Frantz Fanon and C. L. R. James worked by and large within a European tradition, drawing heavily from "the discourses of Western tradition."[45] What is also necessary is a project of construction in which the disenfranchisement of African philosophy is contested through a systematic reworking of philosophies within and across cultures. Chamoiseau conceptualizes a Creole tale, and by extension *Texaco*, as a space "where the symbolic bestiary of Africa—whale, elephant, tortoise, brother rabbit—is introduced by the Storyteller to human or supernatural characters of a more distinctly European influence: the Devil, the Good lord, Cétoute, Ti-jean Horizon."[46] The heavy emphasis he places on African elements in Creole and their transformation in the Caribbean marks a pivotal departure from Euro-centered or Afrocentered discourses. But what is strikingly ironic is that writers like Patrick Chamoiseau, Raphaël Confiant, and Jean Bernabé have emerged not just as important Caribbean writers but also as remarkable French writers who have enriched French "through the structure and vocabulary of creole."[47]

Further compounding this irony is that it is precisely when *créolité* is at its most subversive in affirming all kinds of transgressive border crossings that it recodifies the border of gender. But there is a double edge to this recodification. At the end of the novel, Marie-Sophie persuades the city, with the mayor's help, to absorb Texaco into Fort-de-France's urban landscape. It is significant that the controlling point of view of the novel, Marie-Sophie's, is that of a black woman growing up in twentieth-century Martinique. In encouraging the squatters to arm themselves with sticks, stones, and knives; in affirming violence as a legitimate mode of self-defense; in using vulgar language to intimidate the békés; and in being "unfeminine," Marie-Sophie affirms not the anguish of Fanon's black man but the emergence of a black Martinican female consciousness as central to the sociopolitical efficacy of creolization as a strategy of subversion and resistance.

As Gwen Bergner astutely notes, Fanon's black man, because he speaks specifically about the black man's experience in colonial Antilles, is not a transcendent subject but a masculine subject. Moreover, like Freud, Fanon privileges the visual realm in the construction of gendered subjectivity. It is very disturbing to the black man to be placed in the passive position of the woman, that is, to be in a position where he is made "the recipient of the dismembering gaze that is normatively the male prerogative."[48] In Marie-Sophie's role as narrator and character in *Texaco*, we see a nuanced shift from Fanon's emphasis on the psychic dimension of racialized masculinity toward a broader sociomaterialist understanding of the multiple positionings of a black woman in a complexly stratified Martinique. But this is where we need to distinguish between the genre-circumscribed textuality of *Texaco*'s imaginative explorations of the gendering of Creole society and the entrenched sexism structuring the broader discourse of créolité.

Richard and Sally Price find that because the work of Francophone women writers like Dany Bébel-Gisler, Maryse Condé, and Simone Schwarz-Bartz receives only cursory mention in the Creole discourse of Bernabé, Chamoiseau, and Confiant, the *créolists* end up reifying "essentialist and masculinist notions" of Creole culture, politics, and identity.[49] Often confined to spheres of domesticity, women are not recognized as fully and actively participating in fashioning créolité as a privileged discourse and a new mode of subjectivity. The Prices recount an incident at a literary event, where three important male writers were asked about the status of women writers in Martinique. Their response was that "it posed no problem because their own novels were filled with female characters who actively expressed the women's point of view."[50] It is surprising that the very writers who earnestly seek to counter the power of the colonial, patriarchal unconscious in contemporary Martinique and who, including Chamoiseau, "re-establish the central figure of the storyteller in the narrative life of the French Caribbean"[51] should be so unmindful of their own proclivity to privilege a heterosexual and masculine subject as the pivotal embodiment of the power of the Creole imagination and thus render invisible the presence and role of women in Martinique.[52] Having said this, we need to be careful not to dismiss créolité as an essentially marginalizing discourse and view *Texaco* as yet another example of a colonial wolf in postcolonial sheep's clothing. As I have argued thus far in my reading of *Texaco* as a Creole tale, creolization works along multiple axes of contestation in the imaginative rewriting of Martinican history and recuperation of silenced voices. The class-based and racialized discourse of urbanism and the exercise of governmental power are effectively contested by creolization as the othered spaces of the dispossessed and the poor are reintegrated into the city's official landscape. In such a broad context, which allows for a nuanced reading of the mongrelized idioms of the Caribbean peoples as a rhizomatic discourse of double-coded paradoxes with a tendency toward recidivism, that *Texaco* instantiates the creolized politics of the Caribbean.

In considering the role of the békés and the France-whites as mediators between France and Martinique, I earlier commented on the white bias in the organization of Martinique's social life, a bias signifying the enduring power of whiteness in the Martinican social imagination. Whiteness in the Caribbean is, if I can use Benítez-Rojo's phrase, "a repetition with a difference."[53] Instead of studying how whiteness originated in a specific geopolitical location and the manner in which it gradually attained hegemony in other regions, we need to focus on the multiple points of contact among previously distinct societies interacting within and across noncontiguous zones and points of contrast which engender and solidify the discourse of whiteness not only in the Caribbean but in various parts of the Americas.[54] The question, then, is how whiteness has flowed in the Americas.

The Flow of Whiteness in the Americas

In writing about the anguish of colonized peoples, Frantz Fanon unravels the Manichean dichotomy of a colonial world in which the colonized man—robbed of his history, his culture, and his language and condemned to mimic his masters—turns into a zombie. "Not yet white, no longer wholly black," the colonized man becomes schizoid, his personality fragmented, full of doubt, alienation, and envy.[55] But in Russell Banks's *The Book of Jamaica* (1980) we do not have the anguish of the black colonized man, Fanon's zombie. We have instead the angst of the white man who cannot be colonized. Here is a man who wants to shed his whiteness and cannot. He wants to efface the pigmentation of his skin and cannot. He wants to deny himself the power of all that it symbolizes and cannot. The more he tries to question his own assumptions, play down his privileges, and position himself in *other* ways, the more he finds himself caught up in a discourse of whiteness he cannot disavow. He cannot disengage himself from it because he lives it, he breathes it—he is white.

The central concerns of the novel are these: To what extent can a white American participate meaningfully in the social and cultural life of Jamaica? What does it mean to *be* white, to be born white, to act white? What does whiteness signify? What are its symbols? If one is

white, is one condemned to be a racist? Have our histories so trapped
us that we cannot ever make amends, change our present conditions of
nonequivalence, and speak, write, talk, and communicate across cultures, across the borders of language, race, religion, gender, and nation?
In my discussion of *The Book of Jamaica* and *Rule of the Bone* (1995), I
make two central arguments: First, the novels' fascination with and fetishization of black culture unravel whiteness and blackness as imbricated constructions whose modes of organizing social and cultural life
have a lot to do with the continuing exploitation of those that Europe
and North America have historically defined as others—the exotic and
barbaric native and the "third world" (in the novels' context the Caribbean island countries), which is in need of progress and modernization.
Secondly, while enabling a rethinking of cultural production in the
Americas as a dialectical, interhemispheric process, both novels function as confessional narratives in discourses of whiteness.[56] At this point
a few brief comments on contemporary discourses about whiteness are
in order.

Although whiteness evolved as a descriptive term, with varying degrees of denotations and connotations, it can be generally defined as
"the social construction of both racial and ethnic categorizations" in
relation to the "pan-ethnic experience of whites born in the United
States."[57] While it defines other ethnicities, whiteness remains un-
changed. It is taken for granted because it is deemed the way things are,
the way nature is. But reducing whiteness to light skin color would be
a mistake; it is that, but it is much more. This is why instead of focusing exclusively on how whiteness is produced and theorizing about it
solely from the perspective of nonwhites, contemporary critics have
opted to focus on "the ways that white domination—as a social and
ideological phenomenon—reproduced itself and configures the 'place'
of other racial/ethnic groups in 'centering' itself."[58] In this context,
David Roediger observes that the historical construction of whiteness in
North America embodied the displacing of class anxiety and alienation
into a form of racial solidarity so as to enable the white working class
to earn the "wage," the pleasures and benefits, of whiteness.[59] White-

ness can thus be seen as "the willingness to seek a comfortable place within a system of race privilege."[60] It functioned, writes Valerie Babb, as "a unifying device, defusing class warfare among whites while continually integrating new white immigrants into the white American fabric."[61] Even as the multiple axes of identification and disidentification included language, politics, race, religion, social behavior, and nation, whiteness's mode of differentiating also served as a mode of integrating. Roediger's and Babb's point about the overlapping of class and race makes it difficult to view whiteness as a stable category against which other categories—Asian American, African American, Native American, Hispanic American—can be defined and around which they form their sociocultural and political valences. The power of whiteness also lies in its ability to generate knowledge about all those it deems others. By making itself invisible, whiteness can stake a claim to objectivity and universality, qualities that lend rigor and legitimacy to the knowledge it produces. Speaking specifically about white America's construction of blackness, Toni Morrison calls the knowledge produced by whiteness "American Africanism," by which she means the entire gamut of discourses and knowledges in which black presence is imagined, represented, symbolically mythified, and discoursed about in literatures not written by blacks.[62]

However, whiteness derives part of its affective and cultural force by denying and masking the extent to which it is dependent on all those against which it defines itself. "Positioned as existing outside the political and economic forces that seem to shape other racialized identities," whiteness is always in "conceptual opposition to Blackness."[63] Since it fails to take into account its stark visibility to those identified as nonwhite, to Ruth Frankenberg the invisibility of whiteness is a "white delusion."[64] Because the category is "leaky," in that "race can be seen *only* in relation to other categories such as class, gender, sexuality,"[65] whiteness is already textured as it interacts with and defines itself against other identities.[66] By refusing to "treat white privilege as a fixed and frozen artifact" and by acknowledging that "race derives much of its power from seeming to be a natural or biological category or, at the very least, a coherent social category," we can move beyond the critical impulse to highlight the privileges or losses that whiteness confers on those identified as white and examine its "transformative interests."[67] Whiteness does not possess an unchanging essence that is continually reproduced in society; rather, it changes its forms, alters its symbols, reshapes its structures of privilege, and recreates its social and cultural practices anew. Examining the variegated ways in which whiteness is "continually constructed, reconstructed, and transformed for white people"[68] and "is brought into being as a normative structure, a discourse of power, and a form of identity"[69] is crucial to any endeavor seeking to deconstruct the power of whiteness. The desire for whiteness to be "invisible" and keep transforming its interests makes imperative the need to study and critique its rhetorical strategies, its discursive formations, so that we can see, as Wander et al. note, how it "operate[s] to reinforce [its] historically established hierarchies through a range of strategic devices that mask its true operations."[70]

Because "whiteness has historically enacted a global dominance of itself, [and] that dominance impacts and affects identities and spaces in different ways in different locations as it takes on different meanings in different sites,"[71] we need to address the global dimensions of whiteness. This point is significant here because I discuss Banks's novels in the context of the flow of whiteness across the Americas "through the interlocking axes of power, spatial location, and history."[72] Banks's novels not only dramatize the "transformative interests" of whiteness as it travels across national borders in the Americas, they also embody the contradictions of what Robyn Wiegman refers to as the "reformative" aspects of whiteness, that is, the ways in which whiteness seeks to rehabilitate itself, devoid of its racist and supremacist ideological underpinnings, by having people move "through a range of antiracist positions."[73] As the protagonists of these novels struggle to rehabilitate their lives and their locations in systems of white privilege, the whiteness they reform and affirm is deeply masculinized and thus offers gendered ways of deconstructing and unmasking the ideological machines that sustain its power and legacy. Whiteness in these novels, reformed or otherwise, is a pact that can be agreed upon by men, and it is in the very moment of negotiation, when that pact is drawn up or agreed upon, that racial antagonism is displaced by a transnational ethos of male bonding. A masculinized circuit of whiteness in the Americas forms the novels' structural framework—whiteness reformed through a process of racial homosocialization. By this term I mean the masculinized, male-centered ideas, perspectives, and practices that produce and sustain certain ideological discourses, social structures and institutions, and cultural symbologies that privilege male subjects and their experiences as providing the embryonic space for reforming whiteness, for creating a white consciousness devoid of the taint of prejudice, and for affirming a white culture and identity by effecting a distancing from and disavowal of the power of whiteness in a racialized society.

The protagonists of *The Book of Jamaica* and *Rule of the Bone*, Johnny and Chappie, respectively, confront their whiteness, their identities as whites, not in moments of social upheaval, but in quotidian realities—everyday gestures, conversations, activities in Jamaica.[74] Each travels to Jamaica and is enraptured by its social and cultural ambience; each makes a conscious attempt to immerse himself in Jamaican society; each develops intimate friendships with Rastas; and each, while learning the history of the Maroons, the Ashanti warriors, and their myths and prophecies, develops an acute self-consciousness about his white identity and all its attendant privileges in both the United States and Jamaica.

Living as a tourist with his family in Jamaica, Johnny, the thirty-five-year-old narrator of *The Book of Jamaica*, develops a close relationship with Terron Musgrave, a Rastafarian, and soon finds himself acting as a liaison between two rival Maroon factions from the communities of Gordon Hill and Nyamkopong. But at the end of the novel, as plans to bring together the two Maroon communities fall apart, Johnny hurriedly boards a flight to Miami. The novel had begun on an intimate note with Johnny talking about his close friendship with Terron. But at the end, alienated and frustrated, Johnny leaves with his work unfinished. Some things, however, have changed—Johnny's idea of himself, his conceptions about being white and what it means to be white not just in the United States but in Jamaica, where "the dreamy American had found himself, for the first time in his life, truly alone" (120).[75] But what is this whiteness that Johnny realizes he not only possesses but is completely enmeshed in?

To be white means, to Johnny, not learning or knowing how to survive, because survival "was something one took for granted" (Banks, *Book*, 161). For the first time, his whiteness loses its naturalness as his cherished beliefs in the superiority of reason, order, symmetry, individual achievement, science, research, and honesty make him the "*exotic one, the strange one* . . . and the effort for the first time of having to deal ceaselessly and intimately with such a man was exhausting me" (Banks, *Book*, 167; emphasis added). Such exhaustion is nowhere more evident than in the narrative voice, which changes abruptly from first person to third person in the middle of the novel. As Johnny realizes the difference of his whiteness, its exoticness in a location away from his home in the United States, he loses confidence in the narrative authority of the self-assured psychologized "I." It is as if the narrator cannot trust himself anymore and yields his narrative to the author, trusting in his omniscience and ability to control the uncharted territory of Johnny's whiteness.

Johnny realizes the liminality of whiteness only when he is immersed in the black diasporic culture of the Rastafarians. Jamaica is where he perceives "the almost perfect *reversal* of [his] own world" by which "one can see [one's] otherness" (Banks, *Book*, 193; emphasis added). For instance, during a break at a dance in Kingston, he sees reflected in the mirror his "white face and pale hair" and "shockingly blue eyes and pink hands" and notices how all the other people are "trying not to be staring at [him]" (Banks, *Book*, 206). Johnny experiences his body as, to extend Raka Shome, "a site of difference" through the power of the gaze, which can sometimes function as "a locus of control" (Banks, *Book*, 120).[76] Arguing that racism functions in nonverbal gestures like the gaze, Shome notes that the humiliating power of gazing comes from the desire of the gazer to "mark the nonwhite body for difference";[77] the body becomes the site of otherness. In Johnny's case the gaze becomes inverted, with himself, a white man, as its object. Upon realizing this,

Johnny seats himself for the rest of the dance "in the rear of the room and as far from the others as possible" (Banks, *Book*, 206–7). While Johnny is far removed from the unequal power relation involved when a master gazes at a slave or a white person in a rigidly stratified society gazes at a black or native other, the reversal of positions is nevertheless of importance here because it is the white body that is being gazed at and not the black body.

In the realm of language and communication, Johnny perceives another aspect of whiteness. Rastafarian speech, because of its creolization, which makes it less amenable to phonetic representation, tends to resist "visual representation and exist[s] solely and fully in the speakers' mouths and ears." To whites who are familiar with "written language, conventional English" (Banks, *Book*, 284), learning Rasta speech involves adapting to a new rhythm and syntax that has its roots in orature.

Class presents another problem. Johnny believes that his having been "raised by working people, tenement dwellers, people who for countless generations had worked with their hands and backs . . . counted for something" (Banks, *Book*, 115), as if his working-class roots can somehow gloss over the decidedly superior position that his race gives him over the Rastas. But this is possible only if he elides, not if he takes into account, the implications of his racial positioning. He comments, "[M]y class status . . . permitted me the luxury of remaining detached and untouchable, uncontaminated by these people—in the same way that my race and inability to speak or easily understand their language deprived me of the easy trust and intimacy of the Maroons" (Banks, *Book*, 115). It is striking how notions of purity, detachment, and contamination are deeply imbricated in a reflexive whiteness that continually displaces racial antagonism with an affirmation of class-based solidarity. But whereas *The Book of Jamaica* ends abruptly with this realization, *Rule of the Bone* further extends the implications of its white protagonist's self-reflexivity by raising the question whether one can affirm a white subjectivity without subscribing to a discourse of racism.[78]

When Chappie Dorset, a fourteen-year-old "mall rat," a "homeless kid with a mohawk" (Banks, *Rule*, 100) from Au Sable Forks, upstate

New York, befriends I-Man, a dreadlocked Jamaican Rastafari who had migrated to the United States as a farm worker, Chappie is introduced to a world starkly unlike his world of whiteness—the world of black America. Eventually they both go to Jamaica, I-Man's homeland, where a series of events in quick succession profoundly alters Chappie's ideas of himself and his fascination with Rastafarianism. He meets his father, Paul Dorset, who had abandoned him when he was a little boy and now works as a doctor for the Jamaican government; Chappie lives in I-Man's ant fields in Cockpit Country, where they grow drugs for an international market; and when I-Man is killed, Chappie decides to return to America.

In many ways, Chappie seems an uncanny echo of Huckleberry Finn in Twain's memorable fiction, which is why Robert Niemi calls him a "Huck Finn for the nineties."[79] However, unlike his literary predecessor, Chappie possesses a heightened self-consciousness regarding his strange attraction to I-Man, which makes his desire to become black, or at least a white Rasta, all the more intriguing. In a telling scene after I-Man's death, as Chappie waits for his father in a colonial mansion called the Mothership, he listens to Charles Ives records and ponders the significance of the pieces' titles and themes and the uneven rhythm of the "trumpets and violins coming at [him] from different directions at different speeds and loudness but linked together anyhow" (Banks, *Rule*, 359). Charles Ives (1874–1954), or "Ras I'ves," as Chappie calls him, was a U.S. composer famous for his experimental music. He used polychords (placing several chords against each other), tone clusters without a key center, and fragments of other compositions "with a series of chordal leaps rather than any sort of melodic progression."[80] Although his compositions, in embodying chance and unpredictability, produced dissonances, Ives did not attempt to resolve them, because "the sense of unity is not brought about through exact repetition, either of motifs or of sections, but is established through relationships" or "sound-web[s]."[81] Ives's dissonant music seems to parallel the turbulence of cross-cultural contact in Jamaica.[82] Chappie calls Ives I-Man's "ol' compadre" (Banks, *Rule*, 359) because both of them acknowledge the paradoxical and unstable nature of musical and cultural signification. What Ives does in music, incorporating different musical traditions not so much to achieve a new harmony as to enable different dissonant sounds to be played simultaneously, I-Man does in the realm of cultural production in affirming Chappie as a *white* Rasta. But, as the novel dramatizes, affirmations of hybridization and intermixing of peoples and cultures can also have very real material consequences.

Deeply moved by the murder of I-Man, Chappie, as he listens to the music, experiences a mystic connection with I-Man, who seems to communicate to him a profound truth:

> Maybe that was the message I-Man was sending me, that even though I was a white kid I could still become a true heavy Rasta myself one day but only as long as I didn't ever forget I was a white kid, just like black people could never forget they were black people. He was telling me in a world like ours which is divided into white and black that was how you finally came to know I. (Banks, *Rule*, 360)

But what exactly does it mean not to forget to be a white kid? Consider the title of chapter 18, "Bone Goes Native," which aptly conveys Chappie's desire to identify himself completely with the Rastafarian community in Cockpit Country. When he goes to the "secret Maroon cave fe see in de true lights of I-self" (Banks, *Rule*, 314) and, in a dream sequence, witnesses the brutality of the slave trade and its effects on the Africans, it affirms his immersion into the Rasta community. In other words, Chappie becomes a Rastafarian like I-Man, except that he is a *white* Rasta, not a black one. Or so Chappie would like to assume.

This celebratory impulse to "go native" is completely undermined when, in a swift turn of events, I-Man is murdered by Paul Dorset's henchmen for having slept with Paul's girlfriend, Evening Star. Although Chappie grows dreadlocks and looks and speaks Jamaican, the murderers do not kill him because "he's American. The tourist board'll go nuts." As the killer tells Chappie, "*If you was one of Doc's* [i.e., Paul

Dorset's] *black children you'd be dead meat by now*" (Banks, *Rule,* 339; emphasis added). For all of Chappie's identification with the Rastas and their
acceptance of him as a true Rasta, Chappie is spared his life not because he is his father's son, but because he is his father's *white* son, not
his black son. But why is phenotype so important to becoming an authentic Rasta? As Chappie ponders: "That was the other thing that had
me all twisted up. Whiteness . . . I knew if I wasn't white, if I'd been a
real Rasta-boy like I'd been pretending to be I'd be dead by now"
(Banks, *Rule,* 342). What is important here is that in the discourse of
race, color functions as the fixed sign of otherness, of that which is not
the same. It is a rigid strategy of classifying people into types, distinct
races. To the killers even a mulatto, the product of white and black intimacy, would not be white. Because whiteness is pure, its contamination
should be avoided at all costs. This is Chappie's epiphany—he cannot
ever be a true Rasta so long as his color functions as a rigid organizational mode of classifying people into "us" and "them" and he "enjoys
the benefits of the white race, like still being alive for instance" (Banks,
Rule, 345). In more ways than one, Chappie is not able to return to
"racial innocence"[83] because whiteness cannot be imagined or lived
except in relation to all that is defined and related to as nonwhite. But
besides whiteness enabling Chappie to escape death, what are the "benefits of the white race" in the novel? This question can be approached in
terms both of what Meyer Fortes calls "white bias" in Jamaica and of
the effects of the tourist industry on Jamaican culture and economy.

Although blacks constitute the majority, they "have become almost
entirely assimilated to European cultural patterns"; Jamaican society,
notes Fortes, is basically "oriented towards a European ideal."[84] Color,
which can refer to skin color, skin texture, hair, and other physical features, is "assessed in relation to [its] nearness to European characteristics and distance from the African."[85] Bonham Richardson comments
that "because of the obvious and thoroughgoing domination of the
Caribbean region for centuries by external power-holders who have transformed landscapes and local populations to meet outside market needs,"
the Caribbean continues to be positioned disadvantageously, economi-

cally and politically, in its relationship to North America, Europe, and Asia.[86] Tourism has engendered a range of social and ecological problems in Jamaica, including water pollution, erosion of beaches, and an increase in junk heaps. Because the tourist industry is controlled by multinational corporations and because of Jamaica's dependence on foreign banks, hotel chains, food companies, and travel agencies, the Jamaican government has little control in creating and shaping public policies to ameliorate these detrimental effects.[87] One can only imagine the utter sense of powerless and humiliation native Jamaicans would feel on seeing billboards "reminding (black) local residents to put on happy smiles for white tourists," notes Richardson.[88] To Chappie, that "Jah was actually this African King of Kings named Haile Selassie who drove the whites out of Africa and freed up his people . . . was something white people probably couldn't get" (Banks, *Rule,* 153). Like Johnny in *The Book of Jamaica,* Chappie, through his immersion into Jamaican society and his growing sensitivity to its history of conquest and colonization and its contemporary dependency on international tourism, is able to adopt several antiracist and anticolonial positions in a way that affirms a whiteness that can be socially acceptable as a form of racial identity insofar as it acknowledges and distances itself from its implicatedness in systems of power and privilege. This point leads me to my final argument: that we can situate *The Book of Jamaica* and *Rule of the Bone* in the tradition of what Alastair Bonnett calls "confessional narratives," or the literature or practice of white confession.

Taking a "consciousness-raising" or "awareness-training" approach, which coincides well with the consciousness-raising approaches of the 1970s and the 1980s in the United States, the authors of such narratives aim to inform white readers of their own complicity in perpetuating racial stereotypes and discourses.[89] The impulse is to unravel or make visible "the social construction of race" and how it "perpetuat[es] white privilege."[90] Bonnett observes, "It is tempting to argue that White confessional anti-racism establishes Whiteness as the moral center of anti-racist discourse" as whiteness becomes a "racial community" and a "site of confession," thus leading to "paternalistic concern" rather than a desire to join the realm of "cooperation and participation." The analogy, in this practice of confession, to the idea of "coming out," with its connotations of an essentialized alternative sexuality, is also problematic because there is an assumption that once a declaration of whiteness is made, it may be "lived openly."[91] Furthermore, while *The Book of Jamaica* ends with Johnny's hurried departure from Jamaica, *Rule of the Bone* ends with Chappie's becoming, to use Noel Ignatiev's words, a "race traitor," that is, "someone who is nominally classified as white, but who defies the rules of whiteness so flagrantly as to jeopardize his or her ability to draw upon the privileges of the white skin."[92]

However, what becomes read as whiteness in these texts, reformed or otherwise, is a masculinized whiteness that is able to reform itself through a process of homosocialization—the masculinized, male-centered, male-to-male oriented discourses, sociocultural practices, and modes of racialization that depend on women for their functioning and legitimacy. It is a dependence that is also obscured. In a pivotal scene at the end of *Rule of the Bone*, Chappie, after I-Man is killed by his father's cohorts, returns to the Mothership and has a sexual encounter with Evening Star, his father's girlfriend, to avenge the murder of his "other father," I-Man. To Chappie, identifying I-Man as his other father legitimizes the encounter and seals, in a way, his ability to cross the borders of his whiteness and exact revenge on his father's whiteness by positioning himself as a reformed white Rasta. But to do this, Chappie still needs another kind of whiteness, one embodied in the white female body of Evening Star, to make possible a form of familial transgression, which is also an act of white atonement, to obtain another form of cross-racial identification. Here, then, is an instance of the gendered dynamics of the "transformative interests"[93] of whiteness circling the wagon of reformed Whiteness.

Where Banks's novels depart from traditional confessional narratives is in moving beyond making whiteness the site of confession and acknowledgment. They raise pertinent questions of identify formation in a world in which "points of departure and points of arrival are in cultural flux," where "the invention of tradition (and of ethnicity, kinship and other identity markers) can become slippery, as the search for certainties is regularly frustrated by the fluidities of transnational communication [and patterns of migration]."[94] Rather than affirming an authentic white identity and culture, these novels particularize the flow of whiteness in the Americas even as they underscore the disjunctive processes by which the sociocultural authority of whiteness is differentially and materially produced in the Americas.

This is why we cannot consider whiteness in these novels in its nationalist configuration; we cannot study whiteness exclusively and singularly in terms of U.S. history and nation formation. Instead, we need to focus on the interhemispheric dynamics of whiteness as they are formed in transit as whiteness flows, repetitively and rhizomatically, across the Americas, imbricating itself in the legacies of conquest, colonialism, imperialism, and global tourism.

4 Border Cultures
in the Borderlands

> A border is a dividing line, a narrow strip along a steep
> edge. A borderland is a vague and undetermined place
> created by the emotional residue of an unnatural bound-
> ary. It is in a constant state of transition.
>
> —GLORIA ANZALDÚA

Over the last two decades in North America, the trope of the border
or border crossings to conceptualize contemporary attitudes towards
culture, history, ethnography, and literature, among other things, has
gained enormous critical currency in public and academic discourse,
and border studies has emerged as a legitimate field of study having a
recognizable canon of writers and texts and a panoply of organizational
categories and interpretive frameworks. While it is the U.S. Southwest
that circumscribes the geographic materiality of the field of border studies, sociologically the tendency has been to view the experience of displacement and relocation of Mexicans in the Southwest as paradigmatic
of border societies. This is why several writers and critics, including Gloria Anzaldúa, José David Saldívar, Ramón Saldívar, Norma Alarcón,
Cherríe Moraga, Ana Castillo, and Teresa McKenna, situate border studies in Mexican and Chicano/a historiography. To Anzaldúa, *la frontera*
signals "the coming together of two self-consistent but habitually incompatible frames of reference [which] causes *un choque,* a cultural collision" because "the U.S.-Mexican border *es una herida abierta* where the
Third World grates against the first and bleeds."[1] A study of border culture, notes José David Saldívar, "puts forth a model for a new kind of
US cultural studies, one that challenges the homogeneity of US nationalism and popular culture." It embodies a "synthesis of articulated

development from dissident folklore and ethnography; feminism, literary, critical-legal, and cultural studies; and more recently gender and sexuality studies."[2] Both Anzaldúa and Saldívar, like the other critics mentioned earlier, view Mexican American experience as paradigmatic of border phenomena. Why, then, am I examining Roberta Fernández's *Intaglio: A Novel in Six Stories* and Leslie Marmon Silko's *Almanac of the Dead* and thus bringing together texts dealing with Mexican American and Native Indian experience under the rubric of border studies? Because by doing this I can place Native American history and culture at the heart of border studies and examine how such a centering compels us to reconfigure the borderlands in ways that go beyond the Anglo-Mexican paradigm that has generally dominated the study of border phenomena.

As Scott Michaelsen and David Johnson note, the attempt to identify border cultures as Chicano cultures "serves the dream of purity" because it amounts to a "policing of the border" based on a system of inclusions and exclusions.[3] In a related context, while commenting on how border theorizations may run the risk of reifying existing patterns of marginalization, Amritjit Singh and Peter Schmidt ask, "[T]o what degree will a focus on race and ethnicity obscure the functioning of other axes of affiliation within and across ethnic boundaries—such as class, economic niche, religion, gender, or sexuality?"[4] While recognizing the legitimacy of the historical perspective offered by Chicano/a writers and theorists, I, along with Michaelsen and Johnson and Singh and Schmidt, raise the following questions: Is it theoretically and historically valid to view the borderland phenomenon *solely* through the lens of Mexican American historiography? Are there only three major players in this border drama—the Anglos, the Mexicans, and the Mexicans who eventually become Mexican Americans or Chicanos? What about the interaction among the Anglos, the Chinese, the Mexicans, the Chicanos, the blacks, and the numerous Native Indian peoples in the borderlands—how can we account for their presence and how do they shape our understanding of border cultures and societies in the borderlands? To address these questions, we need to avoid a presentist orientation that views the emergence of border cultures and border studies as the result of post-1960s multiculturalism in the United States. This is why it would be helpful at this point to develop a genealogy of "borderlands"[5] in American historical and literary discourse so that we can chart alternative perspectives to examine border cultures, perspectives that can be sensitive to the fluid and ongoing interactions of multiple groups and communities, and thus move beyond the dominant Anglo-Mexican model to study cultures and literatures formed *on the border* in the borderlands.

Reconfiguring the Borderlands

In *The Spanish Borderlands: A Chronicle of Old Florida and the Southwest* (1921), the historian Herbert Eugene Bolton used the term "Spanish borderlands" to denote what is now the southwestern United States. Attempting to widen the horizons of U.S. American literary history, Bolton focused on the colonial history of Spanish settlement in what before 1848 was northern Mexico. Bolton sought to counter what seemed in American historiography then to be a narrow emphasis on English, Dutch, and French settlements. In writing the history of the Spanish borderlands, Bolton was going against prevalent traditional notions that the Southwest was a land without a history.[6] Because to Bolton the borderlands were "the meeting place and fusing place of two streams of European civilization, one coming from the south, the other from the north,"[7] he argued that these regions had their own unique histories of discovery and settlement. But since the bulk of the documents and texts that formed the historical archives of this region were written in Spanish and thus were not accessible to the English-speaking populace of the United States, Bolton felt that the ideological threads binding the nation with ideals of monolingualism needed to be disentangled. Bolton was thus in many ways addressing the politics of language in the recording of official U.S. history.

Another prejudice that Bolton sought to contest was the *leyenda negra* (Black Legend), an idea firmly embedded in the Anglo-American imagination.[8] According to this legend, the Spaniards, although they traveled deep into the Americas and established large settlements, lacked the necessary acumen to develop out of their New World experience settler societies based on the principles of democracy, progress, and individual liberty. The Spaniards simply did not possess the characteristics that the Anglos were fortunate to be endowed with, namely, a desire for experimentation, exploration, freedom, individualism. These two things—the parochial ethnocentric focus of Anglo historians and the powerful hold of the leyenda negra on the American imagination—formed an ideological grid that Bolton attempted to undermine.

However, the Bolton school, as it came to be called, had its shortcomings. For the most part, following the pattern set Hubert Howe Bancroft in the 1880s, who produced and collected massive volumes of *testimonios*, narratives, and interviews of Southwesterners, Bolton and the numerous writers influenced by him concentrated on recording the large-scale movements or migrations within the region, public achievements of individuals or groups of peoples and individual acts of heroism and bravery, and the establishment of the *presidio*, the *encomienda*, and the mission. As they tended to romanticize and mythicize the Spanish presence in the Southwest, "vilification gave way to sentimentality, and Hispanophilia supplanted Hispanophobia."[9] But in the early decades of the twentieth century, as Weber notes, such a view nonetheless signaled a shift in perspective: the Anglo settlers' descendants, who until then had regarded the Mexicans and Indians of these regions as uncivilized peoples, now began to regard them with interest. The Southwest began to have a special appeal as Spanish culture began to be viewed as exotic, even fascinating, largely because of an interest in the "*peculiar blending* of cultures that characterized the region."[10]

But, as David Thomas observes, a crucial player was missing in the new border history that was beginning to gain official and public respectability—the Native Indian. At best, the Navajos, Apaches, Pueblos, Comanches, Acomas, Hopi, and Zuñi, to name but a few, were "peripheral participants in the borderlands experience."[11] While the revisionary impulses of the Bolton school were indeed salutary, they embodied ambivalence with regard to the status and role of Native Indians in borderland historiography. The dominant view was that the history of the native tribes was more or less the history of the modernization of primitive peoples as they slowly began to ascend the ladder of civilization. It seems as if in countering the hold of the leyenda negra on the American imagination, the Bolton school displaced the notion of inherent inferiority from the Spaniards onto the Native Indians. Weber notes that for all of Bolton's phenomenal efforts, Spanish history in the U.S. Southwest did not gain the kind of official recognition that Bolton had hoped it would. Historians like Earl Pompey, writing in 1955, held that the influence of the Spanish presence in the Southwest was at best an exaggeration. Yet another critic, Howard F. Cline, suggested broadening the framework in order to study the borderlands in the context of Caribbean and Central American histories, and even proposed the term "greater borderlands" to give geographical shape to what seemed to him a narrow field.[12] Weber notes that it was in the 1960s, with the rise of the Chicano movement in the United States, that the history of the Southwest began to gain critical importance, but with a crucial difference: while Bolton had focused exclusively on the Spanish presence, Chicano historians and writers stressed the experiences of Mexicans and their progeny in the Southwest.[13] Today, it is under the rubric of Chicano/a literature that the history of the borderlands is addressed. The preference for "Chicano"[14] instead of "borderlands" suggests the growing sensitivity to issues of race and ethnicity and the ubiquity of identity politics in the post-1960s United States. As Teresa McKenna observes, Chicano literature denotes "literary production by Mexicans or persons of Mexican descent living in the United States. . . . Courses featuring a range of Latino literatures are indeed taught and should be encouraged, but this literature should be addressed under another rubric."[15] It is important to bear in mind that Mexican and Chicana/o experience is central to any analysis of border societies;[16] therefore, the work of Mexican American or Chicano/a critics is invaluable and a welcome change from the narrow perspectives offered by earlier scholarship on the Southwest, in which Anglos are the single most important players in the West and all non-Anglos are either denied agency and voice or relegated to the periphery as marginal peoples. However, the shift from Bolton's emphasis on the Spanish presence in the Southwest to a focus on Mexican Americans or Chicana/os in the United States is not without its problems and challenges.

For example, Gloria Anzaldúa's *conciencia de la mestiza,* which embodies a mode of living in "psychic restlessness" and "states of perplexity"[17] engendered in the meeting of vastly divergent traditions and peoples in the borderlands, while functioning as a powerful trope for contemporary social and cultural formations in the Southwest, is grounded firmly in the archives of a pre-Columbian past. The history of the Cochise, the ancestors of the Aztecs, and the original inhabitants of the Southwest or, more appropriately for the Cochise, Aztlán, is important to Anzaldúa because it is their movement of travel southwards in the twelfth century and later their return to the north, *as a different people,* beginning in the sixteenth century, that marks a pivotal historical moment. While the travelers to the south were pureblooded, the ones who traveled back to Aztlán returned as mixed bloods. The fateful encounter between Spain and the Aztec empire spawned a new race of "hybrid progeny," what José Vasconcelos calls "la raza cósmica" (the cosmic, or fifth, race).[18] When they returned to the Southwest, they came back to Aztlán, their original homeland, but with fundamentally different visions and perspectives of history, culture, and identity. Focusing on the Cochise and the Aztecs enables Anzaldúa to give Aztlán a material presence while also drawing attention to the cultural and sociological effects of the intermingling of European and Amerindian societies in central Mexico and the Southwestern United States. To a large extent this puts into perspective why Anzaldúa's conceptualization of *la mestiza* hinges so centrally on the history of the Cochise and the Aztecs. The numerous references to Aztec myths, traditions, gods and goddesses in her essays and poems underscore the archeological import of her endeavor to trace webs of continuities between the past and the present.[19]

Although to critics like Rafael Pérez-Torres and Benjamin Alire Sáenz such attempts to excavate Aztec myth and culture risk the formation of a narrow vision that, in order to affirm unbroken ties to the past, glosses over historical exigencies and the profound disjunctions they engender,[20] it is worth noting that Anzaldúa's focus on Aztlán displaces the Euro-American focus with a north-south perspective. But what is of concern is that her eloquent poetic evocation of la mestiza as the central trope of border subjectivity and border crossings situates itself, for the most part and in large measure, in Mexican and Chicano/a experience and historiography. To be sure, she does acknowledge Mexican antipathy towards Indians and seems eager to undercut the internalization of this colonial mindset in Chicano/as, but it is hard not to notice that Mexico, Mexicans, Mexican Americans, and Chicano/as play a more central role in her configuration of la mestiza as a border subject. A novel like *Almanac*, as I will later argue, revises Anzaldúa's poetics and politics of the borderlands and la mestiza by reinscribing the history of the Yaquis, their experience in the nation of Mexico, and their vexed relationship with Mexicans as the structural framework within which to envision the final uprising of the dispossessed and marginalized of the Americas. The purpose here is not to delegitimize Anzaldúa's particular narration of border history, but to offer some comments on how a focus on Indian presence in the borderlands revises our reliance on Anglo-Mexican and Spanish-Aztec/Mesoamerican paradigms to conceptualize border experience and thus provides another sociohistorical interface that foregrounds the multiple axes along which diverse societies and cultures have interacted in the borderlands.

I am trying here to contest the premise that the central tension in the borderlands is Mexican resistance to Anglo hegemony. This premise evacuates the complex network of social relations that were formed in the borderlands, networks that gave rise to fundamental disjunctions in the formation of transborder ethnic and racial imaginaries. For instance, this includes the Tohono O'odham Nation of Arizona's attempts to secure border crossing rights for tribal members in Mexico to come to the United States for health care; U.S. Yaquis' concern with the observation of traditional ceremonies that require the presence of Mexican Yaquis in the United States; and Mexican Kickapoos' involvement with the bracero program of the 1950s and 1960s, which led to their working in the United States as migrant laborers.[21] This is why it is important to study the U.S. Southwest as an American Southwest in which, as Eric Anderson observes, "American Indian and Euro-American cultures have been migrating, most often against each other for a very long time."[22] What is important to Anderson is not the Southwest in its homogenous manifestation, but rather how "a variety of Southwests are produced" and where "metaphors and notions of travel, migration and movement appear to be more helpful than metaphors of borders and boundaries." However, this focus is a little problematic given that it is the material creation of border zones in the Southwest that engenders the dispersal and migration of various peoples. Anderson is, however, quick to note that he does not intend substituting "one set of slippery metaphors for another," a statement that aptly conveys the immense difficulty in imaging and imagining the borderlands as a plurality of Southwests that often overlap and intersect.[23]

Like Anderson, Noreen Groover Lape conceptualizes the West, by which she means the Southwest, less in terms of Turner's idea of the frontier as a rite of passage for settler communities and more in terms of Mary Louise Pratt's notion of contact zones, which Pratt defines as "social spaces where disparate cultures meet, clash, and grapple with each other, often in highly asymmetrical relations of domination and subordination—like colonialism, slavery, or their aftermath as they are lived across the globe today."[24] By reconfiguring the West as a material and discursive site that registers the "culturally fluid contexts of the contact zones," Lape is able to bring into focus the historical and social forces that engendered "multiple frontiers [that] were occupied by diverse cultural groups at disparate geographical points."[25] The force of Lape's arguments becomes clear when we take into account the many writers she studies, including John Rollin Ridge, Onoto Watanna, James Beckworth, and Sarah Winnemuca. At first glance this selection may seem representative of the multiracial history of the borderlands. But on closer examination we are unable to sustain our reliance on race and ethnicity to explain the paradoxes that emerge in the borderlands. For example, John Rollin Ridge, a half Cherokee, writes about a Mexican bandit in The *Life and Adventures of Joaquín Murieta,* and Onoto Watanna, a Chinese American, writes about interracial romance in *Miss Numé of Japan* while fashioning for herself a Japanese identity. But the questions Lape raises are interesting: how can we explain why an Indian, or rather a mixed blood, fashions a narrative about a Mexican bandit,[26] or why a Chinese American in the Southwest chooses to pass, not as white, but as Japanese? It is beyond the scope and focus of this chapter to explore Lape's arguments about these writers fully, but the point is clear—the premise that the central tension in the borderlands is Mexican resistance to Anglo hegemony evacuates the complex network of social relations that were formed in the borderlands.

If we reconfigure the Southwest as Indian country and as fluid zones of social and cultural contact, we will be compelled to problematize the war of 1848 as a historical point of reference for theorizing border phenomena and configuring border history. The principal players in the borderlands are no longer Mexicans and Anglos. Instead, the close and often antagonistic interactions among numerous Indian tribes and the Mexicans and the Anglos compel us to redraw, in both a material and a metaphoric sense, the boundaries that have been erected among them at various points in history.[27] In the context of the Indians of the Southwest, to speak of 1848 would be quite parochial because the United States and Mexico did not deign to take Native Indian presence into consideration in 1848. If the Southwest, in Anderson's view, "stand[s] restlessly and paradoxically as a place where alien, migratory cultures have been encountering each other and competing against each other for a very long time,"[28] the nearly 2,000-mile-long border dividing the United States and Mexico becomes not the only border but yet *another* borderline of separation among many others. The borderlands, in other words, are frayed with multiple, permeable borders—the borders that separate presidios and missions from the temporary dwelling places of the Apaches in Arizona and the Yaqui in Sonora and the small-town-like settings of the Pueblos of New Mexico, and the borders that separate Indian reservations and sacred lands from Mexican and American national geographic spaces. What emerges in the borderlands testifies to "a turning of boundaries and limits into the *in-between* spaces through which the meanings of cultural and social authority are negotiated."[29] Border writing and border cultural critiques do not seek teleological and organic forms of social explanation, but strive for the possibility of historical agency in forging a practice of what Guillermo Gómez-Peña calls the "epistemology of multiplicity and a border semiotics."[30] It is within such a particularized retheorization of the relations among the peoples who have historically migrated against each other in the borderlands that I argue that both *Intaglio* and *Almanac* can be viewed as border narratives whose critiques and double-coded affirmations of U.S. and Mexican nationalisms and American, Mexican, and Native Indian cultures and traditions are informed by transnational mythologies and bifocal histories of contact, settlement, conflict, migration, cohabitation, and syncretism in the borderlands.

I begin with Fernández's novel *Intaglio* because it foregrounds a fundamental disruption in Mexican American societal structures with the entry of women into the labor market late in the 1800s and charts the slow emergence of a middle class in the post-1960s United States. Of special significance here is the fraying of the homogenous working-class Chicano identity as women began to exert more control over issues of finance and education in the family, become a little less dependent on men, and gain access to public spaces and spheres hitherto denied them, such as schools and universities, starting of businesses, and ownership of property. While foregrounding the emergence of a Chicano feminist consciousness, the novel subtly and evocatively dramatizes the formation of border culture as a contradictory and multiply encoded process of social and ethnic affiliation.

While the primary issues that the American women's movement in the United States has addressed have been gender and femininity, Chicana feminism has paid attention to the "triple oppression" of women in the United States, obtained by the intersection of race, class, and gender. Women of Mexican descent have had to negotiate the highly mediated nature of their experiences as women whom race and class have positioned as second-class citizens in the United States.[31] Another important focus of Chicana feminism is its concern with the so-called machismo values of Mexican culture. When women internalize hierarchies of gender, it secures the authority of the man and validates a plethora of ideological justifications for the continued marginalization of the woman.[32] However, to Anzaldúa, instead of addressing gender inequity in Mexican American societies by focusing exclusively on a man-woman configuration, a more productive way of undermining gender hierarchies is to affirm the lesbian and gay constructions of human sexuality as well, rather than regarding them as byproducts of or aberrations from heterosexual and patriarchal power. Because the construction of a Mexican American female subjectivity necessarily involves negotiating the material and psychosocial effects of crossing the various borders of language, race, culture, class, and nation in the borderlands, Anzaldúa uses the term "mestiza consciousness" to denote the multiply encoded nature of Chicana border feminism.[33] My discussion, while situating *Intaglio* in this tradition of Chicana feminism and addressing the social and cultural effects of border crossings on Mexican American women and the manner in which they empower themselves by refashioning their roles in both the domestic sphere of home and the public sphere of work, attempts a materialist analysis of border crossings and their effects on border women.

Border Crossings and Mestiza Feminism in the Borderlands

In *Intaglio* Fernández presents six tales of border crossing, relocation, and exile as she charts the travails of a Texas border family struggling to create a sense of home and belonging in the Southwest.[34] While focusing on intergenerational conflicts of migrant families in the borderlands, these six stories stress the enduring presence and influence of Amerindian and Mexican thought patterns and cultural forms in the domestic spaces sanctioned and occupied by border women, and the manner in which they often contest and realign these spaces to register discontent and opposition and, in some cases, overturn traditionally sanctioned codes and conventions designed to position them as either inferior or as products and commodities of a male-dominated social and political economy. Each short narrative, titled after the name of one of the women the narrator, Nenita, describes, foregrounds border women in a variety of roles—as dancers, seamstresses, tarot-card readers, storytellers, historians, and healers. The stories rework several folk tales, signs, and symbols, such as *la curandera, la bruja,* and *la llorona,* as the women cross traditionally sanctioned roles and boundaries designed to place women under systems of hegemony, insert themselves into the public sphere of work and accountability, and refashion their social and gendered roles and identities. It is a reworking that engenders a feminist consciousness, or as Sonia Saldívar-Hull would have it, a "bridge feminism" that seeks to make connections across the divides of race, culture, language, ethnicity, and nation.[35] This feminism does not succumb to the seductive appeal of binary configurations, pure epistemologies, and stable ontologies. Instead, engendered as it is by the "coming together of two self-consistent but habitually incompatible frames of reference," it speaks in a tongue that is forked even as it mongrelizes its cultural affiliations while embracing moments and processes of ambiguity and contradiction.[36] In short, it is a mestiza feminism of the borderlands.

Rather than dealing with each story separately, I will focus on some pertinent issues that the stories address: the effects of the Mexican Revolution of 1910 on the U.S. Southwest; the gradual but inevitable process of Americanization in border families; the attempt by borderlanders to cling to native cultural practices; the continuing yet paradoxical significance of *curanderismo* and archetypal figures like la bruja and la llorona in shaping the worldviews of Nenita as she grows up torn between conflicting traditions and cultures; the desire to remember and record native history; and finally, the affirmation of la conciencia de la mestiza.

In the first story, "Andrea," Nenita, as a little girl and an aspiring dancer, browses through a photo album containing pictures of Tía Consuelo and, more important to Nenita, of Tía Andrea as a dancer. In a picture in which Andrea's demeanor is at odds with Consuelo's solemn and morose appearance, Nenita's aunt Griselda explains away the contradiction as the result of Consuelo having to "adjust to a new culture" (Fernández, 17). But why does Andrea, unlike Consuelo, not have any problem adjusting to American culture? This significant attitudinal difference between the sisters can be better understood in the context of their family's migration to the United States during the Revolution. Consuelo, who is ten years older than Andrea, was born in Mexico, while Andrea was born in Texas after the family migrated to the United States. This fact of history seems to be the fault line between the two sisters. It affects their choice of vocations, mates, and clothing, and also their divergent views about Americanization and native cultural practices.

With the death of their father in the Revolution, Griselda and her daughter Consuelo struggle to eke out a living in San Antonio, and soon Consuelo gets a job as a maid in Mrs. Ernestine Bristol's house. While Andrea, encouraged by the Bristols, begins to fashion a new career as a professional dancer, Consuelo remains a maid for the Bristols. But Consuelo perceives that for all their interest in her sister, the Bristols "never treated Andrea like a real person" and "looked upon her as a cute doll who could do unusual tricks. Take a bow, twirl to the left, give a good *zapateado*. Andrea loved to perform and went along with all the requests" (Fernández, 33). In Consuelo's eyes, Andrea's success as a dancer exacts a toll: "Those experiences pushed her farther away from our reality"; "we were extremely poor and Andrea never seemed connected to our circumstances," "never contributed to the household," and "ignored Mama" (Fernández, 33).

Ironically, the celebration of native culture, instead of drawing the sisters together, only pulls them apart. To Consuelo, Andrea's success as a dancer is the result not so much of the intrinsic richness of Mexican and Spanish dance forms or even of Andrea's talent, but of the Bristols' patronage. Two things result: uneven class formations in the border family and the commodification of Mexican dance. Andrea's success as a dancer eventually positions her as a middle-class American (with money, a comfortable lifestyle, and the ability to travel), while Consuelo is confined to her working-class identity as a maid. This division in class positioning alienates Andrea from what Consuelo considers the roots of their family's past. As Andrea herself notes, "I never had the home

[Consuelo] missed. So, I've always managed to live pretty fully in the present" (Fernández, 27). To Consuelo, home always lay and would lie on the other side, the Mexican side, of the border; home is the memory of becoming "fully formed" (Fernández, 17), of "screaming in the middle of the night," of being "uprooted" (Fernández, 27), and of becoming poor upon their father's death.

By foregrounding the intersection of the Revolution, white patronage, and class formations, this story stresses the insufficiency of ethnicity as a stable marker of identity and the incommensurable historical processes that shape and inform each sister's experience of the borderlands. But some questions arise: Is Andrea American or Mexican American? Is Consuelo Mexican or simply a Mexican who refuses to become American? What does the process of Americanization imply? The experience of travel and relocation in the borderlands occasions, for the sisters, a form of "dwelling . . . in heterogeneous histories."[37] The crucial word here is "dwelling," a mode of living in transit, a way of making a home in the experience of homelessness. But this does not mean that the past is of little or no importance when migrants move from one location to another. Rather, in clinging to the idea of a "lost" home and "liv[ing] in her memories" (Fernández, 26), when Consuelo visits San Luis Potosí she is unable to account for the realities of historical change: "What she found there no longer corresponded to what she remembered" (Fernández, 27). Traveling, notes Trinh T. Minh-ha, "can turn out to be a process whereby the self loses its fixed boundaries" (Minh-ha, 23) and where memory embodies a mode of translation in which identity is constructed, "whose boundaries are *continually repositioned in relation to varying points of reference.*"[38]

It is in these moments that dwelling, as a mode of temporal living in which varying points of references emerge, becomes a translational experience. If border crossing results in the recognition that memory cannot offer a fixed point of reference, it also creates new forms of cultural recovery and practice. In an ironic twist in the narrative, Consuelo becomes more attached to the Carduccis, her sister Andrea's in-laws, learns to speak Italian, becomes a member of the *Figli d'Italia*, participates in the San Giuseppe celebrations, and becomes "quite comfortable with their ways" (Fernández, 31). Her experience of dislocation results not in the revival of Mexican culture but in her affiliating herself with and renewing Italian sociocultural practices! It is possible to view Consuelo's interest in things Italian as a gesture of substitution in which something takes the place of her lost home, Mexico. But the crucial question is, why the Carduccis and Italian language and culture? I am not arguing that by virtue of her Italian interest, Consuelo discards her Mexican-ness and becomes Italian, but rather that Italianness seems to offer a more affirmative response to existing outside of Anglo culture. The issue is further complicated when Nenita dreams of going not to Mexico but to Italy with Consuelo: "While she held me, I imagined the two of us on tour in Rome. . . . Everywhere we went I performed my favorite pieces" (Fernández, 35). But it is as a professional dancer of Mexican dance forms that Nenita imagines herself in this dream, not just as an American or a Mexican.

Whether it is the desire to construct home in foreign locations or to sustain native cultural practices in places away from home, the important question is not so much the affirmation of any stable home or culture as its reconstruction and recovery through a mode of translation that both compels and enables the borderlanders to move in and out of different cultures and languages. Furthermore, as we have seen, the practice of sustaining native culture is intimately connected to the geographical location and class positioning of the borderlanders, which significantly inform their attitudes toward the host society and the degree of their involvement in their native cultures. In the context of this story, the experience of growing up in the borderlands engenders an ethnic border morphology whose multivalent complexity is riven with the disjunctive effects of displacement and migration during the Revolution and its aftermath in the Southwest. In yet another instance of paradoxical forms of cross-cultural and communal identification, the story "Zulema" highlights the subtle reworking of Mexican and American traditions during the Revolution, particularly in reference to border crossing and border experience.

For the revolutionaries, crossing the Mexican border into the United States meant being able to recoup, regather, rearm themselves and their supporters, and collect more resources to enable them to recross the border and renew their fight against the Mexican army.[39] Although to the revolutionaries and migrants the borderline served as a protective cover to thwart the advances of the pursuing Mexican police, border crossing was not a one-time affair. One could cross and recross the border several times a day or a week. In "Zulema" the characters cross the border in two ways: literally and figuratively. As Nenita reminisces about Zulema, her own relationship with her, and Zulema's personal history, we learn that Isabel, Zulema's mother, died while giving birth to Zulema's brother Miguelito in 1914. But unable to bring herself to inform Zulema of her mother's death, Mariana, Isabel's sister, made up the story that Isabel had left Zulema and the newborn Miguelito with her and crossed the border to join her terminally ill sister in San Antonio, Texas. As days turn into months and months turn into years, Zulema can only fantasize about her mother's return as she hears stories of "dozens of people who crossed the bridge with their belongings in wheelbarrows or in suitcases of every sort" (Fernández, 141). Soon Zulema develops the habit of making up stories and inventing "one tale after another with superbly eccentric characters who continued to whirl about" (Fernández, 138). Over the years she and Nenita come to "live in their own special little world, with all [their] cuentos" (Fernández, 147). One significant story is Zulema's version of Sleeping Beauty, in which the prince is captured by the *federales* and his horse is held hostage by the Mexican revolutionary Emiliano Zapata. The prince's castle is destroyed and he is declared a commoner. Without his castle, his horse, and his princely power, he cannot meet Sleeping Beauty and kiss her awake, and she is condemned to remain "out there in the woods forever and forever" (Fernández, 143).

Zulema's narrative may be seen to cross another border, the one that separates literature from history, Mexican culture from Anglo culture. The story of Sleeping Beauty, a hugely popular tale mythologized in western societies, merges with Zulema's quotidian reality—the Mexican

Revolution. The characters in the story, Sleeping Beauty and the prince, are indigenized as the prince is made to represent the Mexicans fighting the revolutionaries, and Sleeping Beauty's predicament becomes, by implication, Zulema's own predicament of waiting for her mother Isabel's return. Zapata is cast not as a heroic figure in this *cuento* but as one who hinders the full development of the story. This cuento embodies a mode of translating Mexican history and Anglo mythology, a translation in which revolutionary heroes are demythologized and an Anglo-Saxon symbology is made to yield to local experience. The casting of the prince as Mexican may have more to do with Zulema's personal experience of living in Mexico during the Revolution. This story, with its reworking of diverse traditions and its interweaving of multiple syncretic narrative forms, underscores the role and function of Mexican culture and beliefs in the borderlands. This leads us to ask, how are Mexican and Amerindian cultural forms and conventions sustained and revived as borderlanders negotiate the threat of cultural imperialism posed by Anglo America? The story "Filomena" dramatizes the implications of this important question.

Significantly, Nenita introduces Filomena in the context of a history of national and international disturbances: Filomena loses her father in the Mexican Revolution, her husband in World War II, and her son, Alejandro, in the Korean War. Faced with raising three children in Texas as a single parent, Filomena decides to recross the border into Mexico and leave her two youngest children with her relatives in Michoacan, hoping she can come back to get them at a later date.

This act of recrossing the border problematizes at least three dominant myths related to the phenomenon of immigration in the United States and borderland experience: one, the myth of reinvention, which involves a reworking of identity through a process of erasing the past and acquiring or assimilating into an American identity; two, the myth of looking back toward home (in this context, Mexico) with a sense of nostalgia, a gesture that results in the creation and evocation of an idealized originary place of belonging, frozen in time and space; and three, the myth that the loss of a native culture is inevitable but is nonetheless offset by significant gains through the acquisition of a public persona and the ability to participate as a citizen in the United States by acquiring English language skills and education, a view explored by Richard Rodriguez in his controversial autobiography, *Hunger of Memory.*[40]

It is a commonplace that migrant peoples, especially when they face opposition or resistance in their place of location, tend to remember the place they left behind as a lost Eden. This pastoral recreation of home, in which they place a heavy emotional and cultural investment, is more often than not far removed from their actual histories and realities. A fundamental discrepancy emerges between what they imagine to happen and what really happens in that place called home. But when migrating peoples exercise some measure of choice in choosing the lands they travel to and the societies in which they live and settle down, home functions less as an idealized place to return to and more as a symbol of what they wanted to leave or even flee from. In the historical context of this story, it would be logical to assume that once people crossed the border from Mexico into the United States, they would not desire to return home. In a sense, only the present and future would matter, not the past. In such a view, Mexico would tend to be conceived of as an inhospitable place, or at best a place to which one could retire after building sufficient financial resources in the United States. But this myth of no return, this desire to shed the old and construct the new in the new land of opportunity called America, is undermined in this story. Filomena's desire to recross the border into Mexico stems not from nostalgia but from the hard reality of a life of poverty in the United States. Her work in Texas "never yielded a sufficient income," and she is unable to obtain her widow's pension due to "bureaucratic stipulations" (Fernández, 66). There is, however, yet another reason why Filomena goes every year to Mexico: to celebrate El Día de los Muertos, the Day of the Dead (to honor Mictlantecuhtli, the lord of the dead). Her yearly pilgrimage keeps alive the memories of her dead father, husband, and son and gives her a sense of belonging, which can be sustained, however, only through the ritualized observance of Amerindian religious forms on the island of Janitzio, the traditional cemetery for the festival.

After Alejandro's death Filomena decides to go to Janitzio along with Nenita and her two children. But this is the last time that they observe this festival in Mexico. Upon their return and for the following three years, Filomena sets up her own *altercitos* in her house to commemorate the festival. On November 2, the same day on which Catholics observe All Souls' Day, sometimes as many as twenty children join Filomena in observing the Tarascan ritual El Día de los Muertos. The contrast between the Catholic festival and the Tarascan ritual lies in their attitude toward death and life and in their use of symbols. All Souls' Day is observed by paying a visit to the cemetery and laying a wreath on the graves and tombs of loved ones. But the Tarascan ritual in Filomena's house is a "joyous and elaborate" event (Fernández, 78). Some children bring skulls made of sugar, candleholders shaped like the tree of life, bamboo flutes, miniature skeleton-musicians made of gesso and painted in bright hues, wooden crosses decorated with chrysanthemums, and richly embroidered napkins. As the ceremony begins and as the incantations reverberate through the little house, a "joyous reverence" (Fernández, 79) envelops Nenita as Kika, the pet Amazon parrot, perches on her shoulder and the image of Alejandro, who died in the Korean War, takes shape right before her eyes.

It is significant that the observance of ritual revitalizes a communal form of native religious practice not in Mexico but in Texas, in Filomena's house. The presence of children at this event can be construed as signaling the possibility that this native Tarascan ritual can retain its vitality even in a land outside of Mexico, where it evolved, and that the rituals can be passed on to a new generation of borderers. Through memory and ritual, a sense of communal identification and home is created as children far removed from their grandparents' histories of migration and displacement are able to regather in Texas and attain a measure of meaningful participation through ritualizing a transplanted Tarascan practice. Whereas to Filomena her adopted home, the United States, is more homely than the land in which she was born, to her children, Lucila and Mateo, their adopted home, Mexico, is more hospitable than an alienating America. As these contradictions emerge within this border family, the interconnecting and overlapping historical processes of change and disruption position different members of the same family on both sides of the border and engender paradoxical constructions of home and belonging.

But in times of regathering, cultural transplantation also involves cultural translation, a process in which that which is transplanted undergoes change. Translation thus engenders a rearticulation of culture that embodies the psychosocial effects of crossing the material and cultural borders in the borderlands and engenders a critical consciousness as borderlanders refuse to immerse themselves unproblematically in native culture. Instead, as the story "Esmeralda" dramatizes, their impulse is to question the assumptions and prejudices of native culture.

In "Esmeralda" Fernández focuses on the experience of rape in the family of Los Lunas and creates a poignant narrative of healing and recovery in which the Luna women, through a process of sharing personal tragedies and family secrets, attempt to restore a semblance of dignity and self-respect to Verónica, a victim of brutal assault. Forced to take up full-time work to support herself and her studies in San Antonio, Verónica takes a job selling tickets at the Palace Theater. She resists the overtures of the Mondragone youths and is abducted and raped. The rest of the story concerns itself with how the Luna women attempt to deal with this bitter experience.

The differences are stark between the response to rape by the Luna women and in what is generally accepted in contemporary American and, in general, Western medical practice. The methods of diagnosis, prescription, and treatment in the practice of medicine and, more particularly, in respect of the evaluation and scientific study of human sexuality in the Euro-American medical discourses form a discursive domain in which an array of psychosocial categories, disciplines, institutions, and vocations are created. School counselors, psychiatrists, hospitals, routine blood and tissue examinations, interviews by psychologists, police reports, legal documents, and privatizing of grief and healing—all these practices, with their emphasis on individual suffering and healing, are displaced in the story by curanderismo.

The Luna women take care of Verónica for several weeks, never leaving her alone. Some bring herbal patches and different kinds of sprigs to be mixed with tea and ointments, while others bring yerba del oso (cow parsnip) and maravilla with baby oil, which they rub into her skin while massaging her battered body. Their treatments include giving her "hot minted baths, mixed with either romerillo or pegapega" (Fernández, 124), burning creosote in clay urns, rubbing palm leaves up and down the length of her body, giving her chamomile tea, and providing *anímala* (cheering up). Although a single curandera[41] is absent in this story, all the women of the family perform the necessary rituals and observe the conventions of curanderismo. Far from succumbing to a nostalgic yearning to celebrate native culture, Fernández dramatizes the enduring influence of native folk healing practices not because they are intrinsically Mexican or Amerindian but because, as Robert Trotter and Juan Chavira note, they use "culturally appropriate methods of dealing with the patients, methods that activate the natural support systems already existing in the community, rather than attempting to develop new or artificial support systems."[42] To a predominantly lower working class of borderlanders who cannot afford costly medical care in the United States, curanderismo provides cheaper alternative methods of dealing with sickness and injuries. Often the healers are members of the patient's family or family network and also come from the same class. Rather than the patient being taken to the hospital, they go to the patient's house; appointments and referrals are not required; bureaucratic procedures do not stall the administration of care and medicine; and rather than there being fees for their services, the patient gives what she can according to her capabilities at that point in her life.[43]

As Verónica gradually responds well to this folk art of healing the mind and the body, their ministrations have a profound impact on the Luna women: "And they cried with me. In fact, one afternoon, Leonor said we were all going to cry together for the *sorrows of all the women* in the family. A wailing session she called. *Lloronas, todas*" (Fernández, 125; emphasis added). Cultural memory is signified by the archetypal figure of la llorona,[44] a mythic figure merging Indian and Spanish popular beliefs. Long considered a ubiquitous haunting presence of the spirit of women wailing for their murdered children, la llorona fuses the Spanish medieval idea of *ánimus en pena*, spirits atoning for their sins in purgatory, with the pre-Columbian Aztec heroine Mocihuaquetzque (who died in childbirth), revered for being born in the afterlife to take the place of warriors. Such was the power of this heroine that sometimes the Aztec warriors took with them into their battles the third finger of a dead Mocihuaquetzque's left hand in the belief that it possessed supernatural powers that would aid them in defeating their enemies, and tribal witch doctors used their hair or their left arms in their healing ceremonies.[45] By weaving curanderismo and the myth of la llorona into her narrative, Fernández foregrounds not only the continuing power of Mexican beliefs and traditions on the borderlanders, but their ability to restore a sense of agency and articulate a form of resistance to male domination. The tales and wailing of other women engender in Verónica a spirit of resilience:

> Hearing [them] gave me the courage to take control of my own situation. So, when my turn came, I spoke in the name of all the women and girls who had experienced sexual violation on the same day I did. On my own behalf, though, I insisted that the wailing stop. "I do not want to become a victim," I said and the others cried for me with relief. (Fernández, 127)

It is through identifying with women suffering a fate similar to hers that Verónica is able to restore to herself a sense of agency and avoid giving in to despair. But the gesture of resistance is not the action of an individual woman who, through knowledge and education and clever manipulation of public institutions like the judiciary and the press, attains a public voice to articulate a demand for respect. Rather, this story foregrounds the negotiation of the recovery of cultural memory and of resisting the demands of a male-dominated society as a complex process of refashioning an already sanctioned space for women—the domestic space of home—as a space harboring oppositional potential.

In the scene where the Luna women gather around Verónica and weep and wail and confess to each other their secret pasts, la llorona both signifies the "fate" of women at the hands of men and gestures toward the possibility of using the very social and material structures used to suppress them—in this context the home and feminine vocation—to register opposition and resistance. Through manipulation, the women are eventually able to get Verónica married to David Baca, a friend of Alfredo's who is a teacher of international business, and thus provide legitimacy for the bastard child of the rape. But Nenita is ambivalent about this act, wondering "what disappointments, if any, lay ahead for all three of them. Looking at the tiny baby I considered whether Verónica had willingly stepped inside an invisible, but nonetheless binding, wall of self-delusion" (Fernández, 131). Obviously she disapproves of the women's deception, considering it simply another form of delusion. Nenita's appreciation for the ameliorative power of native healing is mingled with a deep distrust, since there is always the possibility of delusion in trying to deny the reality of rape, as for instance when Amanda, in referring to the rape, insists that "Verónica had experienced a *great fright*" (Fernández, 124; emphasis added). In Nenita's response, Fernández evokes what is at best an ambiguous attitude toward a native sociocultural practice of healing. It is a mark of borderland experience that while borderers are unable to reconcile fully the tension between native conventions and American practices, they develop a certain kind of critical acumen that enables them to view the debilitating aspects of both Mexican and American traditions. Neither totally affirming nor rejecting either tradition, they develop a critical consciousness that denies to both any intrinsic value. It is, as Anzaldúa notes, la conciencia de la mestiza.[46]

These stories foreground the subtle forms of cultural transformation in the domestic spaces officially sanctioned and reserved for border women and the manner in which they transgress and contest these "natural" spaces. By taking pride in specializing in their vocations and using their skills to manipulate those societal structures that place them at a disadvantage, these border women disturb the familiar division between private and public created by a patriarchal society and literally bring the world into the home and the home into the world. This disturbance "captures something of the estranging sense of the relocation of the home and the world," a relocation in which "the recesses of the domestic space become sites for history's most intricate invasions."[47] It is a disturbance, as we have seen, embodying profound social and cultural disorderliness, and it is in the disorderliness of border experience that we mark the evolution of a mestiza feminist consciousness in the borderlands. While *Intaglio* focuses specifically on Mexican Americans in the borderlands and mestiza cultures formed on the border, as it were, how does a focus on Native Indian presence in the borderlands affect our conceptualization of border communities and border economies?

The Dream of the Fifth World in the Borderlands

Leslie Marmon Silko's *Almanac of the Dead* narrates the continuing saga of Old World–New World contact, in which the prophecies encoded in an ancient Yaqui almanac come to fruition as the marginalized and dispossessed of the Americas dream the birthing of a fifth world.[48] It is not the dream of the ancient mariner seeking to map the *orbis terrarum;* it is not the dream of the rich merchant eager to discover the quickest route to the Indies; it is not the vision of the conquistador eager to subdue resisting natives and plunder the Seven Cities of Cibola; and it is not the greed of the adventurer looking west as he conquers and tames the frontier in search of El Dorado. The dream of the fifth world in *Almanac* is contestatory, its impulse is revenge, and its game plan is the reclamation of stolen land.[49] The dream is a "vivid enactment of the long prophesied collapse of European domination and the simultaneous resurgence of the Native American peoples of much of the continent."[50]

The dream of the fifth world hinges on a central question: How can we negate and overturn the legacy of colonialism and its stultifying effects and contemporary manifestations in the Americas?[51] We cannot fully appreciate the novel's engagement with this question unless we situate it in the transborder social and cultural economy of the U.S. Southwest and read it as a border tale, a narrative that registers the warp and weft of border crossings.

As Bernie Harder notes, the trope of the border is central to the novel:

> The whole novel is concerned with examining the nature of borders and boundaries; state borders, treaty boundaries, and boundaries between white and Native America; between European religion and Native spirituality; between dehumanization and spiritual wisdom. . . . All these borders, and more, such as those defining prisons, reservations, states, and private property, interact with each other; they are *different layers* of the geographical border.[52]

Harder argues that Silko offers a strong critique of oppressive state machineries that seek to impose boundaries on tribal lands, and of the ideology of nationalism, which imposes alien notions of space and time on native peoples. Harder stresses the need to recognize the "alternative views grounded in an older historical reality of the First Nations in North and Central America," including the affirmation of the "spiritual power of Native Americans" and their ability to be in "harmony with the ancestral spirits." Indeed, Harder goes so far as to give primacy to religious beliefs when he notes that "the relationship to society, territory, and the earth is based on understanding the teachings of the *spirits rather than on control based on human ideas.*"[53] But even as Harder critiques the power of national borders, he views Indian spirituality as a discursive border marking the separation between indigenous and nonnative ideas of human interaction with the natural world. While this border or "difference" may have some validity, it risks lending credence to familiar stereotypes of the "noble savage," who, unlike the crass and utilitarian European, lives in instinctual spiritual "harmony with the earth."[54]

More importantly, however, intertribal border conflicts are subsumed within the broader discourse of national border crossings. Thus, Harder is not able to pay attention to the historical realities of cross-racial, cross-cultural, transnational, and intertribal contact in the borderlands. In my focus on New Mexican Apaches and Sonoran Yaquis, I tease out the social, political, and cultural transformations and effects of transborder, intertribal tensions in the border regions. I hope to demonstrate that the grounds on which anticolonial and anti-imperial resistance can be fashioned involve a recognition of the myriad of complex ways in which tribal border crossings are affected by national borders and in which intertribal contact shapes different nationalisms on both sides of the U.S.-Mexican border, albeit with profoundly different effects on Indian communities in the borderlands. It is in this context that *Almanac* seeks to dismantle the ideological structures that have legitimized the writing and inscribing of colonial history by revising its legalistic, legislative, and nationalistic language and codes. Such an endeavor involves acknowledging the various kinds of conflicts the border represents, recognizing the multiple positionings of those who inhabit the myriad contact zones of the West, and negotiating the clash of different value systems in the borderlands. To Virginia Bell, *Almanac* "continues to emphasize the regional and global economic networks in which all the characters are caught."[55] Bell's emphasis on the transnational and the local as interlocked sites of struggle dovetails nicely with my own attempt to read the novel as a border tale. In my study of *Almanac*, I focus particularly on the transborder movement of Native Indians and Mexicans across the U.S.-Mexican border and the impact of these border crossings on the nature of Apache resistance, the formation of intertribal coalitions, and the fashioning of forms of contestation that take into account the multiple and often contradictory positionings of those involved in revolutionary struggles. While situating *Almanac* in this broad framework, I discuss the significance of the novel's dramatization of the clash among several different narratives regarding the capture and death of the Apache warrior Geronimo. Studying these narratives will show how the history of the Apaches of Arizona is intimately tied up with the history of the Yaquis south of the border in Sonora, and how a recognition of the animosity between Mexicans and Yaquis in Mexico provides a historical perspective on the attitudes of Mexican Americans and Chicanos toward people of Indian descent in the United States and Mexico.

Resistance in the Borderlands

The year 1886 marked a turning point in the history of the borderlands. It was the year in which the ever-resisting Apache warrior Geronimo met with two U.S. generals—General George Crook in May and General Nelson Miles in September—to negotiate the terms of his surrender. After eluding U.S. cavalry for several years, escaping from their clutches numerous times, and avoiding a posse of more than five thousand U.S. soldiers, Geronimo had gained a reputation in the American imagination as the "Bad Injun," the perfect embodiment of all the evil the Native Indians were capable of, namely deceit, murder, bloodthirstiness, cunning, and savage brutality. His capture, or rather surrender, in 1886 is significant not because a bandit was ultimately brought in by the long arm of the law, but rather because, as Frederick W. Turner III puts it, "the great adventure" of "making the continent" was over as "the last remnants of the human barriers" to European expansionism in the New World were apprehended.[56] With the "removal" of Geronimo, the Indian Removal Act of 1830 had finally come to complete fruition, and it is not surprising that the historian Frederick Jackson Turner, in a slightly different context, announced the American frontier to have ended in 1890. Just as the wild frontier had finally been tamed, so had the Native Indian, the barbarian of the frontier, also been removed to facilitate the onward march of progress. Civilization had finally triumphed over barbarism. The European race had finally realized its "manifest destiny" and through conquest and imperial practices either subdued those who resisted the advent of modernity in America or domesticated and civilized the unresisting through religious instruction, English-language learning, the establishment of reservations and schools, and introduction to modern technology. Never again would a Native American tribe or leader wage a serious war against the U.S. government.

Geronimo's is a legacy of resistance to the expansionist programs of white settlers in the United States. With dogged persistence, even when the other Apache tribes, including the Chiricahua, Mescalero, Lipan, and Jicarilla, had more or less acceded to the demands of the United States and some Apaches, such as Kieta and Martine, served as scouts for the U.S. soldiers, Geronimo and his army fiercely resisted the American troops and, to avoid capture, would cross with ease across the U.S.-Mexican border into the terrain of the Sierra Madre in Sonora, Mexico. They would also frequently skirmish with Mexican government forces eager to aid in capturing him.[57] After Geronimo eventually surrendered to General Miles in Skeleton Canyon in 1886, he and members of his band were frequently moved from prison to prison and camp to camp until finally they were sequestered at Fort Sill, Oklahoma. After 1907 the remaining survivors were given the option of staying in Oklahoma or being shifted to the Mescalero Reservation in New Mexico.[58] Geronimo and his surrender were of such importance that on March 4, 1905, he rode in the presidential procession of President Theodore Roosevelt, but, as Charles Johnston, who recorded his own account of the event, observes, the native chieftain "did not deign to give" the chief executive "a nod of salutation."[59] Geronimo died on February 17, 1909, in a military hospital at Fort Sill.

Almanac problematizes these versions of Geronimo's capture and the mythic identity he assumed as the U.S. government pursued him relentlessly. Old Yoeme, the Yaqui woman, tells her daughters, Lecha and Zeta, that because she had actually seen photographs of his surrender, she could speak with authority on the matter, and she instructs them to listen carefully to her version of the events and write them down in a notebook by way of updating the ancient almanac. Yoeme narrates the "real" story of Geronimo's capture, and while noting that "there has been too much confusion among white people and their historians" regarding Geronimo, she tells them that "Geronimo" was simply not the real name of the Apache warrior. It was a name given him by the Mexican and U.S. soldiers. Moreover, the man seen meeting with General Miles to negotiate the terms of his surrender in the photograph taken at Skeleton Canyon was "a man who always accompanied the one who performed the feat" (Silko, 129). In Yoeme's story the real Geronimo is not a brave and vengeful warrior but rather a medicine man who could perform "some feats." A few chapters later, Calabaza, a Sonoran Yaqui who is "part of the new generation that the old-time people had scolded for its peculiar interest in 'now' and tomorrow" (Silko, 222) and is involved in smuggling people and commodities across the border, listens to his aunts and elderly Yaquis, specifically Old Mahalawas, telling stories of Geronimo. In these stories the Arizona Apaches and the Sonoran Yaquis overlook the animosities they had prior to the coming of the Europeans and together put up strong resistance to the encroaching Mexicans and Americans. As Calabaza learns, Geronimo could elude General Miles's soldiers because Sonoran Yaquis hid him in the Sierra Madre when he crossed the Arizona border into Mexico. In addition to these stories' stress on the growing intertribal coalitions formed in the borderlands to oppose Mexican and American policies designed to drive the Indians further into the land and eventually dispossess them, the most fascinating thing about Geronimo in them is that the whites never captured the real Geronimo because there was no "real" Geronimo to begin with.

According to Yaqui legends, four Apache warriors were often misidentified as Geronimo—Red Clay (the fourth Geronimo, who died in Oklahoma in 1909), Sleet, Big Pine, and Wide Ledge. These Apaches did not work together as a unit but led separate bands of Indians to conduct raids and attack U.S. troops. The central problem in accepting such an idea is the photographs Miles had taken of Geronimo's surrender at Skeleton Canyon in 1886. But according to Yaqui legends, even when all the warriors were captured at separate times and photographs were taken of them, the images that appeared in the prints did not resemble any of them. Several theories were advanced by the storytellers: the play of light, the polished crystal in the black box used to take the pictures, and the restless soul of an Apache warrior seeking vengeance and imprinting its image on the pictures. The surrender to General Miles was conceived to save the other Apache warriors by an old man, Pancakes, who "spent most of his time dozing under shady trees" (Silko, 230). He tricked Miles into believing that he was the real Geronimo. Although he thought the deceit might soon be recognized, he became caught up in the political intrigues that plagued Washington, and soon the legend of the capture of Geronimo captured the imagination of the American public. Although reporters from the *New York Times* and the *Washington Post* suspected foul play, their photographs of Pancakes showed the same Geronimo who had appeared in earlier photographs, who did not bear any resemblance to any of the other Apaches mistakenly identified as Geronimo. These Yaqui legends not only complicate the veracity of the official account of Geronimo's capture by Miles, they also critique the very notion of representation, which validates the photographs as authentic copies of real events.

According to Wide Ledge, the whites believed that they could give names to people and things, each of which would thus have an unchanging identity and become an identifiable object. They believed that an unmediated process of representation was embodied in photography: that photographs represented in exact detail and form the person or thing being photographed. This is a notion alien to Yaqui thought, which stressed that a person "might need a number of names in order to conduct all of his or her earthly business" (Silko, 227). In a larger sense, the Yaqui conception of reality as a variegated, perpetually changing phenomenon counters the basic premise of U.S. expansionist programs in the borderlands and, by implication, of European endeavors in the Americas: the religiously sanctioned mandate given to Adam, i.e., man, to subdue the earth and establish dominion over nature, an act that defined the very essence of Europe and its peoples. The Indian worldview did not allow the absolute separation between humans and nature that the European worldview hinged on. As Frederick W. Turner III notes, Thoreau's fascination with the Indians was based on his respect for the way they did not view the land as nature to be subdued but desired to "offer [themselves] to it in order to live with it." They viewed human beings "as participating with the natural world in the huge cycle of life"[60] and were inclined to regard themselves not as opposed to nature but as active players along with the earth in a cosmic drama in which man's future and well being were directly proportional to the manner in which he treated and respected the earth and its resources. Thus, the Yaqui idea that the photographs were not able to "capture" the presence of Geronimo through a static process of representation coincides with their conception of the natural order of things, in which the souls of the departed played an active part in human affairs and in which reality could not be arrested in any chain of signification.

But what is at issue here? The novel does not just point out that in broad terms the European and Indian worldviews differed. Rather, by complicating the narrative of the removal of the Indians and the conquest of the frontier, the novel inserts in the public imagination a long tradition of native resistance to white settlers in the borderlands. It is not enough to note that whatever the Indian perspective, there is no denying that Geronimo was indeed captured and thus the Americans had finally subdued the Apaches. The purpose here is not to disprove this fact but to call into question its *import*—if the Apaches do not think that Geronimo is captured, then fact or fiction, fancy or magic realism, for all practical purposes there is no end to the war between the United States and the Apaches since the terms of engagement are understood in fundamentally different ways. David L. Moore views the multiple Indian narratives of Geronimo as a "performance of semiotic play" that contests "colonial projections," which in this context can refer to the value and importance given to non-Indian historiography about Indians.[61]

In a similar vein, in her short story "A Geronimo Story," Silko underscores the shaping power of language and narrative as alternative modes of contesting domination. Andy, a young Laguna man, accompanies his uncle Siteye as a scout on an expedition with U.S. army officers to hunt for the Apache warrior. Although they fail to lead the army officers to Geronimo, the story, as Helen Jaskoski notes, "resonate[s] with the theme of Andy's initiation."[62] Andy learns about techniques of riding, corralling, saddling, and feeding horses; the ancient bed of lava in Navajo myths; the colonizing impulses of white settlers; and the desperate anger of Apache warriors. Thus, the hunting expedition for Geronimo turns into a rite of passage for this young Laguna, especially as Siteye narrates to his nephew stories of his past, of the mesa and the harshness of the desert, the dryness of rocks, the secret caves filled with food and water for hunters and wanderers. In more ways than one, the story of Geronimo is not really about Geronimo the man but about the emergence of various narratives of his life and deeds, particularly his stringent opposition to U.S. efforts to dispossess Indian tribes in the Southwest, that begin to circulate among the Indians. The power of Geronimo lies precisely in his absence, in the traces and tracks he leaves behind. These can be read as a meaningful text of resistance and strategic contestation only by Indians such as Andy, who learns the power of language, how it functions as a fluid, open-ended, and paradoxical process of representation, and how it can be used both to track the history of the past and to imprint the meaning of the present on individual and tribal consciousness.

This is why, to Silko, tracking the one true and official story of Geronimo is a task best suited for constructing narratives of conquest and settlement, not narratives of sustaining of tribal subjectivity. The tribal impulse in narrating and listening to the many narratives of Geronimo becomes an act of remembrance. Learning to "destroy [the] enemy with words" and to "remember the way, the beauty of the journey"[63] comprise Andy's rite of manhood. Interestingly, Silko's choice, in the title of the story, to use not the determinative article "the" but instead the partially signifying "a" points to other Geronimo stories waiting to be told and heard and demonstrates the transformative power of narrative to empower and reintegrate members into a tribal community.

These alternative narratives of Geronimo, then, both in the short story and in *Almanac*, authorize continued Apache resistance to the Americans and the Mexicans and also validate the relevance of Laguna, Navajo, and Yaqui mythology in the formation of a border consciousness whose gaze is multiply encoded. This border consciousness looks both ways, north and south, toward the United States and Mexico, toward the past and the present, in order to negotiate the terms of its territorial, cultural, and political sovereignty in the present. Such a perspective affirms Yaqui resistance as embodying productive practices of opposition and reclamation that *Almanac* underscores as the new American drama for the millennium.

But it is important to bear in mind that what I am referring to as the "new American drama" is not postnationalist in the sense of assuming that the nation-state as both a category of analysis and a socializing force in contemporary society has become irrelevant in the new millennium. In mapping an alternative, tribal historiography, the novel avoids this teleological impulse for reasons that become clear only if we pay attention to the formation of Apache and Yaqui tribal coalitions to thwart U.S. and Mexican attempts to subsume them within a national imaginary. Historically, however, it is the forced relocation of Yaquis within Mexican national space that makes myopic any perspective that dismisses the nation as a relic of the twentieth century. The Apache resistance to U.S. policies of nation formation and the Yaqui opposition to Mexican practices of nationalization are not meant to be affirmed as an idealization of a pantribal American identity in which the nation and national borders lose their determinative power. They are meant to foreground the nation as an ideological apparatus that legitimates particular forms of colonization grounded in racialized discourses of separatism and dispossession. What, then, do we make of the Yaquis in Arizona? When did they become border crossers and relocate in the United States? What historical events precipitated their migration from Sonora to Arizona? The crossing of national borders does not mean that national borders do not matter anymore. Rather, it is precisely the historical event of Yaquis migration north of the U.S.-Mexican border that engenders a process of intratribal othering and varied affirmations of pantribal identity in the Americas.

Yaquis in the Borderlands

The "almanac" in the title of the novel is a "notebook," a collection of "thin sheets of membrane . . . stretched and pressed out of horse stomachs" on which are inscribed stories, sayings, proverbs, diagrams, instructions, pictures, poems, and songs of the Yaqui and other Native Indian tribes. Yoeme, a "wild old Yaqui woman" (Silko, 125), gives the almanac to her granddaughters, Lecha and Zeta, for safekeeping. The almanac, as Bell notes, "repeatedly and overtly reminds" us that it "move[s] between the hands and unnamed historical persons and tribes" and is "not the property or even the process of just one imagined community."[64] The history of the Yaquis in the borderlands aptly bears out Bell's observation. In the early 1900s, pursued by the federales in Sonora, thousands of Yaquis fled across the border into Arizona and moved into other parts of the U.S. Southwest. The almanac survives because a group of boys and girls succeeded in their assigned task of smuggling it across the border, although some of the pages were lost or were used for various purposes by members of the group. The almanac, which is eventually passed back to Yoeme, thus testifies to the resilience of the Yaquis and their desperate attempts to avoid surrendering to the Mexicans, and also, in the novel's context, to Indian resistance to U.S. hegemony: "Even then, when the heart of every Yaqui was crying out, no Yaqui ever said 'surrender.' It was the same war they had been fighting for more than four hundred years" (Silko, 234).

The almanac is important not only because it contains information about agricultural methods, harvesting techniques, the weather, floods, plagues, and famines, but also because it tells about the "days yet to come" (Silko, 137), in a future the novel gestures toward as the time of the birthing of the fifth world, embodying the reclamation of native land. The almanac is thus central to the novel's thematic concern—the fulfillment of the ancient prophecy encoded in its brittle pages. The question arises, why did Silko foreground Yaqui history so centrally in her novel? Numerous Indian tribes have histories of dispossession and conquest that could have fit just as well as the Yaquis'. A study of Yaqui history, however, reveals a range of issues that are crucial not only to the program of reclamation Silko affirms in the novel, but also to the manner in which this program is conceived of and envisioned. A brief illumination of these issues will help in contextualizing the centrality of Yaqui history to the novel's thematic concerns.

Evelyn Hu-DeHart notes that from the time of first contact with the Europeans in the sixteenth century right up to the early decades of the twentieth century, Yaquis were able to maintain a distinct identity both as an ethnic group and as a tribal nation.[65] Until the Jesuits were expelled from northern Mexico in 1767, the Yaquis and the missionaries maintained strong relationships of interdependence, and the period was "one of peaceful acculturation and material development."[66] As Edward Spicer notes, the attitude of the Yaquis was "not that of a conquered people, nor was it that of a tribe too lacking in policy or organization to resist infiltration."[67] With the Jesuits the Yaquis were able to maintain a strong position from which to negotiate their terms of contact, and oftentimes their involvement with the Jesuits was voluntary. The missionaries did not conquer them as did the secular Spaniards who subdued and exploited other native tribes in central Mexico; indeed, the missionaries often helped the Yaquis resist Spanish attempts to expel them and claim their land. By the expulsion of the Jesuits, secular Spain hoped to hasten the process of conquest.[68]

From the time of Mexico's independence from Spain in 1821, the Mexican government spared no effort in trying to convince the Yaqui people to join the new republic and become part of Mexico. In 1902, during the era of Porfirio Díaz, the Yaquis were subjected to "their most violent repression"[69] as Díaz initiated a brutal campaign of terror and intimidation. Thousands of Yaquis were systematically hunted down like animals, rounded up, and sent to Yucatan. Employers of Yaquis also incurred the wrath of the Mexican police, who created a special force—the Eleventh Rural Corps, or the Special Auxiliary Force—for the express purpose of tracking down Yaquis in residential areas and businesses. The business owners were threatened with fines and destruction of property if they refused to give information regarding their Yaqui employees or continued to hire them. By the time this program of re-location was officially called off in 1908, thousands of Yaquis had lost their homes and become separated from their families, a fact that "finally succeeded in breaking the spirit of the Yaquis, rebels as well as pacíficos."[70] While thousands of Yaquis were relocated to Yucatan, thousands more, as noted above, fled across the border into Arizona and into other southwestern states, where they found refuge and employment because American businesses were eager to hire cheap labor and hardworking people. Their usefulness to businesses in the Southwest was so significant that during Díaz's relocation program several newspapers published detailed accounts of the Mexican government's cruel policy toward the Yaquis, while businesspeople petitioned the American embassy in Mexico and tried to persuade Secretary of State Elihu Root to discuss the matter with the Mexican ambassador in Washington.[71] This relocation marked a turning point in the history of the Yaquis as a nation. The last revolt against the Mexican government took place in September 1926, when several Yaquis attempted to meet Álvaro Obregón, who had just retired from the presidency and whom the Yaquis had supported during the tumultuous years of the Mexican Revolution. Unfortunately, Obregón tricked the Yaquis and called in government troops. More than twenty thousand federal troops entered Yaqui territory and carried out a massacre, while airplanes bombed their pueblos. Today the Yaquis can no longer lay claim to their own land and are a "'wandering tribe,' a people in exile, burning eternal candles to a lost idea of a homeland." Moreover, the deportation of the Yaquis "forced a greater and more permanent exodus of Yaquis across the border, to southwestern and western United States. . . . Consequently, Yaquis became the *most widely dispersed native people of North America*, covering a thirty-five hundred mile expanse from southern Mexico to southern California."[72]

These Yaqui border crossings engendered a new Yaqui border consciousness that registered the effects of their forced dispersal and their attempts to fashion a new life in the United States. Soon Yaquis on either side of the border would begin to differentiate themselves. Edward

Spicer notes that in the nineteenth and twentieth centuries Sonora Yaquis used the word "Yoeme" ("we most human of people") to refer to themselves.[73] Use of this self-referential term would denote group inclusivity, and nonuse would signify exclusion from the group based on familiarity with the language. Those who did not speak Yaqui were automatically excluded from the group. Language was thus central to group identification among Sonora Yaquis.

The Arizona Yaquis, however, used the word "Yaqui" to refer to themselves. They did not speak the language but were in some way connected to Yaqui culture and Yaqui people and thus identified themselves as Yaquis since they, to some degree or another, participated in Yaqui life. A person who spoke the language would be termed "muy Yaquis" (very Yaqui), while one who, while still related to them, did not speak the language and had only a rudimentary understanding of Yaqui life would simply be called "Yaqui." Another related word is "Yori," used to refer to the Mexicans, who, in Yaqui myth, originated from the Yaquis. It means "light color," or "ash color." "Yoeme" signified deeper immersion than "Yori" in Yaqui culture, philosophy, and religion.[74] As is evident, language both registers the impact of border crossings on the Yaquis and shapes their understanding of the differences that emerge between them on both sides of the border. It is precisely the changes and readjustments of tribal society during exile, in the time of dislocation, and in the anxious moments of migration that are significant for our study. I want to focus on that which emerges as "new" and "other" and "different" as peoples cross the borders of tribe, language, and nation.

The Yaquis, as we have seen, were adept at the art of survival, and the attempt to negotiate the tension of affirming Yaqui identity and heritage on both sides of the boundary engenders a Yaqui border subjectivity. Silko's use of the almanac, however, shifts our focus away from the tenacity of a single Indian tribe and toward the forms of contact between the Yaquis of Sonora and the Maya of Yucatan. It is during their stay in the Yucatan peninsula, where they had been relocated by the Díaz regime, that the Yaquis come into contact with the Maya, and that is also where the almanac, which is modeled after Mayan codices, as Joni Adamson points out, passes hands and falls into the hands of the Yaquis, who later move north, some of them eventually into the United States.[75] That the almanac could still exist in the twentieth century, so long after the Mayan civilization's rise and decline (ca. 300–900 AD) and eventual disintegration upon contact with the conquistadors in the sixteenth century, testifies to its enduring power, which lies in its having survived the exigencies of migration and relocation through a process of transformation. The almanac as an authentic Mayan document holds little value to the Yaquis. Even as they use the information it contains, they make their own additions to it, thus altering its status as an incontrovertible sign of indigenous history, culture, and society. The almanac becomes a hybrid text, in script, form, status, and genre, whose meanings and interpretations are constantly changing as its preservers struggle to maintain a sense of continuity in the face of European domination and, hundreds of years later, to maintain a sense of autonomy against jingoistic attempts to subsume the Yaquis and the Maya into the Mexican national imaginary. As Adamson perceptively notes, it is a "text that insists that indigenous people and their environments are not the ground and matrix of Euro-American action, but live, responsive, resistant, and capable of articulating their own perspectives about the world and their place in it."[76] And while, as Ami M. Regier observes, it "exists in the narrative as a pantribal grouping of indigenous writings from various periods and tribal groups,"[77] the almanac is also a text of resistance and signals the possibility of adaptation and survival. Interestingly enough, in light of one possible etymology of the word "almanac," which traces it to the thirteenth-century Iberian Arabic "al-manakh" (define or determine),[78] Silko's grounding of the novel in the traditional mythos of the Maya, and specifically the Yaquis, underscores the importance of preconquest Euro-Arabian histories of travel and transatlantic migration in conceptualizing the multiple forms of allegiances that the almanac engenders across national and hemispheric boundaries and across the borders of imagined communities struggling to determine their destinies and futures as they negotiate the legacy of conquest and the power of the nation-state. Thus, the novel encodes its narrative heterology in, as Daria Donnelly notes, "the prophetic mode with all its weird and disruptive energy,"[79] while also traversing, as Caren Irr sees it, the "transitive ground between past and future," even as it seeks to forge hemispheric and global forms of social and political association.[80] But what forms do resistance and opposition take in the borderlands?

The Yaquis, as one of the few Indian tribes that have persisted and partially succeeded in maintaining their unique sense of identity for hundreds of years, well into the early twentieth century, serve in the context of the novel as a useful model for configuring native resistance to the legacy of colonialism. Hu-DeHart notes that from the time of first contact the Yaquis responded variously to the Jesuits and later to the Spaniards and Mexicans. At a very general level their responses followed three impulses: "acceptance, acquiescence, or accommodation; the autonomous or self-reliant Yaqui rebellion; and alliance with, or incorporation into, a larger political party or movement. Within each pattern of type are variations, again according to the conditions of the times. *This flexibility has consistently characterized Yaqui history.*"[81]

While recuperating tribal histories and cultures in order to construct contemporary forms of social agency and gain economic and political power is an important concern in *Almanac,* the significance of its alternative mapping of history and modernity lies in its sensitivity to the power of neocolonial networks that privilege native elites and the resiliency of local events and forces in shaping and determining the impact of globalization in the hemispheres.[82] Thus, transnational indigeneity offers no easily discernible divisions between oppressor and oppressed, powerful and dispossessed. Neither, as most theories in border studies tend to do, does it prioritize a Mesoamerican heritage in order to draw parallels among different marginalized peoples in the Americas; view Anglo-Americans as the primary antagonists; or even consider Eurocentrism the most significant threat to the formation of a transborder social and cultural imaginaire. It is a mark of Silko's achievement that she refrains from giving in to sentimental and nostalgic longings for a pre-Columbian era, when life in the Americas was

Edenic and all the native peoples lived in harmony, with only occasional conflicts and disturbances. The dream of the fifth world is not so much a return to a lost paradise as the forging of a "one world/many tribes" in which organic notions of ethnic and tribal identity, *sangre pura,* and national conceptions of time and history yield to the determining power of transborder processes and the unpredictable nature of local forces acting upon the international flow of people and cultural commerce in the Americas.

Most of the characters in the novel who are actively involved in subverting and contesting hegemonic pressures are, in some way and to some degree, products of the very system they are eager to resist. Gregory Salyer's perceptive comment regarding "Western and Native abuses of technology"[83] in the novel can just as well be applied to the novel's characters. Roy, a Vietnam veteran, works for Triggs's plasma center and recruits homeless people; Tacho, an Indian, works as a chauffeur for Menardo, a Mexican businessman, who lusts after wealth and will go to any extreme to realize his dreams. The female protagonists are equally solipsistic and individualistic. Lecha abandons her son Ferro; Zeta is incapable of love and both sisters become drug addicts; Algeria and Angelita La Escapia sometimes indulge themselves to suit their own ends. While the novel, as Janet St. Clair views it, "critiques the entire worldview of Western Europe, in a general sense, a worldview that cherishes a capitalism-at-all-costs, unchecked individualism, and rampant commodity fetishism,"[84] Salyer pointedly notes that "the characters of *Almanac,* whether native or European, embody decadence that is rarely matched in American fiction."[85] The characters come with all their human frailties, and all of them are self-absorbed and utilitarian to some degree. Structurally, as well, the novel embodies a sense of disorder and a tangled existence. Silko herself notes: "It was as if you had shattered a two-hour movie. Some of it didn't have dialogue. Like if you took two hours of a feature film and tore it or chopped it up and mixed it all up."[86] Sometimes, with its constant piling up of sentences with the same word order, the syntax of the narratives almost numbs the reader into a state of vertigo. Thematically, structurally, and stylistically, the novel embodies the struggles and conflicts of the borderlands. Yet rather than give in to despair and hopelessness, it reconfigures the very notion and terms of resistance and rebellion by linking postcolonial discourse analysis and programs of decolonization with postmodern insights into the instability of language and representation and the signifying nature of power and knowledge, all of which underscore an important idea—that there is no outside space that the resisting subject can inhabit from which to launch or initiate resistance.

The Dream of the Fifth World as a Practice of Negotiating

Almanac foregrounds the contradictions and complex negotiations that emerge in anticolonial resistance. Roy, the Vietnam veteran, begins working for Triggs in recruiting homeless vets as organ and blood donors, but after befriending Triggs's secretary, Peaches, and realizing his employer's insidious plans, he begins to form an army of the homeless for a final confrontation. Clinton, the black Indian, focuses on the interracial animosities that threaten to tear apart their plans to stage confrontation with the government and the law. To Clinton, being a minority or a victim of discrimination does not automatically make a person incapable of racist practices; racism and oppression come in many guises and are not confined to any single racial or ethnic group. Angelita La Escapia, a Cuban Marxist, teaches Marxism to peasants and villagers in Mexico, with a view to inciting them to revolt. She does not dismiss Marx and his ideas for not being native. To Angelita, Marxist thought is intimately connected with the particular circumstances of their struggle for autonomy and land, and although Marx "as a European had misunderstood a great deal," he nonetheless had a "primitive devotion to the worker's stories" (Silko, 520) and understood and appreciated the power of oral tradition and stories to shape reality itself. Angelita even turns against her lover and comrade, Bartolomeo, because he "falsely discredited and endangered the people's army for the sake of cheap Marxist propaganda" and believed that the Indians were "[j]ungle monkeys and savages [who had] no history" (Silko, 525). According to

Tamara M. Teale, Marxist thought appeals to Angelita because it views history as the discursive terrain on which an alternative worker-conscious, anticapitalist historiography can be inscribed. However, her embrace of Marxism is tempered by her sensitivity to how the common value of both Marxism and capitalism, the industrial development of the earth, is antithetical to indigenous thought.[87] The twins, Lecha and Zeta, are not model law-abiding American citizens; along with Ferro and his accomplice Paulie, they smuggle drugs, weapons, and people across the U.S.-Mexican border. The Korean Awa Gee, an expert in telecommunications and computers, disrupts telephone lines, intercepts official electronic signals such as the emergency warning signal, hacks into government records to alter and delete confidential information, and even creates new identities for illegal aliens. Interested in "the perfection of complete disorder and disintegration," Awa Gee dreams of creating a computer program "that would destroy all existing computer networks" so the U.S. "blackout would be complete" (Silko, 690). Like Angelita, Awa Gee does not reject computer technology on nativist grounds; he will take whatever is at hand, master it, and then use it against the oppressors.

All of these characters are deeply implicated in the social structures and institutions that they seek to contest. But their realization of the manner in which they have become cogs in a capitalist machine run amok, and of the marginalization of their history, language, and culture, leads them to form strategies of resistance and survival across racial divisions and national borders, a mode of resistance that Gayatri Spivak views as the practice of negotiating.[88]

As our discussion of *Almanac* shows, the stakes for the inhabitants of the borderlands are very high: "it's about time, and what's called history, and story, and who makes the story and who remembers."[89] And it's also about fundamental shifts in realigning hegemonic geopolitical boundaries and their normative ideologies. The aim is to create alternative centers, alternative historical perspectives, alternative aesthetics, and alternative politics.

The large map spreading across the first two pages of the novel contains the names of numerous characters, positioned according to the places they inhabit or from which they originate. Rather than the U.S. Southwest, the map shows parts of Arizona and Sonora. Tucson, the social and cultural center of the novel, is positioned right in the middle of the map, with several arrows pointing toward it from various places— San Diego, the Laguna Pueblo Reservation, New Jersey, Albuquerque, El Paso, Tuxtla Gutiérrez, Mexico City. Other arrows point toward Buenos Aires and south to Cartagena. All of these places ultimately lead to and close in upon Tucson, which is the center, the place where the oppressed peoples of the Americas will converge and launch their final offensive. Haiti and Cuba are also shown, along with the names of the characters who hail from there. Silko's gesture in including them reminds us of José Martí, in the late nineteenth century, and Roberto Fernández Retamar, in the late twentieth century, who sought to establish Havana as an alternative center in the Americas to enable Latin American countries to contest U.S. hegemony. Such a repositioning would allow them to establish an oppositional standpoint, in a very material sense, from which to deflect the flow of power from north to south. From that standpoint they would be able to conceptualize an alternative politics and poetics of the Americas that would give voice to marginalized native tribes, the poor, the disenfranchised, and the dispossessed. As Arnold Krupat perceptively notes, such a repositioning of centers, by prioritizing the south-north interconnections in the Americas, seeks to subvert the Eurocenteredness of the hegemonic east-west paradigm traditionally used to configure American thought and culture.[90]

The ending of the novel, as we will see, nicely dramatizes the historical, cultural, and political stakes in such a repositioning of centers. The novel begins with the banishment of Sterling from the Laguna Reservation in Arizona for his alleged conspiracy with a Hollywood film crew to allow them to film the sacred land of the stone snake. Over eighty years before, white U.S. government officials had betrayed the Lagunas by stealing their idols and displaying them in a museum as rare cultural artifacts. The tribal council, viewing Sterling's betrayal as even more severe because he is a Laguna, banishes him from the tribe. Sterling boards a bus to Santa Fe but accidentally gets off at Tucson, where eventually, and just as purposelessly, he joins Ferro's drug-trafficking gang.

In the 1940s the U.S. government, wanting to dig uranium mines to help in the war, pressured the Lagunas to open up their lands. While the older people considered this sacrilegious, the younger ones, while not eager, were heartened by the employment and economic stability that would come. As a result, the Laguna were the first of the Pueblo tribes to benefit, in some measure and ironically, from the devastation of native land.

The novel ends with Sterling pondering the implications of the "last big Indian war" (Silko, 756) when he returns to the reservation to be "alone with the earth" (Silko, 757) and the giant stone snake. His earlier skepticism regarding "religions and spirits had meant nothing" because he had constructed his worldview by reading magazines like *Reader's Digest* and *Police Detective*. But now the ancient prophecy of the eventual reclamation of the Americas seem to be coming true, which means that the "old-time ways" and "old beliefs" (Silko, 762) are not dying out. Sterling turns to his own tribe's oral traditions while recognizing that, as St. Clair observes, "wholeness comes from acts of remembrance."[91]

Sterling's return can be viewed as marking his spiritual and cultural "arrival," that is, as a moment that "ends" his forced migration. In insisting on such a return, the novel undermines the influence of what Manuel Luís Martínez refers to as "movement discourse" in border studies, a discourse that "articulates the American faith in 'mobility' as being ultimately redemptive and progressive."[92] Whereas border studies tends to view border crossing and travel, and therefore mobility itself, for whatever reason, as the structuring principle of border cultures and societies, *Almanac* raises the question of collective and individual desire not for a different kind of or access to mobility but for a halt, deflection, and sometimes even reversal of direction of the flow of ideas, peoples, and memories in the borderlands. To put it another way, movement, like fixity, as Martínez notes, is a "function of power,"[93] and as we have already seen in this chapter's focus on Apache rebellion and Yaqui migration, it would be more productive to study the power of the nation-state to enforce and create the national boundaries that result in enforced migration, and of nationalism to lend credence to such an exercise of power, in relation to the continuing influence of intertribal forms of contact in the borderlands. Pantribal identity and commonality can be assumed only insofar as European experience in the Americas becomes the central vantage point in the writing and conceptualizing of history in the Americas. But as the history of the Yaquis makes clear, when we study the Indian tribes' different responses to European colonies and communities in the Americas, the assumption of a pantribal consciousness becomes problematic. Native Indian patterns of social and cultural movement in the Americas predate European arrival, and while it is important to acknowledge that intertribal rivalry often resulted in forced relocation and migration, numerous Indian tribes lived a nomadic life that was dependent on seasonal change and the availability of natural resources for daily sustenance. Thus, Sterling's return to the reservation has just as much to do with the Laguna tribe's attempts to deal with the legacy of European colonialism, which sometimes position them in antagonistic relations with other Indian tribes, as it has to do with the continuing attempt of corporate businesses to use their land without their consent and often to the detriment of their health and well being. While *Almanac* does insist on a certain kind of return or "arrival," it does so not so much to affirm the recuperation of an authentic Laguna spirituality as to point out that the border subject in this instance is not an Anglo settler or a Mexican migrant but an Indian who recrosses, not the U.S.-Mexican border, but the border of the Laguna Reservation. This recrossing contests the primacy of national borders to shape and influence tribal sovereignty and cultural history. In this sense the novel gestures toward reimagining tribal history, culture, and identity in their transnational and transtribal dimensions.

But as we have also seen, *Almanac*'s focus on Mexican antipathy to Yaqui presence in Mexico, the formation of U.S. and Mexican Yaqui communities, and the influence of Mayan culture and history on the Yaquis in Yucatan compels us to resituate transnational, intertribal, and transborder forms of movement and political allegiance within a larger

network of intercontinental sociocultural and economic commerce linking Mesoamerica to the Iberian peninsula. Thus, in one sense the borderlands mark the site of the "local" in a hemispheric, global economy,
but, in more ways than one, the terms in which the local can be read as
"local" and in which Sterling's return to the Laguna reservation can be
read as an "arrival" hinge on what Sadowski-Smith refers to as "transnational indigeneity," which departs from the current emphasis in border
studies on bloodlines and a common Mesoamerican heritage.[94]

However, as Eric Cheyfitz points out, the "national" in the transnational, and other related terms like "tribe," "nation," and "sovereignty,"
emerge as part of an official language of federal Indian legal discourse
and thus necessitate a fundamental revision of their meaning and usage.[95]
Tribal movement in the borderlands should also be viewed in the context
of Indian nomadism, not just within the context of national border
crossing. This view also complicates governmental focus on individual
ownership and productivity of land as the only substantive evidence
for incorporation into the national body politic.[96] Thus, affirming a
transnational indigeneity as Sadowski-Smith does should also involve
acknowledging *Almanac's* exploration of the continuing significance of
kinship-based social relations, clan formations, nomadism, and bloodlines in shaping Pan-Indian anti-imperial, anticolonial political endeavors in the Americas. Sterling's return or "arrival" is also a moment that
portends a different kind of future for the oppressed people of the
Americas, a future in which they must revisit the archives of the past in
order to renarrate the contemporary meaning and significance of the
histories of psychic dismemberment, forced migration, dispossession,
exile, and border crossings and thus literally fashion a new symbology
to suit the needs of the present. Sterling acknowledges the power of the
spirit world and the authority of indigenous traditions, and he waits,
along with the stone snake, eagerly looking southward, hoping to see in
the distant horizon the regathering of native peoples of the Americas
readying themselves for a final uprising and the birthing of the fifth
world in the borderlands.

ACKNOWLEDGMENTS

I must have been around ten when my father, Nana, called out to me one day as he stood by a shelf stacked with books and papers. He pulled out a book from the shelf, held it in his hand, and asked, "How would you define eternity?" I did not know what he was up to but replied, "Forever and forever . . . thousand times forever." He said, "Look at this picture and read the first paragraph. See how eternity is being defined here. Isn't it fascinating?" In the picture was a bird perched on a mountaintop. It had lowered its head to sharpen its beak against the mountain. The first paragraph said that once every thousand years, this bird would fly across the oceans and rest for a few moments on the mountaintop. The time it would take for the mountain to erode from the bird's sharpening its beak would amount to just one single day of eternity. I was stunned. I told my father that this was unimaginable—it would take forever for the mountain to erode. "Yes," he replied. And we both kept looking at the picture. I would return to that book several times over the years just to open its pages and peer closely at the bird and let my imagination fly along with it. I do not remember the writer, the title of the book, or the kind of bird.

But another picture has been even more memorable to me than the one of the bird. It is the picture of a book, a father, and a son, and how they were all wrapped in wonder. The wonder for me was not only about a bird defining eternity; it was about my father calling out to me while I was playing, showing me something from his very important but very different world, and then sharing an outlandish tale with me so that we could both wonder about the world, about life, about eternity.

We were wondering together; we were learning together; we were being together. And it was a book and a picture that made it all happen.

My mother had a different way with books. She listened to my stories about what I read but would ask me things about them that often left me flustered. The expanded idea of the world that I thought books gave me would begin to shrink when I talked to her about them. "Tell me what the book is *not* saying," she would say. It sounded weird to my young mind that I could learn from knowing what was absent in the books, and that the knowledge I obtained through books was only a little part of the world, not the final measure of learning. That sense of wonder, of moving into worlds beyond my own, could never lead to a mastery of the unknown. It could only give me more fragments to deal with and to wonder about. In *Reworlding America*, there is a whole lot of wondering about America and a whole lot of fragmenting of received ideas and traditions of America. And I hope at least some measure of learning too. This note is a very special word of thanks to Mom and Nana for their love and for what they did with books and with me.

At Loyola University Chicago, my professors Paul Jay, Harveen Mann, and Susanna Cavallo, among others, held me to high standards of scholarship. Paul listened with an open mind and encouraged me to try out things on my own. Harveen often suggested cutting out big chunks of text, sometimes several pages, and insisted on not sacrificing clarity for complexity. Susanna never hesitated to share her books and engage in lengthy discussions with me about my work. With them, learning was an opportunity to explore multiple lines of inquiry while adhering to the integrity of an argument. Among my colleagues at the University of Southern Maine (USM), Kathleen Ashley and Lorrayne Carroll have been especially generous with their friendship. I benefited greatly from Ann Dean's and Nancy Gish's careful reading of two chapters of this book and from their insightful suggestions. Willard Rusch's, Lisa Walker's, and Benjamin Bertram's hospitality has been exemplary. By processing book requests, extending deadlines, or searching stacks in a timely and professional manner, the staff of the Albert Brenner Glickman Library at USM helped me balance the demands of teaching and research. I am grateful to them for their commitment to their work: Loraine Lowell, Kristina Edwards, John Plante, William (Bill) Sargent, David Vardeman, and Casandra Fitzherbert.

Over the last few years, my students at USM have taught me a lot, and they continue to do so. Their passion for learning and sometimes their struggles to obtain a college education have been humbling experiences. With insight and patience, they help me better understand Paulo Freire's emphasis on relating learning to democratic and civil engagement. I will always be in their debt, and gladly so. At Ohio University Press, a conscientious editor, David Sanders, set the tone and pace over the last year for revising this book in ways that helped me recognize the importance of writing for multiple audiences and of having an editor who cares deeply about the books he reads. I am grateful to John Morris, also at OU Press, for his careful reading of the manuscript and for making copyediting a learning experience. I was privileged to have two anonymous readers of the manuscript who raised substantive questions for me to wrestle with but tempered their criticisms with encouragement. I am indebted to Sumitra and Willie Simpson, my aunt and uncle, without whose love and support my experience of intercontinental migration and relocation would be bereft of the rich and complex tensions of learning to live between cultures and straddle traditions. Whenever the demands of writing kept me detached from the world and I lost perspective, Hannah, my wife, always translated, albeit in a different register, Edward Said's insistence on making secular criticism yield to the obligations, demands, and needs of the world. For this, I cannot thank her enough.

NOTES

Preface

1. See National Commission on Terrorist Attacks upon the United States, *The 9/11 Commission Report* (New York: W. W. Norton, 2004), 47–70; Michael Scheuer, *Imperial Hubris: Why the West Is Losing the War on Terror* (Washington, DC: Brassey's, 2004), 59–102; Paul Williams, *Al Qaeda: Brotherhood of Terror* (Parsippany, NJ: Alpha, 2002), 105–25.

2. See Rod McGuirk, Associated Press, "Iraqi Exiles around World Vote in Election," *ABC News,* January 30, 2005, http://abcnews.go.com/International/print?id=455018 (accessed May 5, 2005). Iraqi exiles in Syria, the United States, Australia, Jordan, Iran, the United Arab Emirates, and the United Kingdom, among other countries, voted in the Iraqi election of 2005. That the U.S. government actively encouraged exiles who were also U.S. citizens to vote in the Iraqi elections raises the issue of double belonging in the cultural sense and dual citizenship in the political sense. The twist here is that the state is encouraging this dual affirmation of identity and culture so that its own interests can be well served. What happens when the state does not do so, such as when peoples in diaspora attempt to sustain their traditions and form social and economic networks that the state may view as a threat, complicates our understanding of minority communities' process of Americanization or non-Americanization, making it hard to view Americanization as simply a cultural or psychosocial process that has little or no bearing on the workings of the nation-state.

3. The kind of intercontinental networks formed by global software alliances doing global software work are not just a neat extension of

American economic power outside of U.S. national boundaries. These networks have several layers and offshoots—for example, India, Ireland, and Israel form one significant network that faces increasing competition from China, the Philippines, and Russia. Sahay Sundeep, Brian Nicholson, and S. Krishna, *Global IT Outsourcing: Software Development across the Borders* (Cambridge: Cambridge University Press, 2003), xi, 12. How American culture circulates among these networks and what kinds of cross-cultural encounters take place that affect social and personal identities can become important factors in examining the socioeconomic and cultural dynamics interconnecting America with these global networks.

4. See "U.S. Jobs Going Overseas Becomes Election 2004 Issue," *PBS Newshour Extra*, March 10, 2004, http://www.pbs.org/newshour/extra/features/jan-june04/outsource_3–10.html (accessed June 4, 2005).

5. See U.S. Census Bureau, PHC-T-1, table 3, April 2, 2001, http://www.census.gov/population/cen2000/phc-t1/tab03.pdf (accessed May 5, 2005); U.S. Census Bureau, "Hispanic and Asian Americans Increasing Faster than Overall Population," press release, June 14, 2004, http://www.census.gov/Press-Release/www/releases/archives/race/001839.html (accessed May 5, 2005).

6. Nicolás C. Vaca, *The Presumed Alliance: The Unspoken Conflict between Latinos and Blacks and What It Means for America* (New York: HarperCollins, 2004), 16. Vaca candidly explores the stereotypical knowledge and prejudices that have influenced, albeit in limited ways, historical patterns of involvement and cooperation between blacks and Latinos. His argument—that instead of a model of shared interests, which downplays profound group differences, we should adopt a model of strategic coalitions, which takes into account divergent group interests in order to develop and pursue clear goals—does not shy away from critiquing the ideals of essentialism and the anti-Anglo paradigm that have come to determine the norms and boundaries of public discourse about race relations in the United States.

7. Sharon Ann Navarro and Armando Xavier Mejia, eds., *Latino Americans and Political Participation* (Santa Barbara, CA: ABC-CLIO, 2004), 3.

8. Wai Chee Dimock, "Literature for the Planet," *PMLA* 116, no. 1 (2001): 177.

9. Azar Nafisi, *Reading Lolita in Tehran: A Memoir in Books* (New York: Random House, 2003), 6 (emphasis added).

10. Edward Said, *The World, the Text, and the Critic* (Cambridge, MA: Harvard University Press, 1983), 227.

11. The appropriation of a text like *Reading Lolita in Tehran* and an author like Azar Nafisi by a large corporation to promote itself underscores the paradoxical links between global economic and cultural flows. Nafisi is featured in Audi's 2004 "Never Follow" advertising campaign along with David Bowie, William H. Macy, and Freddy Adu, and the copy in the frame featuring Nafisi reads, "Teacher, writer, visionary. Azar Nafisi stands for freedom of imagination and the pursuit of happiness for all people." http://www.neverfollow.com/flash.html (accessed June 22, 2005). The contradiction here is that while the memoir dislocates America from its national context to highlight the transnational pressures brought to bear on the text's global circulation, the Audi ad Americanizes, through a form of corporate sponsorship, both the book and the author in a discourse of freedom and individualism, ideas that have almost mythic power in traditional American history and contemporary society. The ad claims particularity and universality at the same time, seeming to invoke both an American and a universal drama by threading ideas of America, Nafisi, freedom, and a phrase lifted from the Declaration of Independence. Absent a critique of such appropriations, the memoir and the writer run the risk of becoming yet more cultural artifacts exported by big businesses to a world market, and of recodifying notions of America as a symbol for freedom and Iran or the non-West as a symbol for oppression. Nafisi's appearance in the Audi ad, and the fact that Audi is a German company, give a certain cultural legitimacy to the machinery of global capitalism, but critical attention is much needed toward such confluences of interests between practices of academic knowledge production and dissemination and multinational businesses, which link, as Román de la Campa perceptively observes, "citizenship with consumption, thereby comprising new forms of distributing and packaging the symbolic capital necessary to enter middle class." Román de la Campa, "Latin, Latino, American: Split State and Global Imaginaries," in *Globalization and the Humanities*, ed. David Leiwei Li (Hong Kong: Hong Kong University Press,

2004), 113. De la Campa offers a critique of the nexus between cultural globalization and media technology in which "America" becomes a site for performing and claiming individual consumerist desire.

12. Marc Shell and Wernor Sollors, *The Multilingual Anthology of American Literature* (New York: New York University Press, 2000), do a fine job of making available numerous narratives, poems, pictographs, etc., written in non-English languages and in some way or another related to Americans, American experiences, and the idea of America. Because their historical contexts question and redraw the boundaries of a U.S.-centric and English-only American studies, these literatures cannot be added to an already existing canon in order to make it more multicultural and diverse.

13. Charles Bright and Michael Geyer, "Where in the World Is America? The History of the United States in the Global Age," in *Rethinking American History in a Global Age*, ed. Thomas Bender (Berkeley: University of California Press, 2002), 72.

14. Robyn Wiegman, "Introduction: The Futures of American Studies," *Cultural Critique* 40 (1998): 5.

15. Paul Giles, *Virtual Americas: Transnational Fictions and the Transatlantic Imaginary* (Durham, NC: Duke University Press, 2002), 261 (emphasis added). Giles makes a strong case for locating the transatlantic imaginary at the center of American studies because it renders suspect nationalism's isomorphic tendencies by refusing to participate in its tautological dance of self-affirmation. The virtualization of America embodies a process of refraction and dislocation, both symbolic and material, in the construction of the national imaginary. Giles's examination of the transatlantic virtualization of America demonstrates how the nation's armature teeters and collapses to reveal not its foundational structures but a gritty, elliptical assemblage of ideological bric-a-brac.

Chapter 1

1. Gayatri Chakravorty Spivak, "The Rani of Sirmur," in *Europe and Its Others*, ed. Francis Barker, Peter Hulme, Margaret Iversen, and Diana Loxley (Colchester: University of Essex Press, 1985), 1:141, 133.

2. Arif Dirlik, "American Studies in the Time of Empire," *Comparative American Studies* 2, no. 3 (2004): 288.

3. Ibid., 291.

4. Susan Gillman, Kirsten Silva Greusz, and Rob Wilson, "Worlding American Studies," *Comparative American Studies* 2, no. 3 (2004): 262 (emphasis in original).

5. Peter Jennings and Todd Brewster, *In Search of America* (New York: Hyperion, 2002), ix (emphasis added).

6. Niall Ferguson, *Empire: The Rise and Demise of the British World Order and the Lessons for Global Power* (New York: Basic Books, 2003), 370.

7. Ferguson, *Colossus: The Price of America's Empire* (New York: Penguin, 2004), 292.

8. José E. Limón, "Translating Empire: The Border Homeland of Rio Grand City, Texas," *American Quarterly* 56, no. 1 (2004): 31.

9. Spivak, "Rani," 133.

10. Samuel P. Huntington, *Who Are We? The Challenges to America's National Identity* (New York: Simon and Schuster, 2004), 17–19.

11. Ibid., 18.

12. Ibid., 67.

13. Ibid., xvii (emphasis added).

14. Dirlik, "American Studies," 288.

15. Huntington, *Who Are We?* xvii.

16. Charles F. Richardson, *American Literature (1607–1885): The Development of American Thought* (New York: G. P. Putnam's Sons, 1887), 1.

17. Ibid., 2 (emphasis added).

18. Ibid., 12.

19. Ibid., 16.

20. Ibid., 22.

21. John Seely Hart, *Manual of American Literature* (Philadelphia: Eldredge and Brother; repr., New York: Johnson Reprint, 1969), 25. Citations are to the Johnson Reprint edition.

22. Charles Angoff, *A Literary History of the American People,* vol. 1, *From 1607 to the Beginning of the Revolutionary Period* (New York: Alfred A. Knopf, 1931), 6, 3.

23. Robert E. Spiller, *The Cycle of American Literature* (New York: Free Press, 1955).

24. Donald E. Pease, "New Americanists: Revisionist Interventions into the Canon," *Boundary 2* 17, no. 1 (1990): 2.

25. Ronald Takaki, *A Different Mirror: A History of Multicultural America* (Boston: Little, Brown, 1993), 15.

26. Malini Johar Schueller and Edward Watts, eds., introduction to *Messy Beginnings: Postcoloniality and Early American Studies* (New Brunswick, NJ: Rutgers University Press, 2003), 2.

27. Jan Radway, "What's in a Name?" in *The Futures of American Studies,* ed. Donald E. Pease and Robyn Wiegman (Durham, NC: Duke University Press, 2002), 72.

28. In rejecting the unifying, homogeneous meaning of "America" and its obsession with all things European, Saldívar seeks to foreground the Americas not as homogeneous entities but as a set of interlinked continents whose histories of conquest and settlement embody the emergence of a mestizo American culture: "a culture of hybrid Americans, ethnic and cultural descendants of aborigines, Africans and Europeans." Such a focus, he notes, "redirects the *Eurocentric focus* of earlier scholarship," to foreground a "distinctive, postcolonial, pan-American consciousness." José David Saldívar, *The Dialectics of Our America* (Durham, NC: Duke University Press, 1991), xi–xii (emphasis added).

29. Paul Jay, "The Myth of America and the Politics of Location: Modernity, Border Studies, and the Literature of the Americas," *Arizona Quarterly* 54, no. 2 (1998): 172.

30. José Martí, *The America of José Martí: Selected Writings,* trans. Juan de Onís (New York: Funk and Wagnalls, 1954), 149.

31. Frantz Fanon, *The Wretched of the Earth* (New York: Grove Weidenfeld, 1963), 37.

32. Martí, *America of José Martí,* 143.

33. Perhaps the Venezuelan writer Andrés Bello, writing in the early 1800s, can be seen as Martí's precursor. Bello founded the *Reportorio Américano* to encourage philosophical conversations between Europe and South America. Mary Louise Pratt notes that Bello "made himself a conduit and filter for European writings that might be useful to the nation building process" and that Bello sought the help of the English to counter Spanish hegemony. Pratt, *Imperial Eyes: Travel Writing and Transculturation* (London: Routledge, 1992), 172. Interestingly, both Bello and Martí lived for

extended periods outside of their native countries. Bello spent about nineteen years in London, and Martí wrote his most pungent critique of North America while living in the United States. But while Bello focused on Euro-American linkages and histories, Martí stressed the rise of the United States and, by extension, North America as a dominating power in north-south relations. Crucial to my discussion is the role of the mediator and conduit played by people like Bello and Martí in the intercontinental flow of ideas and commodities between Europe and the Americas.

34. William Shakespeare, *The Tempest,* ed. Stephen Orgel (Oxford: Clarendon Press, 1987), 1.2.362–63.

35. Roberto Fernández Retamar, *Caliban and Other Essays* (Minneapolis: University of Minnesota Press, 1989). Retamar also sought to establish Havana as an alternative center in order to encourage Latin American artists and writers to create new forms of social and cultural expression. He founded the Casa de las Américas to promote the publication of journals and formed literary organizations to encourage artistic and intellectual endeavor. Over the years, judges on the committee of the prestigious Casa de las Américas Award have included such notables as Alejo Carpentier, Julio Cortázar, Carlos Fuentes, Gabriel García Márquez, Edward Kamau Brathwaite, and the North American beat poet Allen Ginsberg, and recipients have included Rolando Hinojosa (U.S.), Roqué Dolton (El Salvador), and Rígoberta Ménchu (Guatemala). In this sense Havana "not only re-centers an expanded cultural field for American studies but also establishes an oppositional critical standpoint both within and beyond it, one that represents the socialist cultural politics of Latin America as part of the global struggle." Carolyn Porter, "What We Know That We Don't Know: Remapping American Literary Studies," *American Literary History* 3 (1994): 506.

36. Porter, "What We Know," 510.

37. Ibid. (emphasis added).

38. Jay, "Myth of America," 172.

39. Ibid., 167.

40. Nelly Richard, "Postmodernism and Periphery," in *Postmodernism,* ed. Thomas Docherty (New York: Columbia University Press, 1993), 466.

41. It is significant that Richard pushes the historical time frame of modernity back into the sixteenth and seventeenth centuries, the time of European settlement in the Americas. Habermas had emphasized the eighteenth century, which marked the evolution of the Enlightenment project, characterized by the self-sufficiency of reason. Richard's time frame allows her instead to link the idea of modernity, as suggesting an abrupt break from the past, with the rhetoric of progress and civilization.

42. This humanism is a precursor to the humanism of the eighteenth century. Here there is a gradual shift away from the view that a divine being directly influenced the cosmos and that the cosmos was entirely intelligible toward a view that man's imperative was to render the unintelligible world intelligible. As Louis Dupré notes, man becomes a "meaning-giving 'subject'" and since it "now fell upon the human mind to interpret a cosmos," the "mind became the spiritual substratum of all reality." *Passage to Modernity* (New Haven: Yale University Press, 1993), 3. However, the notion that the universal man is the European subject is tellingly dramatized in the debates concerning the humanity of the Amerindian. Two prominent writers who debated this issue are Bartolomé de Las Casas (*Apologia*, 1548–50), who argued against the colonization of the natives on the ground that the Amerindians and the Europeans possessed a common humanity, and Juan Ginés de Sepúlveda (*The Just Causes of War against the Indians*, 1548), who argued that European colonialism could be justified by the subhuman nature of the Amerindian peoples. Both texts are included (in Spanish) in *Apologia [de Juan Ginés de Sepúlveda contra Fray Bartolomé de las Casas y de Fray Bartolomé de las Casas contra Juan Ginés de Sepúlveda]*, ed. Angel Losada (Madrid: Editora Nacional, 1975). In addition, conjunctive with the elevation of the human mind as a meaning-producing mechanism is the reworking of the medieval view of history and its valuation of the past. But in the fifteenth and sixteenth centuries the past became less of an idealized repository and began to be used to "legitimate human efforts towards shaping the future." The past was "irreversibly past" and could not be repeated, and each "period presents itself as irreducibly different." Dupré, *Passage to Modernity*, 146. Here again we have the idea of a break from the past, marking the point of the emergence of difference in the epochal or periodizing sense. By the eighteenth century, man begins to emerge as the center of all things, the sole meaning-

making subject in the world, and history begins to operate on the principle of eschatology.

43. Edmundo O'Gorman, *The Invention of America* (Bloomington: Indiana University Press, 1961), 124, 46.

44. Paul Gilroy, *The Black Atlantic: Modernity and Double Consciousness* (Cambridge, MA: Harvard University Press, 1993), 15.

45. Ibid., 16–17, 14.

46. Edouard Glissant, *Caribbean Discourse: Selected Essays*, ed. and trans. J. Michael Dash (Charlottesville: University of Virginia Press, 1989), 146.

47. Ibid., 149.

48. Ibid., 150.

49. Jay, "Myth of America," 168 (emphasis in original).

50. Ibid.

51. Ibid., 179.

52. Oscar Martínez, *Border People* (Tucson: University of Arizona Press, 1994), 5.

53. Gloria Anzaldúa, *The Borderlands/La Frontera* (San Francisco: Aunt Lute Books, 1987), 4–5.

54. Claudia Sadowski-Smith, ed., introduction to *Globalization on the Line: Culture, Capital, and Citizenship at the U.S. Borders* (New York: Palgrave, 2002), 1.

55. Guillermo Gómez-Peña, "Documented/Undocumented," in *Multi-Cultural Literacy*, ed. Rick Simonson and Scott Walker (Minneapolis: Graywolf Press, 1988), 130.

56. José David Saldívar, *Border Matters* (Los Angeles: University of California Press, 1997), 160.

57. John Carlos Rowe, "Post-Nationalism, Globalism, and the New American Studies," *Cultural Critique* 40 (1998): 21.

58. Ibid., 17.

59. Amy Kaplan, "Left Alone with America," in *Cultures of United States Imperialism*, ed. Amy Kaplan and Donald E. Pease (Durham, NC: Duke University Press, 1993), 4.

60. Ibid., 15.

61. Rowe, "Post-Nationalism," 23.

62. Ibid., 14 (emphasis added).

63. O'Gorman, *Invention of America*, 124.

64. Stephen Greenblatt, ed., introduction to *New World Encounters* (Los Angeles: University of California Press, 1993), vii.

Chapter 2

1. Beatriz Pastor Bodmer, *The Armature of Conquest: Spanish Accounts of the Discovery of America, 1492–1589*, trans. Lydia Longstreth Hunt (Stanford: Stanford University Press, 1992), 3.

2. Ibid., 4.

3. Frederick Jackson Turner, *The Frontier in American History* (New York: Henry Holt, 1920), 3–4, 22–24. Coincident with the frontier process of exploration and settlement, sectionalism also shaped the American imagination, argues Turner: "We in America are in reality a federation of sections rather than of states." Turner, "Sections and Nation," in *Frontier and Section: Selected Essays of Frederick Jackson Turner*, ed. Ray Allen Billington (Englewood Cliffs: Prentice Hall, 1961), 141. For Turner, these sections, each with its specific topography, are New England, the Middle States, the Southeast, the Southwest, the Middle West, the Great Plains, the Mountain States, and the Pacific Coast. Turner, "Sections and Nation," 136–37. The inhabitants of each section share certain social and political beliefs, formed in large part during the settling of the frontier as the settlers confronted the topography of that section. Thus, the Southwest, with its vast deserts, shaped an American character distinct from that in New England, whose coastal topography propelled its industrialization at a faster rate. Often class and regional interests crossed state borders to develop pansectional political coalitions, which in turn exercised their clout to shape domestic policy at the congressional level. In this way, writes Billington, Turner complicates his own frontier thesis by drawing attention to factors other than the frontier experience; the study of these factors necessitates an interdisciplinary approach. Ray Allen Billington, introduction to Turner, *Frontier and Section*, 4.

4. Turner, *Frontier and Section*, 11.

5. To Alistair Hennessy, the frontier, as social phenomenon and mythic construction, follows a different trajectory in Latin American history. If Turner's frontiers are racially circumscribed and delineated, the

sharp divisions between insider and outsider, foreigner and native, are not easily afforded in South America, due, Hennessy argues, to the high rate of interracial intimacies among the indigenous peoples, the Europeans, and the slave populations from Africa. In opposition to North American patterns, which form what he calls "frontiers of exclusion," South American patterns form "frontiers of inclusion." Hennessy, *The Frontier in Latin American History* (Albuquerque: University of New Mexico Press, 1978), 19.

6. Gregory H. Nobles, *American Frontiers: Cultural Encounters and Continental Conquest* (New York: Hill and Wang, 1997), 9–11, 13.

7. Annette Kolodny, "Letting Go Our Grand Obsessions: Notes toward a New Literary History of the American Frontiers," in *Subjects and Citizens: Nation, Race, and Gender from Oroonoko to Anita Hill,* ed. Michael Moon and Cathy N. Davidson (Durham, NC: Duke University Press, 1995), 11 (emphasis in original).

8. Howard Lamar and Leonard Thompson, eds., introduction to *The Frontier in History: North America and Southern Africa Compared* (New Haven: Yale University Press, 1981), 7.

9. Ibid., 7.

10. Kolodny, "Letting Go," 17.

11. Ibid.

12. Ibid., 20–21. Kolodny also comments that just as European contact gave rise to hybridized forms of expression, the presence of African slaves in the Americas played a significant role in syncretizing cultural and religious traditions. In addition, one should also pay attention to precolonial frontier processes as Indian tribes speaking about 550 dialects and languages came into contact with each other, thus engendering cross-cultural and linguistic formations. Ibid., 15–16.

13. Stephen Greenblatt, introduction to *New World Encounters* (Los Angeles: University of California Press, 1993), vii.

14. Djelal Kadir, *Columbus and the Ends of the Earth: Europe's Prophetic Rhetoric as Conquering Ideology* (Berkeley: University of California Press, 1992), x–xi.

15. Homi Bhabha, ed., *Nation and Narration* (New York: Routledge, 1990), 297.

16. Ibid.

17. Kadir, *Columbus*, 4.

18. Ibid., 5–6 (emphasis in original).

19. Ibid., 70.

20. Inga Clendinnen, "'Fierce and Unnatural Cruelty': Cortés and the Conquest of Mexico," in *New World Encounters*, ed. Stephen Greenblatt (Los Angeles: University of California Press, 1993), 12.

21. S. L. Cline, introduction to *Conquest of New Spain: 1585 Revision*, by Bernardino de Sahagún, ed. S. L. Cline, trans. Howard F. Cline (Salt Lake City: University of Utah Press, 1989), 4.

22. Ibid.

23. Ibid., 6.

24. Ibid., 8.

25. Sahagún, *Conquest of New Spain*, 28.

26. Cline, introduction to *Conquest*, 9.

27. Bernal Díaz del Castillo, *The Conquest of New Spain*, trans. J. M. Cohen (London: Penguin, 1963). Hereafter cited in text.

28. Davíd Carrasco, "Toward the Splendid City: Knowing the Worlds of Moctezuma," in *Moctezuma's Mexico: Visions of the Aztec World*, ed. Davíd Carrasco and Eduardo Matos Moctezuma (Niwot: University Press of Colorado, 1992), 100.

29. In 1943 the ethnologist Paul Kirchoff introduced the term "Mesoamerica," which he used, notes Davíd Carrasco, to denote " a distinctive pattern of cultural traits in Mexico and parts of Central America that was indicative of urban civilizations. . . . Mesoamerica was inhabited by a wide spectrum of social groups with various levels of social integration, but the city-state was the most influential unit." The topography of Mesoamerica included what is now southern Mexico, Guatemala, El Salvador, Belize, and regions of Nicaragua, Honduras, and Costa Rica. Ibid., 191.

30. Francisco López de Gómara, *Cortés: The Life of the Conquerer*, ed. and trans. Lesley Byrd Simpson (Berkeley: University of California Press, 1964), 4.

31. Lesley Byrd Simpson, introduction to López de Gómara, *Cortés*, xxii–xxiii.

32. Rolena Adorno, "History, Law, and the Eyewitness Protocols of Authority in Bernal Díaz del Castillo's *Historia verdadera de la conquista de la Nueva España,*" in *The Project of Prose in Early Modern Europe and the New World,* ed. Elizabeth Fowler and Roland Greene (Cambridge: Cambridge University Press, 1997), 154.

33. Ibid., 161.

34. Adorno also argues that Díaz sought to present an "understanding of the conquest from the inside." Ibid., 171. The sweeping reforms introduced by the crown, owing in large measure to the anticolonial efforts of people like Las Casas and codified in 1526, made it increasingly difficult for old conquistadors like him to petition the courts or the crown for redress and reparations. In writing his narrative, Díaz was in many ways up against a Spain reluctant to give leeway to explorers in settling the New World. His audience needed to be convinced that his own involvement with the Cortés expedition was in accordance with the codified ordenanzas issued *after* the conquest. He was writing both as an eyewitness involved in the conquest and as a witness whose testimony could be recognized as just and legal by standards of jurisprudence and morality even if his experiences directly contradicted these standards.

35. Gayatri Chakravorty Spivak, "The Rani of Sirmur," in *Europe and Its Others,* ed. Francis Barker, Peter Hulme, Margaret Iversen, and Diana Loxley (Colchester: University of Essex Press, 1985), 1:141, 133.

36. Tzvetan Todorov, *The Conquest of America: The Question of the Other,* trans. Richard Howard (New York: Harper and Row, 1984), 248.

37. Homi Bhabha, *The Location of Culture* (New York: Routledge, 1994), 171.

38. Enrique Dussel, *The Invention of the Americas,* trans. Michael D. Barber (New York: Continuum, 1995), 11.

39. Michel de Certeau, *The Writing of History,* trans. Tom Conley (New York: Columbia University Press, 1988), 215–66 (emphasis added).

40. José Rabasa, *Writing Violence on the Northern Frontier: The Historiography of Sixteenth Century New Mexico and Florida and the Legacy of Conquest* (Durham, NC: Duke University Press, 2000), 22.

41. Clendinnen, "'Fierce and Unnatural Cruelty,'" 41.

42. Greenblatt, *New World Encounters,* xvi.

43. Mary Louise Pratt, *Imperial Eyes: Travel Writing and Transculturation* (London: Routledge, 1992), 4.

44. Lamar and Thomson, *Frontier in History*, 7.

45. William H. Prescott, *History of the Conquest of Mexico and History of the Conquest of Peru* (New York: Random House, 1936), 350.

46. Francis Jennings, *The Invasion of America: Indians, Colonialism and the Cant of Conquest* (Chapel Hill: University of North Carolina Press, 1975), vii.

47. Karen Ordahl Kupperman, ed., introduction to *America in European Consciousness: 1492–1750* (Chapel Hill: University of North Carolina Press, 1995), 1–3.

48. Ibid., 5.

49. Janet Whatley, introduction to *History of a Voyage to the Land of Brazil, Otherwise Called America*, by Jean de Léry, trans. Janet Whatley (Berkeley: University of California Press, 1990), xv.

50. Frank Lestringant, "The Philosopher's Breviary: Jean de Léry in the Enlightenment," in *New World Encounters*, ed. Stephen Greenblatt (Los Angeles: University of California Press, 1993), 129.

51. Léry, *History*, 69–77. Hereafter cited in text.

52. As Whatley notes, extending the Calvinist Urbain Chauveton, to Léry "America is the providential gift of a 'tableau tout neuf'—a wholly new picture—to reanimate our jaded sense of wonder and revivify our adoration of God." Whatley, introduction to *History*, xxvii.

53. Peter Mason, *Deconstructing America: Representations of the Other* (New York: Routledge, 1990), 20 (emphasis added).

54. Ibid., 34.

55. Laurette Séjourné, *Burning Water: Thought and Religion in Ancient Mexico* (New York: Grove Press, 1960), 11.

56. Alfred Soman, ed., preface to *The Massacre of St. Bartholomew: Reappraisals and Documents* (The Hague: Martinus Nijhoff, 1974), vii–viii.

57. Garry Hogg notes that "the practice of eating human flesh was noted in almost every part of the world, except Europe, as a recognized ingredient of the accepted social order." Quoted in Richard Sartore, *Humans Eating Humans* (Notre Dame, IN: Cross Cultural Publications, 1994), 6.

58. Hans Askenasy, *Cannibalism: From Sacrifice to Survival* (New York: Prometheus Books, 1994), 62.

59. William Arens, "Rethinking Anthropophagy," in *Cannibalism and the Colonial World*, ed. Francis Barker, Peter Hulme, and Margaret Iversen (Cambridge: Cambridge University Press, 1998), 42, 40.

60. Peter Hulme, introduction to Barker et al., *Cannibalism*, 10.

61. Sartore, *Humans Eating Humans*, viii.

62. Whatley, introduction to *History*, xxviii.

63. Michel Eyquem de Montaigne, *The Essays of Montaigne*, trans. E. J. Trechmann (1927; repr., London: Oxford University Press, 1946), 63. Citations are to the 1946 edition.

64. Ibid., 209.

65. Ibid., 210.

66. Lestringant, "Philosopher's Breviary," 129.

67. The word "savage" in Léry's chronicle does not connote animal-like ferociousness or savagery but "living in a state of nature." For instance, wildflowers in French are referred to as "fleurs sauvages." Whatley, introduction to *History*, 232.

68. Frank Lestringant, *Cannibals: The Discovery and Representation of the Cannibal from Columbus to Jules Verne*, trans. Rosemary Morris (Berkeley: University of California Press, 1997), 9. This book offers a genealogy of anthropophagy from Columbus to Jules Verne.

69. To Whatley, *Voyage* dramatizes the tension "at the intersection of two great axes of early modern European experience: the Protestant Reformation and the discovery of America." Whatley, introduction to *History*, xvi. Léry seeks to portray himself and his companion as sincere reformists like Luther who refuse to succumb to the pressures of Catholicism even in a landscape as strange and unfamiliar as America. Calvinist theology provides Léry with a theological model for assimilating the non-Christian pagan into the fold of humanity. In this sense, to Whatley *Voyage* embodies the "Protestants staking out their ground of moral and intellectual influence over how the experience of discovery and expansionism in the New World would be assimilated by Europe." Ibid., xxi.

70. John H. Elliott, "Renaissance Europe and America: A Blunted Impact?" in *First Images of America*, ed. Fredi Chiappelli (Berkeley: University of California Press, 1976), 20.

71. Hugh Honour, *The New Golden Land: European Images of America from the Discoveries to the Present Time* (New York: Pantheon Books, 1975), 3.

72. According to legend, during the reconquest of Spain from the Arabs in the early thirteenth century, Cabeza de Vaca's maternal forefather marked a secret pass in the mountains of Sierra Morena, in northern Seville, with a cow's skull to enable the Christian king to pass through undetected and rout the Muslim armies. As a token of appreciation, the king bestowed the title "Cabeza de Vaca" (cow's head) on the shepherd family. Morris Bishop, *The Odyssey of Cabeza de Vaca* (New York: Century, 1933), 4. Family pride may thus explain Cabeza de Vaca's use of his maternal family's name, which also enabled him to find favor among the rich and royal subjects of his time.

73. Although Pastor Bodmer characterizes Cortés as the "model conqueror" (*Armature of Conquest*, 50), I think Cabeza de Vaca's pacifism and benign colonialism, which contrast directly with Cortés's ideology of militarism, certainly make him a more deserving candidate for this title.

74. He is the same man who was sent by the governor of Cuba to subdue the recalcitrant Cortés in 1520. Cortés defeated him, seized his weapons and ships, persuaded his men to accompany him to wage war with the Aztecs, and returned to Moctezuma's palace. This marked a turning point in the campaign against Moctezuma.

75. The exact trail of the Spaniards is the subject of many debates. Cleve Hallenbeck discusses this issue at length and focuses on the merits and problems of various routes proposed by critics and historians, including Bandelier, Bancroft, Ponton and M'Farland, Baskett, Read, Twitchell, and Davenport and Wells. These critics disagree on the location of the numerous Amerindian communities and the size and location of the rivers, inlets, bays, and mountain ranges the travelers encounter. Hallenbeck, *Álvar Núñez Cabeza de Vaca: The Journey and Route of the First European to Cross the Continent of North America: 1534–36* (Glendale, CA: Arthur H. Clark, 1940), 243. However, the general area of Cabeza de Vaca's travels stretched from Florida into the present-day U.S. Southwest and northern Mexico.

76. Ibid., 13.

77. Ibid., 14.

78. David Howard, *Conquistador in Chains: Cabeza de Vaca and the Indians of the Americas* (Tuscaloosa: University of Alabama Press, 1997), 195.

79. Rolena Adorno and Patrick Charles Pautz, eds., *Álvar Núñez Cabeza de Vaca: His Account, His Life, and the Expedition of Pánfilo de Narváez* (Lincoln: University of Nebraska Press, 1999), 1:xvi.

80. Rolena Adorno, "The Negotiation of Fear in Cabeza de Vaca's *Naufragios*," in *New World Encounters*, ed. Stephen Greenblatt (Los Angeles: University of California Press, 1993), 52, 76.

81. Ibid., 49.

82. Ibid., 55.

83. Álvar Núñez Cabeza de Vaca, *Relación*, trans. Rolena Adorno and Patrick Charles Pautz, in Adorno and Pautz, *Álvar Núñez Cabeza de Vaca*, vol. 1 (Lincoln: University of Nebraska Press, 1999). Hereafter cited in text.

84. Bhabha, *Location*, 72.

85. Ibid., 89.

86. Also see Kadir's discussion of Gonzalo Fernández de Oviedo's accounts of cannibalism. *Columbus*, 118–20.

87. José Rabasa, "Allegory and Ethnography in Cabeza de Vaca's *Naufragios* and *Commentarios*," in *Violence, Resistance, and Survival in the Americas*, ed. William B. Taylor and Franklin Pease G.-Y. (Washington, DC: Smithsonian Institution Press, 1994), 51.

88. Bishop, *Odyssey*, 69.

89. Rabasa, "Allegory," 53.

90. Upon returning to Spain, Cabeza de Vaca was soon appointed, by royal decree, governor of La Plata in South America, where Spanish settlements included regions of present-day Argentina, Paraguay, Bolivia, and Brazil. However, due to his nonmilitaristic approach to establishing settler communities and the political intrigues of other Spanish explorers, he was charged with treason, captured, and, after a formal hearing before the Council of the Indies, indicted and banished from the Indies. Bishop, *Odyssey*, 285; and see map on 174. On March 18, 1551, he was sentenced to serve the king in Oran, North Africa, but his sentence was rescinded and his banishment from the Indies was restricted to the Río de la Plata. Howard, *Conquistador in Chains*, 190.

91. Rabasa, "Allegory," 48.

92. Adorno and Pautz, *Álvar Núñez Cabeza de Vaca*, xix.

93. Rabasa, "Allegory," 53.

94. Ibid., 63.

95. Rabasa, *Writing Violence*, 42.

96. Ibid., 70.

97. Haniel Long, *Interlinear to Cabeza de Vaca* (Santa Fe: Writer's Editions, 1936). Hereafter cited in text.

98. Kun Jong Lee, "Pauline Typology in Cabeza de Vaca's *Naufragios*," *Early American Literature* 34 (1999): 242.

99. Ibid., 242.

100. Ibid., 253.

Chapter 3

1. Paule Marshall, *The Chosen Place, The Timeless People* (New York: Harcourt, Brace and World, 1960), 13.

2. J. Michael Dash, *The Other America: Caribbean Literature in a New World Context* (Charlottesville: University of Virginia Press, 1998), 3.

3. Silvio Torres-Saillant, "The Cross-Cultural Unity of Caribbean Literature: Toward a Centripetal Vision," in *A History of Literature in the Caribbean*, vol. 3, ed. A. James Arnold (Philadelphia: John Benjamins, 1997), 58.

4. David Lowenthal, *West Indian Societies* (New York: Oxford University Press, 1972), xiii.

5. Torres-Saillant, "Cross-Cultural Unity," 61–62.

6. Richard D. E. Burton, *Afro-Creole: Power, Opposition, and Play in the Caribbean* (Ithaca: Cornell University Press, 1997), 1–2.

7. Edouard Glissant, *Caribbean Discourse: Selected Essays*, ed. and trans. J. Michael Dash (Charlottesville: University of Virginia Press, 1989), 62 (emphasis added).

8. Torres-Saillant, "Cross-Cultural Unity," 57, 59 (emphasis added).

9. Dash, *Other America*, xi–xii.

10. Ibid., 5.

11. Ibid., x–xi. Dash's use of the phrase "the other America," although taken from Michael Harrington's book on urban poverty in the United States, refers to the Caribbean and echoes José Martí's sentiments in that Dash, like Martí, focuses on the Caribbean's "process of self-definition"

(xi), a process whose centrifugal and centripetal impulses connect the intellectual and cultural traditions of Europe, Africa, Asia, and America. Unlike Martí, however, Dash uses the term to configure a Pan-Caribbean poetics, thus localizing Martí's much broader Pan-American focus.

12. Antonio Benítez-Rojo, *The Repeating Island: The Caribbean and the Postmodern Perspective,* trans. James Maraniss (Durham, NC: Duke University Press, 1996), 103.

13. Keith Alan Sprouse, "Chaos and Rhizome: Introduction to Caribbean Poetics," in Arnold, *History,* 81.

14. Benítez-Rojo, *Repeating Island,* 7, 9.

15. Ibid., 18.

16. Ibid., 27 (emphasis added). But in Benítez-Rojo's use of "wandering" as a paradigmatic metaphor for the experiences of Caribbean peoples, Torres-Saillant detects a "carefree, unencumbered theoretical stance" ("Cross-Cultural Unity," 67), which tends to gloss over the material consequences of wandering and cultural interaction in the Caribbean. He also faults Benítez-Rojo, given his evidently intimate knowledge of poststructuralist thought and postmodern discourse, for his excessive reliance on Western philosophers and critics. Indeed, the subtitle of *The Repeating Island* promises a "postmodern perspective." For a more pungent assessment of Benítez-Rojo in relation to Glissant, see Román de la Campa, "Resistance and Globalization in Caribbean Discourse: Antonio Benítez-Rojo and Edouard Glissant," in Arnold, *History,* 87–116. But Dash calls Benítez-Rojo's book the "best work so far by a Latin Americanist that explores the Caribbean as a *zone of indeterminacy and metamorphosis.*" Dash, *Other America,* 9 (emphasis added). It is this focus. I think, that makes Benítez-Rojo's work central to any attempt to configure a Pan-Caribbean poetics.

17. Sprouse, "Chaos and Rhizome," 85–86.

18. Glissant, *Poetics of Relation,* trans. Betsy Wing (Ann Arbor: University of Michigan Press, 1997), 14.

19. Ibid., 12.

20. Glissant, *Caribbean Discourse,* 16.

21. Ibid., 18–23.

22. Ibid., 22.

23. Patrick Chamoiseau, *Texaco*, trans. Rose-Myriam Réjouis and Val Vinokurow (New York: Pantheon Books, 1997). Hereafter cited in text.

24. James Holston and Arjun Appadurai, "Cities and Citizenship," *Public Culture* 8 (1996): 187.

25. Ibid.

26. Ibid., 188 (emphasis added).

27. Dash, *Other America*, 8.

28. Juris Silenieks, review of *Texaco*, by Patrick Chamoiseau, *World Literature Today* 67, no. 4 (1993): 1.

29. Dash, *Other America*, 143.

30. Ibid., 144.

31. Mariam K. Slater, *The Caribbean Family: Legitimacy in Martinique* (New York: St. Martin's Press, 1977), 59. In contemporary Martinique the békés are not a homogeneous group, notes Fred Constant. They can be differentiated along the lines of class, education, and work into the *grands békés*, who are very small in number and own large portions of land; the large group of middle-class békés, who occupy governmental positions, are a little more open minded than the older békés, and seek to develop multiethnic cooperatives and businesses; and the *petits blancs*, who are employed by the grands békés. Constant, "French Republicanism under Challenge: White Minority (Béké) Power in Martinique and Guadeloupe," in *The White Minority in the Caribbean*, ed. Howard Johnson and Karl Watson (Princeton: Markus Wiener, 1998), 176–78. Hereafter cited in text.

32. Slater, *Caribbean Family*, 59–60.

33. Fernando Henrique's term, quoted in Slater, ibid., 60.

34. Quoted in Slater, ibid., 58.

35. Michel Giraud, "Dialectics of Descent and Phenotypes in Racial Classification in Martinique," in *French and West Indian: Martinique, Guadeloupe and French Guiana Today*, ed. Richard D. E. Burton and Fred Reno (Charlottesville: University of Virginia Press, 1995), 79. In a related context, Constant notes that the relationship between the French and the békés was not always uniform. It was very ambiguous and ambivalent, depending on the specific pressures of the international market and the implementation of governmental regulations perceived as detrimental to each province's own interests. Constant, "French Republicanism," 177.

36. Shalini Puri, "Canonized Hybridities, Resistant Hybridities: Chutney Soca, Carnival, and the Politics of Nationalism," in *Caribbean Romances: The Politics of Regional Representation*, ed. Belinda J. Edmondson (Charlottesville: University of Virginia Press, 1999), 12–13 (emphasis in original). When such displacement happens, comments Puri, hybridity can end up *"securing* rather than disrupting the status quo." Ibid., 14 (emphasis in original). She further notes that *"refusing* some of these hybridities and border crossings may have less to do with a modernist nostalgia for secure origins than a will to physical survival and a struggle for political self-determination." Ibid., 15 (emphasis in original). In a related context, reviewer Jonathan Foreman comments that the novel's straddling of French and Creole linguistic systems results in a prose that is "ponderous, self-indulgent, and overwhelmingly mediocre." While to some critics *Texaco*'s Creole may seem to be an enabling form of hybridity, Foreman sees only "failed metaphors" because the author is "very, very French," which is precisely the argument the créolists make against Césaire and, to some extent, Glissant. Foreman, "Take Magical Realism—Please!" review of *Texaco*, by Patrick Chamoiseau, *National Review* 49, no. 8 (1997): 1–3.

37. Quoted in Puri, "Canonized Hybridities," 13.

38. Ibid.

39. Patrick Chamoiseau, *Creole Folktales*, trans. Linda Coverdale (New York: New Press, 1994), xii.

40. Edward W. Soja, *Postmodern Geographies: The Reassertion of Space in Critical Social Theory* (New York: Verso, 1989), 12.

41. Ibid., 35.

42. Burton, *Afro-Creole*, 138 (emphasis added). Although Creole emerged in the meeting of French and African culture in the Americas, the use of the term can be extended to include not just French language and its inventive reworking by slaves in the Americas but also, as Burton notes, "autochthonous creation[s], combining a diversity of elements (principally European and African but also Indian and Amerindian) in a manner that is entirely distinctive sui generis—rather than a set of African survivals or a mimetic vision of the culture of metropolitan France" (137). Burton rightly stresses Creole culture and language as distinctive sociocultural processes having their own rhythms and internal

consistencies and as variants of things European and African in the Americas.

43. Glissant, *Caribbean Discourse*, 20.

44. Paget Henry, "Fanon, African and Afro-Caribbean Philosophy," in *Fanon: A Critical Reader*, ed. Lewis R. Gordon, T. Denean Sharpley-Whiting, and Renée T. White (Cambridge, MA: Blackwell, 1996), 221.

45. Ibid., 241.

46. Chamoiseau, *Creole Folktales*, xii.

47. Burton, *Afro-Creole*, 159.

48. Gwen Bergner, "Who Is That Masked Woman? or, The Role of Gender in Fanon's *Black Skin, White Masks*," *PMLA* 110, no. 1 (1995): 80.

49. Richard Price and Sally Price, "'Shadowboxing in the Mangrove': The Politics of Identity in Postcolonial Martinique," in Edmondson, *Caribbean Romances*, 126–31.

50. Ibid., 140–41.

51. Caryl Phillips, "Unmarooned," review of *Texaco*, by Patrick Chamoiseau, *New Republic* 216, no. 17 (1997): 3–4.

52. See these writers' manifesto: Jean Bernabé, Patrick Chamoiseau, and Raphaël Confiant, *In Praise of Creoleness*, trans. M. B. Taleb-Khyar (Paris: Gallimard, 1990). Unable to restrain their Creole profusions, they characterize créolité as a universal discourse heralding the emergence of a "new dimension of man, whose prefigured shadow we are." Ibid., 88. Having thus validated the homogenizing centrality of créolité and affirmed their roles as Creole prophets paving the way for a global phenomenon of dizzying cultural and linguistic hybridization, it is hardly surprising to note their self-importance when they arrogate to themselves the authority to speak for women and women writers through the power of their Creole speech and writing.

53. Benítez-Rojo, *Repeating Island*, 3.

54. Howard Johnson notes that revisionist scholarship's exclusive stress on minorities or the powerless would lead to distorting the complex interplay of other minorities and racial groups that have influenced and continue to influence Caribbean societies. Thus it is very important to focus on the white minority, which exerts a powerful force in various parts of the Caribbean to this day. An exclusive focus might lead to the monolithification of a certain version of history as the canvas became

limited and the participants of large-scale social processes became restricted to the lower class or marginalized. Johnson, introduction to Johnson and Watson, *White Minority*, ix–xvi.

55. Frantz Fanon, *Black Skin/White Masks* (New York: Grove Weidenfeld, 1967), 138.

56. Alastair Bonnett, "Constructions of Whiteness in European and American Anti-racism," in *Debating Cultural Hybridity*, ed. Pnina Werbner and Tariq Modood (London: Zed, 1997), 183.

57. Judith N. Martin, Robert L. Krizek, Thomas K. Nakayama, and Lisa Bradford, "What Do White People Want to Be Called? A Study of Self-Labels for White Americas," in *Whiteness: The Communication of Social Identity*, ed. Thomas K. Nakayama and Judith N. Martin (London: SAGE, 1999), 29 (emphasis in original).

58. Philip C. Wander, Judith N. Martin, and Thomas K. Nakayama, "Whiteness and Beyond: Sociohistorical Foundations of Whiteness and Contemporary Challenges," in Nakayama and Martin, *Whiteness*, 22. Wander et al. note that the naturalistic tradition of the eighteenth and nineteenth centuries, which provided the basis for the classification of humans into types based on skin color, texture, height, and even "cranial capacity," assumed "that the physical world had an intrinsical hierarchical order in which whites were the last and most developed like in 'the great chain of being.'" Ibid., 15. In 1800 Georges Cuvier, a botanist, and Arthur de Gobineau, a zoologist, proposed a race hierarchy with the white or (Caucasian) coming in first, the Mongoloid second, and the Negro third. Toward the end of the nineteenth century these findings were used to explain variations in behavior and inequalities in social existence. Ibid. This led to the rise of race theory.

59. David R. Roediger, *The Wages of Whiteness: Race and the Making of the American Working Class* (New York: Verso, 1991), 13.

60. Noel Ignatiev, "Treason to Whiteness Is Loyalty to Humanity," in *Critical White Studies: Looking Behind the Mirror*, ed. Richard Delgado and Jean Stefancic (Philadelphia: Temple University Press, 1997), 609.

61. Valerie Babb, *Whiteness Visible: The Meaning of Whiteness in American Literature and Culture* (New York: New York University Press, 1998), 41.

62. Toni Morrison, *Playing in the Dark: Whiteness and the Literary Imagination* (Cambridge, MA: Harvard University Press, 1992), 6.

63. Bonnett, "Constructions of Whiteness," 173, 177.

64. Ruth Frankenberg, "Mirage of an Unmarked Whiteness," in *The Making and Unmaking of Whiteness*, ed. Birgit Brander Rasmussen, Eric Klinenberg, Irene J. Nexica, and Matt Wray (Durham, NC: Duke University Press, 2001), 73.

65. Wander et al., "Whiteness and Beyond," 15 (emphasis in original).

66. Christina W. Stage, "We Celebrate 100 Years: An 'Indigenous' Analysis of the Metaphors That Shape the Cultural Identity of Small Town U.S.A," in Nakayama and Martin, *Whiteness*, 71.

67. Martha R. Mahoney, "The Social Construction of Whiteness," in Delgado and Stefancic, *Critical White Studies*, 330.

68. Ibid., 331.

69. Vron Ware and Les Back, introduction to *Out of Whiteness: Color, Politics, and Culture* (Chicago: University of Chicago Press, 2002), 13.

70. Wander et al., "Whiteness and Beyond," 23. Also see Mike Hill, *After Whiteness: Unmaking an American Majority* (New York: New York University Press, 2004), 12. Hill examines "how an emergent post-white national imaginary figures into public policy issues, into the habits of sexual intimacy, and into changes within public higher education, at a moment when white racial change has declared its ambivalent debut."

71. Raka Shome, "Whiteness and the Politics of Location," in Nakayama and Martin, *Whiteness*, 109.

72. Ibid.

73. Robyn Wiegman, "Whiteness Studies and the Paradox of Particularity, " *Boundary 2* 26, no. 3 (1999): 124.

74. Jamaica, which was "discovered" by Columbus in 1494, remained a Spanish colony for about 150 years, until Oliver Cromwell captured the island from the Spaniards in 1655. For more than three hundred years, until 1962, Jamaica was under British rule. During its long and torturous history, Jamaican demographics underwent significant changes. To speak about a native Jamaican is indeed a problem: in about a century from the arrival of the Spanish adventurers, the Arawak population declined from an estimated 60,000 to 74 due to disease, ill treatment by the settlers, suicide, and overwork. Fernando Henriques, *Family and Color in Jamaica* (Bristol: Macgibbon and Kee, 1953), 23. By the time the British conquered the island, Barry Floyd notes, "not a single pure-blooded

Arawak remained." *Jamaica: An Island Microcosm* (New York: St. Martin's Press, 1979), 31. Floyd further observes that as the Arawaks declined in number, Negro slaves began to be imported, first being seen on the island about twenty years after the Spanish conquered it. Soon slavery was firmly established, and it continued under British rule until 1833, when the Emancipation of Slavery Bill was passed in the British Parliament; within about a year the law was effective in the empire. The importation of labor from Asia, particularly from India and China, was one of the effects of Emancipation: as the newly freed slaves refused to work for paltry wages and demanded better treatment, business owners were forced to look elsewhere for cheap labor. Because the East Indians and Chinese who came as indentured laborers were willing to work under the very conditions the slaves had previously worked under, there was much animosity toward them among the native coloreds and blacks. Colored people with light pigmentation trafficked between the blacks and the whites and gained immense advantage and social standing. I have elaborated on this aspect not only to foreground the great racial heterogeneity of Jamaica, but to underscore the black-white framework as a historically viable context in which to situate the hegemony of whiteness in this island.

75. Russell Banks, *The Book of Jamaica* (New York: HarperCollins, 1980), 120. Hereafter cited in text.

76. Shome, "Whiteness," 120. Shome borrows Laura Mulvey's theorization of the "male gaze," which fragments the female body for visual pleasure.

77. Ibid., 122.

78. Banks, *Rule of the Bone* (New York: HarperCollins, 1995). Hereafter cited in text.

79. Robert Niemi, *Russell Banks* (New York: Twayne, 1997), 170.

80. Henry Cowell and Sidney Cowell, *Charles Ives and His Music* (New York: Oxford University Press, 1955), 155, 159.

81. Ibid., 173, 155.

82. Some of Ives's important works include "Paracelsus," "In the Night," and "Harvest Home Chorales" (ibid., 155–56), and "Ann Street," "The Housatonic at Stockbridge," "The Cage," "Psalm 90," and "General William Booth Enters Heaven." Larry Starr, *A Union of Diversities: Style in the*

Music of Charles Ives (New York: Schirmer, 1992), 80, 129. It is significant that Ives's music incorporates the syncopation of minstrel music, the Charleston rhythm, and the rumba rhythm of Afro-Cubans (Cowell and Cowell, *Charles Ives*, 167–69).

83. Frankenberg, "Mirage," 74.

84. Meyer Fortes, *Family and Color in Jamaica* (London: Macgibbon and Kee, 1968), 22, 173.

85. Ibid., 54.

86. Bonham C. Richardson, *The Caribbean in the Wider World, 1492–1992: A Regional Geography* (Cambridge: Cambridge University Press, 1992), 3.

87. Ibid., 125–66.

88. Ibid., 127.

89. Bonnett, "Constructions of Whiteness," 182.

90. Stephanie M. Wildman, "Reflections on Whiteness: The Case of Latinos(as)," in Delgado and Stefancic, *Critical White Studies*, 324.

91. Bonnett, "Constructions of Whiteness," 182–83.

92. Ignatiev, "Treason to Whiteness," 607.

93. Mahoney, "Social Construction," 330.

94. Arjun Appadurai, "Disjuncture and Difference in the Global Cultural Economy," in *Colonial Discourse and Post-Colonial Theory*, ed. Patrick Williams and Laura Chrisman (New York: Columbia University Press, 1994), 355.

Chapter 4

1. Gloria Anzaldúa, *The Borderlands/La Frontera* (San Francisco: Aunt Lute Books, 1987), 78, 3.

2. José David Saldívar, *Border Matters* (Los Angeles: University of California Press, 1997), ix–xii.

3. Scott Michaelsen and David E. Johnson, eds., "Border Secrets: An Introduction," in *Border Theory: The Limits of Cultural Politics* (Minneapolis: University of Minnesota Press, 1997), 18.

4. Amritjit Singh and Peter Schmidt, introduction to *Postcolonial Theory and the United States*, ed. Singh and Schmidt (Jackson: University Press of Mississippi, 2000), 41.

5. By linking the U.S. Southwest to Mexico's northern provinces, the term "borderlands" provides a transnational focus and is thus more helpful than the term "Southwest" for referring to the states on both sides that abut the U.S.-Mexican border.

6. David Weber, "The Idea of the Spanish Borderlands," in *Columbian Consequences*, vol. 3, ed. David Hurst Thomas (Washington: Smithsonian Institution Press, 1991), 4.

7. Herbert Eugene Bolton, "The Borderlands in American History," in *Bolton and the Spanish Borderlands*, ed. John Francis Bannon (Norman: University of Oklahoma Press, 1964), 59.

8. William Maltby notes that Julián Juderías coined the term in 1912 to refer to a corpus of writings dating from the sixteenth century to the present that embodied the idea of the Spanish as a nasty and brutish people. Because Spain, a powerful colonial power in the sixteenth and seventeenth centuries, sought to extend its dominion across the Atlantic by conquering and converting the Indians, other European powers experiencing the throes of the Reformation sought to denigrate the Spanish and check their growing power. This gave rise to anti-Hispanic sentiment, which, ironically, was fueled by the "apostle of the Indians," the Dominican friar Bartolomé de Las Casas, whose writings, most notably the *Brevísima Relación de la Destrucción de las Indias* (1551), against the encomienda and other Spanish colonial practices seemed to prove beyond dispute the inhumanity of the Spaniards and their lack of interest in creating societies based on the ideals of Renaissance humanism. In pointing to how the way in which the English incorporated the legend into their writings over the last few centuries differed from the way in which the Dutch, the French, and the Italians assimilated and reworked the legend, Maltby helps to undermine monolithic constructions of the leyanda negra. Maltby, *The Black Legend in England: The Development of Anti-Spanish Sentiment, 1558–1660* (Durham, NC: Duke University Press, 1971), 3, 4, 12.

9. Weber, "Idea," 6.

10. Noggle, quoted in Weber, "Idea," 6.

11. Thomas, *Columbian Consequences*, 3:5.

12. Howard F. Cline, quoted in Weber, "Idea," 10–12.

13. Ibid.

14. Pablo Vila observes that "Chicano," far from being a term with a stable descriptive meaning, has been used in several different ways, often with contradictory connotations, by people located in diverse places in the Southwest. Generally, U.S.-born people of Mexican descent opt to use the term, but not those born in Mexico who immigrated to the United States. Language also plays a crucial part: people of Mexican ancestry who were born and brought up in the United States and speak English and not Spanish (not fluently or not at all) are quick to call themselves Chicano. Contrary to common assumptions, the term did not originate in the 1960s; it was used early in the twentieth century as an ethnic slur to refer to Mexicans, particularly poor blue-collar workers from Mexico who had recently immigrated to the United States in search of better opportunities. Gradually, the term began to be used to refer to all Mexicans, regardless of when they arrived in the United States. It is now used as an in-group marker of identification, a means of establishing a sense of commonality and solidarity. In public, however, outside the group, other terms, such as "Mexican American" and "Hispano," are preferred. "Chicano" began to gain positive meaning in the 1960s and the 1970s during the struggle for representation and equality by minority groups. Consonant with the desire to contest discriminatory practices was the impulse to restore and sustain Mexican culture and identity. But to some the term sometimes evokes fears of ethnic ghettoization, which would lead to further isolation from the larger public and other minority peoples. Vila notes that a productive way of approaching the term is not just to see how it has been used historically, but to understand the various struggles for identity and representation that it has been made to configure at different periods in history and view "the symbolic struggle around the label Chicano as part of a broader struggle to define a particular experience, that of people of Mexican descent living in the United States." Vila. "The Competing Meanings of the Label 'Chicano' in El Paso," in *The U.S.-Mexico Border: Transcending Division, Contesting Identities*, ed. David Spener and Kathleen Staudt (Boulder: Lynne Rienner, 1988), 189.

15. Teresa McKenna, *Migrant Song* (Austin: University of Texas Press, 1997), 139.

16. The emergence of a Mexican American working class in the Southwest is a central issue in borderland historiography. As Mario Bar-

rera observes, the dynamics of a growing capitalist American economy provided the "underlying structure of interests" that ultimately led to the war of 1848, which resulted in the U.S. annexation of Mexico's northern provinces. Barrera, *Race and Class in the Southwest* (Notre Dame, IN: University of Notre Dame Press, 1979), 5. To an expanding industrial Midwest and North, points out Ramón Saldívar, the South became a source of cheap raw material because the production of "industrial metals and agricultural products . . . required only an unskilled labor force" of railroad workers, farm workers, and smelter mine laborers. Saldívar, *Chicano Narrative: The Dialectics of Difference* (Madison: University of Wisconsin Press, 1990), 19. In a related context, Norman Graebner argues, "From the beginning, travelers, traders, and officials who concerned themselves with the coastal regions had their eyes trained on ports. The goal of American policy was to control the great harbors of San Francisco, San Diego, and Juan de Fuca Strait. With their acquisition, expansion on the coastline ceased." Graebner, *Empire on the Pacific* (New York: Ronald Press, 1955), vi. I point out these issues because the factors influencing U.S. expansionist programs leading to the war of 1848 play a significant role to this day in giving rise to what Saldívar refers to as a Mexican American working-class consciousness in the Southwest. Saldívar, *Chicano Narrative,* 23. In the twentieth century, U.S. governmental initiatives like the bracero program (1940–50) and the establishment of the maquiladoras (1960s) along the U.S.-Mexican border testify to the increasing influence of American economic interests, which create a disposable labor force across the border in Mexico and significantly affect the phenomenon of border crossing from Mexico into the United States and vice versa, not only by Mexicans but by peoples from different South American countries and even Asia, Europe, and Africa. The establishment of border patrols, the billions of dollars poured into the INS and its affiliated agencies to "protect America," the increase in drug trafficking across the border, and the popular stereotyped image of Mexicans as potential drug lords, traffickers, or, at best, lawnmowers, dishwashers, domestic helpers, and per diem workers—these are the effects of a range of social and economic interests set in motion more than one hundred and fifty years ago whose repercussions continue to this day in the borderlands.

17. Anzaldúa, *Borderlands,* 78.

18. Quoted in ibid., 77.

19. The politics of language become central to the endeavor of reviving and recovering Mexican American presence in the Southwest. According to Genaro Padilla, one needs to move between languages—Spanish and English—in order to engage the dynamics of Chicano history productively. Padilla, *My History, Not Yours: The Formation of Mexican American Autobiography* (Madison: University of Wisconsin Press, 1993), 4, 20. In the context of the official U.S. historical and literary discourse of Mexicans in the Southwest, it would be fruitful to study the numerous essays and autobiographical narratives in Spanish—the Bancroft Collection is a massive storehouse of these. Hubert Howe Bancroft, Henry Lebbeus Oak, William Nemos, and Frances Fuller Victor, *History of California*, 7 vols. (San Francisco: A. L. Bancroft, 1884–90). This necessarily complicates any easy binarisms because these discourses evolved in relation to each other and not in distinct social and cultural spaces. Thus, we cannot automatically regard the work of Bancroft or Bolton as more authoritative than works written in Spanish by people of Mexican descent. It is such multilingual coding of Mexican American literary history that makes bilingualism central to border discourse.

20. Pérez-Torres underscores the importance of reading Aztlán less as symbolizing a return to origins and more as a discursive sign. "Refiguring Aztlán," in Singh and Schmidt, *Postcolonial Theory*, 104. Sáenz finds Anzaldúa's "fetishi[zing of] Aztec and Indian culture" "disturbing" because it "offers very little" to borderlanders who "live mostly in urban settings." Sáenz, "In the Borderlands of Chicano Identity, There Are Only Fragments," in Michaelsen and Johnson, *Border Theory*, 85.

21. Eileen M. Luna-Firebaugh, "The Border Crossed Us: Border Crossing Issues of the Indigenous Peoples of the Americas," *Wicazo Sa Review* 17, no. 1 (2002): 159, 167–68.

22. Eric Anderson, *American Indian Literature and the Southwest* (Austin: University of Texas Press, 1999), 187.

23. Ibid., 4, 9.

24. Mary Louise Pratt, *Imperial Eyes: Travel Writing and Transculturation* (London: Routledge, 1992), 4

25. Noreen Groover Lape, *West of the Border: The Multicultural Literature of the Western American Frontiers* (Athens: Ohio University Press, 2000), 3.

26. In similar vein, in his deconstructive reading of *Joaquin Murieta*, John Carlos Rowe argues against viewing the text as a clear instance of Mexican subaltern opposition to American presence in the Southwest. While it overtly adopts an anti-American tone, the text, Rowe notes, affirms the American myth of individualism and uses American ideals to displace an emphasis on nationality and ethnicity in order to inscribe individual sanctity and privacy in the narrative as the primary loci from which to conceptualize a "multicultural and multi-regional" subjectivity in the Southwest. Rowe, *Literary Culture and U.S. Imperialism: From the Revolution to World War II* (New York: Oxford University Press, 2001), 115. Similarly, Laura Browder notes that by appropriating accepted symbols and practices of ethnicity, those who "impersonate" ethnicity manipulate the "idea of ethnicity as performance" through a "strenuous performance of American authenticity." Browder, *Slippery Characters: Ethnic Impersonators and American Identities* (Chapel Hill: University of North Carolina Press, 2000), 11, 53. The Asian appropriation of Mesoamerican mythology in the borderlands that Sadowski-Smith emphasizes in her reading of Karen Tei Yamashita's *Tropic of Orange* aptly demonstrates both the problem of relying on Chicanismo philosophy to theorize border societies and the usefulness of Browder's theory of ethnicity as performance. Sadowski-Smith, "The U.S.-Mexico Borderlands Write Back: Cross-Cultural Transnationalism in Contemporary U.S. Women of Color Fiction," *Arizona Quarterly* 57, no. 1 (2001): 91–112.

27. Cecil Robinson argues that William Faulkner, Allen Tate, Mark Twain, and Mary Austin are some of the canonized American writers who have woven the unique mestiza culture of the Southwest into their writings. It would be fruitful, then, to study these writers alongside Chicano writers in the context of border phenomena rather than treating them as outsiders and therefore inauthentic. Robinson, *No Short Journeys* (Tucson: University of Arizona Press, 1991).

28. Anderson, *American Indian Literature*, 3.

29. Homi Bhabha, introduction to *Nation and Narration* (New York: Routledge, 1990), 4.

30. Guillermo Gómez-Peña, "Documented/Undocumented," in *Multi-Cultural Literacy*, ed. Rick Simonson and Scott Walker (Minneapolis: Graywolf Press, 1988), 130.

31. Beatriz M. Pesquera and Denise A. Segura, "With Quill and Torch: A Chicana Perspective on the American Women's Movement and Feminist Theories," in *Chicanas/Chicanos at the Crossroads*, ed. David R. Maciel and Isidro D. Ortiz (Tucson: University of Arizona Press, 1996), 232, 237.

32. Adelaida R. Del Castillo, "Gender and Its Discontinuities in Male/Female Domestic Relations: Mexicans in Cross-Cultural Context," in Maciel and Ortiz, *Chicanas/Chicanos*, 214.

33. Anzaldúa, *Borderlands*, 77.

34. Roberta Fernández, *Intaglio: A Novel in Six Stories* (Houston: Arte Publico Press, 1990). Hereafter cited in text.

35. Sonia Saldívar-Hull, "Feminism on the Border: From Gender Politics to Geopolitics," in *Criticism in the Borderlands: Studies in Chicano Literatures, Culture, Ideology*, ed. Héctor Calderón and José David Saldívar (Durham, NC: Duke University Press, 1991), 203–20.

36. Anzaldúa, *Borderlands*, 78.

37. Iain Chambers, "Leaky Habitats and Broken Grammars," in *Travellers' Tales: Narratives of Home and Displacement*, ed. George Robertson (New York: Routledge, 1994), 246.

38. Trinh T. Minh-ha, "Other than Myself/My Other Self," in Robertson, *Travellers' Tales*, 20.

39. Oscar Martínez, *U.S.-Mexico Borderlands* (Wilmington: Jaguar Books, 1996), 107.

40. To Rodriguez it is futile, and ultimately detrimental, to hold on to native practices in the United States because doing so only slows down one's inevitable Americanization. Assimilation into American society is, according to him, not only inevitable but something to be desired by immigrants if they want to make their presence felt in American society and attain a public voice. Rodriguez, *Hunger of Memory* (New York: Bantam Books, 1982). There have been near-hysterical dismissals of Rodriguez's positions, in which he has been called a "betrayer" and a "traitor" to his race and culture. Michaelsen and Johnson note that several critics, including Norma Alarcón, José Saldívar, Ramón Saldívar, and Rosaura Sánchez, have excluded Rodriguez from the Chicano canon. These critics "essential[ize] Chicano identity around the figure of resistance: in short, there will be no Chicano assimilation." Michaelsen and Johnson, *Border*

Theory, 18. One could just as well dismiss *Intaglio* with the same charges, but the crucial difference perhaps lies in Rodriguez's emphasis on loss and Fernández's emphasis on sustaining native traditions.

41. Like the curandera, la bruja, a literary/mythic figure generally associated with the spirit world, has special healing powers. However, while la bruja is a spiritual healer and can predict the future and know the past, the curandera specializes in healing the body. Ana Castillo, *Massacre of the Dreamers* (Albuquerque: University of New Mexico Press, 1994), 156–57.

42. Robert T. Trotter and Juan A. Chavira, *Curanderismo* (Athens: University of Georgia Press, 1981), 2.

43. Ibid., 3. As Trotter and Chavira note, curanderismo generally functions as a supplementary system of health care. By tapping into resources already existing within the family, it significantly reduces financial and psychological burdens, thus furthering the process of recovery.

44. Ana María Carbonell differentiates between la llorona, who "wails and weeps," and la gritona, who "shouts and hollers." Carbonell, "From Llorona to Gritona: Coatlicue in Feminist Tales by Viramontes and Cisneros," *MELUS* 24, no. 2 (1999): 72. Frequently associated with water imagery, la llorona is a multidimensional figure signifying both the destructive and nourishing aspects of water. Ibid., 61. In addition, while embodying the contradictions of both death and rebirth, the figure of la llorona, notes Carbonell, also "resembles feminist psychoanalytic definitions of the female 'self-in-relation,' an *interdependent* versus a *dependent* or *independent* self." Ibid., 57 (emphasis in original). It is this notion of interdependency that Fernández weaves into the story.

45. Tey Diana Rebolledo, *Women Singing in the Snow: A Cultural Analysis of Chicana Literature* (Tucson: University of Arizona Press, 1995), 62–63.

46. Anzaldúa, *Borderlands*, 77.

47. Homi Bhabha, *The Location of Culture* (New York: Routledge, 1994), 9.

48. Leslie Marmon Silko, *Almanac of the Dead* (New York: Simon and Schuster, 1991). Hereafter cited in text.

49. In her discussion of the novel, Ann Folwell Stanford argues that medicine as practice, social structure, and institution and as vocation, belief, myth, and scientific discourse is questioned and forced to acknowledge its own complicity in dispossessing the poor and those without access

to power. The crucial problem, as Stanford observes, is that "not all bodies are rendered fodder for scientific and medical gain, but predictably, those that are deemed worthless (and Other) by the dominant society," including the homeless, drug addicts, prostitutes, minorities, illegal immigrants, and the victims of war, all of whom are part of the indigenous pantribal coalitions envisioned in the novel. Stanford, "'Human Debris': Border Politics, Body Parts, and the Reclamation of the Americas in Leslie Marmon Silko's *Almanac of the Dead*," *Literature and Medicine* 16, no. 1 (1997): 32.

50. Sven Birkerts, "Apocalypse Now," *New Republic* 205, no. 19 (1991): 39.

51. To Janet St. Clair, the effects of colonialism in the Americas amount to a "nightmarish wasteland" engendered by the "misogynist, arrogantly hierarchical, and egocentric traditions of Western liberal individualism," characterized by "insane solipsism and phallocentric avarice." St. Clair, "Death of Love/Love of Death: Leslie Marmon Silko's *Almanac of the Dead*," *MELUS* 21, no. 2 (1996): 141.

52. Bernie Harder, "The Power of Border in Native American Literature: Leslie Marmon Silko's *Almanac of the Dead*," *American Indian Culture and Research Journal* 24, no. 4 (2000): 98 (emphasis added).

53. Ibid., 96, 99.

54. Ibid., 104.

55. Virginia E. Bell, "Counter Chronicling and Alternative Mapping in *Memoria del fuego* and *Almanac of the Dead*," *MELUS* 25, nos. 3–4 (2000): 27.

56. Frederick W. Turner III, introduction to *Geronimo: His Own Story*, ed. S. M. Barrett (New York: E. P. Dutton, 1970), 44–45.

57. Britton Davis, *The Truth about Geronimo* (Chicago: Lakeside Press, 1951), xxxix, li.

58. Ibid., lvii

59. Charles H. L. Johnston, *Famous Indian Chiefs* (Boston: L. C. Page, 1909), 308.

60. Turner, introduction to *Geronimo*, 14, 18.

61. David L. Moore, "Silko's Blood Sacrifice: The Circulating Witness in *Almanac of the Dead*," in *Leslie Marmon Silko: A Collection of Critical Essays*, ed.

Louise K. Barnett and James L. Thorson (Albuquerque: University of New Mexico Press, 2001), 166.

62. Helen Jaskoski, *Leslie Marmon Silko: A Study of the Short Fiction* (New York: Twayne, 1998), 62.

63. Leslie Marmon Silko, "A Geronimo Story," in *Come to Power: Eleven Contemporary American Indian Poets,* ed. Dick Lourie (New York: Crossing Press, 1974), 92, 94.

64. Bell, "Counter Chronicling," 26.

65. Evelyn Hu-DeHart, *Yaqui Resistance and Survival: The Struggle for Land and Autonomy, 1821–1910* (Madison: University of Wisconsin Press, 1984).

66. Elizabeth Warner Giddings, *Yaqui Myths and Legends,* ed. Harry Behn (Tucson: University of Arizona Press, 1974), 6.

67. Edward H. Spicer, *The Yaquis: A Cultural History* (Tucson: University of Arizona Press, 1980), 16.

68. Ibid., 4–6.

69. Hu-DeHart, *Yaqui Resistance,* 155.

70. Ibid., 182.

71. Ibid., 173.

72. Ibid., 172, 202 (emphasis added).

73. Spicer, *Yaquis,* 306.

74. Ibid., 307.

75. Joni Adamson, *American Indian Literature, Environmental Justice, and Ecocriticism: The Middle Place* (Tucson: University of Arizona Press, 2001), 142–43.

76. Ibid., 144. The relevance of the birthing of the fifth world in the sense in which *Almanac* dramatizes it becomes clearer in light of recent events in Chiapas, Mexico, an issue that Joni Adamson addresses in detail. She draws attention to the attempts of Mayan rebels who, in 1994, led by a non-Mayan, Subcomandante Marcos, and calling themselves Zapatistas, led public protests demanding that the Mexican government initiate land reform policies, including land redistribution in the state of Chiapas. The government's response was swift—it suppressed the rebellion by sending in the military and accused the Zapatistas of pandering to the machinations of a non-Mayan and foreigners. Adamson, *American Indian Literature,* 128–36. Adamson argues that the government's response was grounded in essentialisms about Mayan identity and

that, more importantly, it misconstrued the forms of political action initiated by the Zapatistas. By going beyond tribal forms of affiliation and building an international network of supporters, the Mayans affirmed nontraditional and non-Indian forms of solidarity to achieve their local, social, and political goals. While noting that the government relented and began to make concessions by investing in the development of the state's economy and infrastructure, Adamson observes that this incident is a form of "syncretic resistance" (152), an idea that is closely related to my own argument about how *Almanac* gestures toward the formation of postnational and transborder subjectivities and the dynamics of political involvement in the borderlands.

77. Ami M. Regier, "Material Meeting Points of Self and Other: Fetish Discourses and Leslie Marmon Silko's Evolving Conception of Cross-Cultural Narrative," in Barnett and Thorson, *Leslie Marmon Silko*, 201.

78. Moore, "Silko's Blood Sacrifice," 177.

79. Daria Donnelly, "Old and New Notebooks: *Almanac of the Dead* as Revolutionary Entertainment," in Barnett and Thorson, *Leslie Marmon Silko*, 246.

80. Caren Irr, "The Timeliness of *Almanac of the Dead*, or a Postmodern Rewriting of Radical Fiction," in Barnett and Thorson, *Leslie Marmon Silko*, 226.

81. Hu-DeHart, *Yaqui Resistance*, 5 (emphasis added).

82. Sadowski-Smith, "U.S.-Mexico Borderlands," 106–8. The trope of the border and of border crossings to imagine new forms of transnational affiliation and transborder activism gains greater significance when viewed through the refractory optics of the diasporic imagination, an optics that frustrates the search for the transparent vision by unsettling the balance afforded by a stable, hermeneutic ontology. This is why, to Sadowski-Smith, the diaspora becomes a primary category of analysis to theorize an alternative global politics and subversive border cultures in the borderlands. She reads *Almanac* as foregrounding the historical and contemporary effects of "diasporic displacements" while engendering "new modes of cross-cultural and transnational mythmaking" in the Americas. Ibid., 91–92.

83. Salyer, *Leslie Marmon Silko* (New York: Twayne, 1997), 114.

84. St. Clair, "Death of Love," 141–42.

85. Salyer, *Leslie Marmon Silko*, 98.

86. Silko, interview, in *Winged Words*, ed. Laura Coltelli (Lincoln: University of Nebraska Press, 1990), 150.

87. Tamara Teale, "The Silko Road from Chiapas, or Why Native Americans Cannot be Marxists," *MELUS* 23, no. 4 (1998): 157–58.

88. Gayatri Chakravorty Spivak, *The Post-colonial Critic: Interviews, Strategies, Dialogues*, ed. Sarah Harasym (New York: Routledge, 1990), 72.

89. Silko, interview, 151.

90. Arnold Krupat, *The Turn to the Native: Studies in Criticism and Culture* (Lincoln: University of Nebraska Press, 1996), 51.

91. St. Clair, "Death of Love," 154.

92. Manuel Luís Martínez, "Telling the Difference between the Border and the Borderlands: Materiality and Theoretical Practice," in *Globalization on the Line: Culture, Capital, and Citizenship at U.S. Borders*, ed. Claudia Sadowski-Smith (New York: Palgrave, 2002), 54.

93. Ibid., 60.

94. Sadowski-Smith, "U.S.-Mexico Borderlands," 94.

95. Eric Cheyfitz, "The (Post)Colonial Predicament of Native American Studies," *Interventions* 4, no. 3 (2002): 408.

96. Valerie Karno, "Legal Hunger: Law, Narrative, and Orality in Leslie Marmon Silko's *Storyteller* and *Almanac of the Dead*," *College Literature* 28, no. 1 (2001): 2.

BIBLIOGRAPHY

Adamson, Joni. *American Indian Literature, Environmental Justice, and Ecocriticism: The Middle Place.* Tucson: University of Arizona Press, 2001.

Adorno, Rolena. "History, Law, and the Eyewitness Protocols of Authority in Bernal Díaz del Castillo's *Historia verdadera de la conquista de la Nueva España.*" In *The Project of Prose in Early Modern Europe and the New World,* edited by Elizabeth Fowler and Roland Greene, 154–75. Cambridge: Cambridge University Press, 1997.

———. "The Negotiation of Fear in Cabeza de Vaca's *Naufragios.*" In *New World Encounters,* edited by Stephen Greenblatt, 48–84. Los Angeles: University of California Press, 1993.

Adorno, Rolena, and Patrick Charles Pautz, eds. *Álvar Núñez Cabeza de Vaca: His Account, His Life, and the Expedition of Pánfilo de Narváez.* 3 vols. Lincoln: University of Nebraska Press, 1999.

Anderson, Eric. *American Indian Literature and the Southwest.* Austin: University of Texas Press, 1999.

Angoff, Charles. *A Literary History of the American People.* Vol. 1, *From 1607 to the Beginning of the Revolutionary Period.* New York: Alfred A. Knopf, 1931.

Anzaldúa, Gloria. *The Borderlands/La Frontera.* San Francisco: Aunt Lute Books, 1987.

Appadurai, Arjun. "Disjuncture and Difference in the Global Cultural Economy." In *Colonial Discourse and Post-Colonial Theory,* edited by Patrick Williams and Laura Chrisman, 324–39. New York: Columbia University Press, 1994.

Arens, William. "Rethinking Anthropophagy." In *Cannibalism and the Colonial World,* edited by Francis Barker, Peter Hulme, and Margaret Iversen, 39–62. Cambridge: Cambridge University Press, 1998.

Askenasy, Hans. *Cannibalism: From Sacrifice to Survival.* New York: Prometheus Books, 1994.

Babb, Valerie. *Whiteness Visible: The Meaning of Whiteness in American Literature and Culture.* New York: New York University Press, 1998.

Bancroft, Hubert Howe, Henry Lebbeus Oak, William Nemos, and Frances Fuller Victor. *History of California.* 7 vols. San Francisco: A. L. Bancroft, 1884–90.

Bandelier, Adolph Francis. Introduction to *The Journey of Álvar Núñez Cabeza de Vaca and His Companions from Florida to the Pacific, 1528–1536,* by Álvar Núñez Cabeza de Vaca, Marco da Nizza, and Antonio de Mendoza, edited by Adolph Francis Bandelier, translated by Fanny Bandelier, xix–xxxvi. New York: A. S. Barnes, 1905.

Banks, Russell. *The Book of Jamaica.* New York: HarperCollins, 1980.

———. *Rule of the Bone.* New York: HarperCollins, 1995.

Barrera, Mario. *Race and Class in the Southwest.* Notre Dame, IN: University of Notre Dame Press, 1979.

Bell, Virginia E. "Counter Chronicling and Alternative Mapping in *Memoria del fuego* and *Almanac of the Dead.*" *MELUS* 25, nos. 3–4 (2000): 6–30.

Belnap, Jeffrey Grant, and Raúl A. Fernández, eds. *José Martí's "Our America": From National to Hemispheric Cultural Studies.* Durham, NC: Duke University Press, 1999.

Benítez-Rojo, Antonio. *The Repeating Island: The Caribbean and the Postmodern Perspective.* Translated by James Maraniss. Durham, NC: Duke University Press, 1996.

Bercovitch, Sacvan. "America as Canon and Context: Literary History in a Time of Dissensus." *American Literature* 58, no. 1 (1986): 99–107.

Berdan, Frances F. *The Aztecs of Central Mexico: An Imperial Society.* New York: CBS College, 1982.

Bergner, Gwen. "Who Is That Masked Woman? or, The Role of Gender in Fanon's *Black Skin, White Masks.*" *PMLA* 110, no. 1 (1995): 75–88.

Bernabé, Jean, Patrick Chamoiseau, and Raphaël Confinat. *In Praise of Creoleness.* Translated by M. B. Taleb-Khyar. Paris: Gallimard, 1990.

Bhabha, Homi. *The Location of Culture.* New York: Routledge, 1994.

———, ed. *Nation and Narration.* New York: Routledge, 1990.

Billington, Ray Allen, ed. *Frontier and Section: Selected Essays of Frederick Jackson Turner,* 1–9. Englewood Cliffs, NJ: Prentice Hall, 1961.

Birkerts, Sven. "Apocalypse Now." *The New Republic* 205, no. 19 (1991): 39–41.

Bishop, Morris. *The Odyssey of Cabeza de Vaca.* New York: Century, 1933.

Bolton, Herbert Eugene. "The Borderlands in American History." In *Bolton and the Spanish Borderlands,* edited by John Francis Bannon, 4–32. Norman: University of Oklahoma Press, 1964.

Bonnett, Alastair. "Constructions of Whiteness in European and American Anti-racism." In *Debating Cultural Hybridity,* edited by Pnina Werbner and Tariq Modood, 173–92. London: Zed Books, 1997.

Bright, Charles, and Michael Geyer. "Where in the World Is America? The History of the United States in the Global Age." In *Rethinking American History in a Global Age,* edited by Thomas Bender, 63–99. Berkeley: University of California Press, 2002.

Browder, Laura. *Slippery Characters: Ethnic Impersonators and American Identities.* Chapel Hill: University of North Carolina Press, 2000.

Burton, Richard D. E. *Afro-Creole: Power, Opposition, and Play in the Caribbean.* Ithaca: Cornell University Press, 1997.

———. "The Idea of Difference in Contemporary French West Indian Thought: Négritude, Antillanité, Créolité." In *French and West Indian: Martinique, Guadeloupe and French Guiana Today,* edited by Richard D. E. Burton and Fred Reno, 137–66. Charlottesville: University of Virginia Press, 1995.

Cabeza de Vaca, Álvar Núñez. *Relación.* Translated by Rolena Adorno and Patrick Charles Pautz. In *Álvar Núñez Cabeza de Vaca: His Account, His Life, and the Expedition of Pánfilo de Narváez,* edited by Adorno and Pautz, vol. 1. Lincoln: University of Nebraska Press, 1999.

Cabeza de Vaca, Álvar Núñez, Marco da Nizza, and Antonio de Mendoza. *The Journey of Álvar Núñez Cabeza de Vaca and His Companions from Florida to the Pacific, 1528–1536.* Edited by Adolph Francis Bandelier. Translated by Fanny Bandelier. New York: A. S. Barnes, 1905.

Calvin, John. *Institutes of the Christian Religion.* Edited by John T. McNeill. Translated by Ford Lewis Battles. Philadelphia: Westminster Press, 1960.

Caponnetto, Antonio. *The Black Legends and Catholic Hispanic Culture.* Translated by José R. López and Rosa M. López. New Hope, KY: St. Martin de Porres Lay Dominican Community, 1991.

Carbonell, Ana María. "From Llorona to Gritona: Coatlicue in Feminist Tales by Viramontes and Cisneros." *MELUS* 24, no. 2 (1999): 53–74.

Carrasco, Davíd. "Toward the Splendid City: Knowing the Worlds of Moctezuma." In *Moctezuma's Mexico: Visions of the Aztec World*, edited by Davíd Carrasco and Eduardo Matos Moctezuma, 99–148. Niwot: University Press of Colorado, 1992.

Castillo, Ana. *Massacre of the Dreamers.* Albuquerque: University of New Mexico Press, 1994.

Castro, Américo. *The Spaniards: An Introduction to Their History.* Translated by Willard F. King and Selma Margaretten. Berkeley: University of California Press, 1971.

Certeau, Michel de. *The Writing of History.* Translated by Tom Conley. New York: Columbia University Press, 1988.

Chambers, Iain. "Leaky Habitats and Broken Grammars." In *Travellers' Tales: Narratives of Home and Displacement,* edited by George Robertson, 245–49. New York: Routledge, 1994.

Chamoiseau, Patrick. *Creole Folktales.* Translated by Linda Coverdale. New York: New Press, 1994.

———. *Texaco.* Translated by Rose-Myriam Réjouis and Val Vinokurow. New York: Pantheon Books, 1997.

Chevigny, Bell, and Gari Laguardia. *Reinventing the Americas.* Cambridge: Cambridge University Press, 1986.

Cheyfitz, Eric. "The (Post)Colonial Predicament of Native American Studies." *Interventions* 4, no. 3 (2002): 405–27.

Clendinnen, Inga. *Aztecs: An Interpretation.* Cambridge: Cambridge University Press, 1991.

———. "'Fierce and Unnatural Cruelty': Cortés and the Conquest of Mexico." In *New World Encounters,* edited by Stephen Greenblatt, 12–47. Los Angeles: University of California Press, 1993.

Cline, S. L. Introduction to *Conquest of New Spain: 1585 Revision,* by Bernardino de Sahagún, edited by S. L. Cline, translated by Howard F. Cline, 1–21. Salt Lake City: University of Utah Press, 1989.

Cohen, J. M. Introduction to *The Conquest of New Spain,* by Bernal Díaz del Castillo, 7–12. London: Penguin, 1963.

Constant, Fred. "French Republicanism under Challenge: White Minority (Béké) Power in Martinique and Guadeloupe." In *The White Mi-*

nority in the Caribbean, edited by Howard Johnson and Karl Watson, 169–79. Princeton: Markus Wiener, 1998.

Cowell, Henry, and Sidney Cowell. *Charles Ives and His Music.* New York: Oxford University Press, 1955.

Dash, J. Michael. *The Other America: Caribbean Literature in a New World Context.* Charlottesville: University of Virginia Press, 1998.

Davis, Britton. *The Truth about Geronimo.* Chicago: Lakeside Press, 1951.

De la Campa, Román. "Latin, Latino, American: Split States and Global Imaginaries." In *Globalization and the Humanities,* edited by David Leiwei Li, 101–17. Hong Kong: Hong Kong University Press, 2004.

———. "Resistance and Globalization in Caribbean Discourse: Antonio Benítez-Rojo and Edouard Glissant." In *A History of Literature in the Caribbean,* vol. 3, edited by A. James Arnold, 87–116. Philadelphia: John Benjamins, 1997.

Del Castillo, Adelaida R. "Gender and Its Discontinuities in Male/Female Domestic Relations: Mexicans in Cross-Cultural Context." In *Chicanas/Chicanos at the Crossroads,* edited by David R. Maciel and Isidro D. Ortiz, 207–30. Tucson: University of Arizona Press, 1996.

Díaz del Castillo, Bernal. *The Conquest of New Spain.* Translated by J. M. Cohen. London: Penguin, 1963.

Dickason, Olive Patricia. *The Myth of the Savage and the Beginnings of French Colonialism in the Americas.* Edmonton: University of Alberta Press, 1984.

Dimock, Wai Chee. "Literature for the Planet." *PMLA* 116, no. 1 (2001): 173–88.

Dirlik, Arif. "American Studies in the Time of Empire." *Comparative American Studies* 2, no. 3 (2004): 287–302.

Donnelly, Daria. "Old and New Notebooks: *Almanac of the Dead* as Revolutionary Entertainment." In *Leslie Marmon Silko: A Collection of Critical Essays,* edited by Louise K. Barnett and James L. Thorson, 245–59. Albuquerque: University of New Mexico Press, 2001.

Dupré, Louis. *Passage to Modernity.* New Haven: Yale University Press, 1993.

DuRivage, Françoise. "*Texaco:* From the Hills to the Mangrove Swamp." *Thamyris* 6, no. 1 (1999): 35–42.

Dussel, Enrique. *The Invention of the Americas.* Translated by Michael D. Barber. New York: Continuum, 1995.

Elliott, John H. *The Discovery of America and the Discovery of Man.* London: Oxford University Press, 1972.

———. "Renaissance Europe and America: A Blunted Impact?" In *First Images of America,* edited by Fredi Chiappelli, 11–23. Berkeley: University of California Press, 1976.

Fanon, Frantz. *Black Skin/White Masks.* New York: Grove Weidenfeld, 1967.

———. *The Wretched of the Earth.* New York: Grove Weidenfeld, 1963.

Ferguson, Niall. *Colossus: The Price of America's Empire.* New York: Penguin, 2004.

———. *Empire: The Rise and Demise of the British World Order and the Lessons for Global Power.* New York: Basic Books, 2003.

Fernández, Roberta. *Intaglio: A Novel in Six Stories.* Houston: Arte Publico Press, 1990.

Floyd, Barry. *Jamaica: An Island Microcosm.* New York: St. Martin's Press, 1979.

Foreman, Jonathan. "Take Magical Realism—Please!" Review of *Texaco,* by Patrick Chamoiseau. *National Review* 49, no. 8 (1997): 1–3.

Fortes, Meyer. *Family and Color in Jamaica.* London: Macgibbon and Kee, 1968.

Frankenberg, Ruth. "Mirage of an Unmarked Whiteness." In *The Making and Unmaking of Whiteness,* edited by Brigit Brander Rasmussen, Eric Klinenberg, Irene J. Nexica, and Matt Wray, 72–96. Durham, NC: Duke University Press, 2001.

Giddings, Elizabeth Warner. *Yaqui Myths and Legends.* Edited by Barry Behn. Tucson: University of Arizona Press, 1974.

Giles, Paul. *Virtual Americas: Transnational Fictions and the Transatlantic Imaginary.* Durham, NC: Duke University Press, 2002.

Gillman, Susan, Kirsten Silva Greusz, and Rob Wilson. "Worlding American Studies." *Comparative American Studies* 2, no. 3 (2004): 259–70.

Gilroy, Paul. *The Black Atlantic: Modernity and Double Consciousness.* Cambridge, MA: Harvard University Press, 1993.

Giraud, Michel. "Dialectics of Descent and Phenotypes in Racial Classification in Martinique." In *French and West Indian: Martinique, Guadeloupe and French Guiana Today,* edited by Richard D. E. Burton and Fred Reno, 75–85. Charlottesville: University of Virginia Press, 1995.

Glissant, Edouard. *Caribbean Discourse: Selected Essays.* Edited and translated by J. Michael Dash. Charlottesville: University of Virginia Press, 1989.

———. *Poetics of Relation.* Translated by Betsy Wing. Ann Arbor: University of Michigan Press, 1997.

Gómez-Peña, Guillermo. "Documented/Undocumented." In *Multi-Cultural Literacy,* edited by Rick Simonson and Scott Walker. Minneapolis: Graywolf Press, 1988.

———. "1995—Terreno Peligroso/Danger Zone: Cultural Relations between Chicanos and Mexicans at the End of the Century." In *Borderless Borders,* edited by Frank Bonilla, Edwin Mélendez, Rebecca Morales, and María de los Angeles Torres, 131–38. Philadelphia: Temple University Press, 1998.

Graebner, Norman A. *Empire on the Pacific.* New York: Ronald Press, 1955.

Greenblatt, Stephen, ed. Introduction to *New World Encounters,* vii–xvii. Los Angeles: University of California Press, 1993.

Greenblatt, Stephen, and Giles Gunn, eds. Introduction to *Redrawing the Boundaries: The Transformation of English and American Literary Studies,* 1–11. New York: Modern Language Association of America, 1992.

Habermas, Jürgen. "Modernity—an Incomplete Project." In *Postmodernism,* edited by Thomas Docherty, 98–109. New York: Columbia University Press, 1993.

Hallenbeck, Cleve. *Álvar Núñez Cabeza de Vaca: The Journey and Route of the First European to Cross the Continent of North America: 1534–36.* Glendale, CA: Arthur H. Clark, 1940.

Harder, Bernie. "The Power of Border in Native American Literature: Leslie Marmon Silko's *Almanac of the Dead." American Indian Culture and Research Journal* 24, no. 4 (2000): 95–106.

Hart, John Seely. *Manual of American Literature.* Philadelphia: Eldredge and Brother; repr., New York: Johnson Reprint, 1969.

Hennessy, Alistair. *The Frontier in Latin American History.* Albuquerque: University of New Mexico Press, 1978.

Henriques, Fernando. *Family and Color in Jamaica.* Bristol: Macgibbon and Kee, 1953.

Henry, Paget. "Fanon, African and Afro-Caribbean Philosophy." In *Fanon: A Critical Reader,* edited by Lewis R. Gordon, T. Denean Sharpley-

Whiting, and Renée T. White, 220–43. Cambridge, MA: Blackwell, 1996.

Hill, Mike. *After Whiteness: Unmaking an American Majority.* New York: New York University Press, 2004.

Holston, James, and Arjun Appadurai. "Cities and Citizenship." *Public Culture* 8 (1996): 187–204.

Honour, Hugh. *The New Golden Land: European Images of America from the Discoveries to the Present Time.* New York: Pantheon Books, 1975.

Howard, David. *Conquistador in Chains: Cabeza de Vaca and the Indians of the Americas.* Tuscaloosa: University of Alabama Press, 1997.

Hu-DeHart, Evelyn. *Yaqui Resistance and Survival: The Struggle for Land and Autonomy, 1821–1910.* Madison: University of Wisconsin Press, 1984.

Hulme, Peter. Introduction to *Cannibalism and the Colonial World,* edited by Francis Barker, Peter Hulme, and Margaret Iversen, 1–38. Cambridge: Cambridge University Press, 1998.

Huntington, Samuel P. *Who Are We? The Challenges to America's National Identity.* New York: Simon and Schuster, 2004.

Ignatiev, Noel. "Treason to Whiteness Is Loyalty to Humanity." In *Critical White Studies: Looking Behind the Mirror,* edited by Richard Delgado and Jean Stefancic, 607–12. Philadelphia: Temple University Press, 1997.

Irr, Caren. "The Timeliness of *Almanac of the Dead,* or a Postmodern Rewriting of Radical Fiction." In *Leslie Marmon Silko: A Collection of Critical Essays,* edited by Louise K. Barnett and James L. Thorson, 223–44. Albuquerque: University of New Mexico Press, 2001.

Jaskoski, Helen. *Leslie Marmon Silko: A Study of the Short Fiction.* New York: Twayne, 1998.

Jay, Gregory. "The End of 'American' Literature: Toward a Multicultural Practice." *College English* 53 (1991): 264–81.

Jay, Paul. *Contingency Blues.* Madison: University of Wisconsin Press, 1997.

———. "The Myth of America and the Politics of Location: Modernity, Border Studies, and the Literature of the Americas." *Arizona Quarterly* 54, no. 2 (1998): 165–92.

Jennings, Francis. *The Invasion of America: Indians, Colonialism and the Cant of Conquest.* Chapel Hill: University of North Carolina Press, 1975.

Jennings, Peter, and Todd Brewster. *In Search of America.* New York: Hyperion, 2002.

Johnson, Howard. Introduction to *The White Minority in the Caribbean*, edited by Howard Johnson and Karl Watson, ix–xvi. Princeton: Markus Wiener, 1998.

Johnston, Charles H. L. *Famous Indian Chiefs*. Boston: L. C. Page, 1909.

Kadir, Djelal. *Columbus and the Ends of the Earth: Europe's Prophetic Rhetoric as Conquering Ideology*. Berkeley: University of California Press, 1992.

———. "Introduction: America and Its Studies." *PMLA* 118, no. 1 (2003): 9–24.

Kaplan, Amy. "Left Alone with America." In *Cultures of United States Imperialism*, edited by Amy Kaplan and Donald E. Pease, 3–21. Durham, NC: Duke University Press, 1993.

Karno, Valerie. "Legal Hunger: Law, Narrative, and Orality in Leslie Marmon Silko's *Storyteller* and *Almanac of the Dead*. *College Literature* 28, no. 1 (2001): 1–10.

Kingdon, Robert M. *Myths about the St. Bartholomew's Day Massacres: 1572–1576*. Cambridge, MA: Harvard University Press, 1988.

Kolodny, Annette. "Letting Go Our Grand Obsessions: Notes toward a New Literary History of the American Frontiers." In *Subjects and Citizens: Nation, Race, and Gender from Oroonoko to Anita Hill*, edited by Michael Moon and Cathy N. Davidson, 9–26. Durham, NC: Duke University Press, 1995.

Krupat, Arnold. *The Turn to the Native: Studies in Criticism and Culture*. Lincoln: University of Nebraska Press, 1996.

Kupperman, Karen Ordahl, ed. Introduction to *America in European Consciousness: 1492–1750*, 1–29. Chapel Hill: University of North Carolina Press, 1995.

Lamar, Howard, and Leonard Thompson, eds. Introduction to *The Frontier in History: North America and Southern Africa Compared*, 3–13. New Haven: Yale University Press, 1981.

Lape, Noreen Groover. *West of the Border: The Multicultural Literature of the Western American Frontiers*. Athens: Ohio University Press, 2000.

Lauter, Paul. *Canons and Contexts*. New York: Oxford University Press, 1991.

Lee, Kun Jong. "Pauline Typology in Cabeza de Vaca's *Naufragios*." *Early American Literature* 34 (1999): 241–62.

León-Portilla, Miguel, trans. and ed. *The Broken Spears: The Aztec Account of the Conquest of Mexico*. Boston: Beacon Press, 1962.

Léry, Jean de. *History of a Voyage to the Land of Brazil, Otherwise Called America.* Translated by Janet Wheatley. Berkeley: University of California Press, 1990.

Lestringant, Frank. *Cannibals: The Discovery and Representation of the Cannibal from Columbus to Jules Verne.* Translated by Rosemary Morris. Berkeley: University of California Press, 1997.

————. "The Philosopher's Breviary: Jean de Léry in the Enlightenment." In *New World Encounters*, edited by Stephen Greenblatt, 127–38. Los Angeles: University of California Press, 1993.

Limón, José E. "Translating Empire: The Border Homeland of Rio Grande City, Texas." *American Quarterly* 56, no. 1 (2004): 25–32.

Livermore, Harold V. Introduction to *Royal Commentaries of the Incas*, by Garcilaso de la Vega, translated by Harold V. Livermore, xv–xxxi. Austin: University of Texas Press, 1966.

Long, Haniel. *Interlinear to Cabeza de Vaca.* Santa Fe: Writer's Editions, 1936.

López de Gómara, Francisco. *Cortés: The Life of the Conquerer.* Edited and translated by Lesley Byrd Simpson. Berkeley: University of California Press, 1964.

Losada, Angel, ed. *Apologia [de Juan Ginés de Sepúlveda contra Fray Bartolomé de las Casas y de Fray Bartolomé de las Casas contra Juan Ginés de Sepúlveda].* Madrid: Editora Nacional, 1975.

Lowenthal, David. *West Indian Societies.* New York: Oxford University Press, 1972.

Luna-Firebaugh, Eileen M. "The Border Crossed Us: Border Crossing Issues of the Indigenous Peoples of the Americas." *Wicazo Sa Review* 17, no. 1 (2002): 159–81.

Mahoney, Martha R. "The Social Construction of Whiteness." In *Critical White Studies: Looking Behind the Mirror*, edited by Richard Delgado and Jean Stefancic, 330–33. Philadelphia: Temple University Press, 1997.

Mailloux, Steven. "Making Comparisons: First Contact, Ethnocentrism, and Cross-Cultural Communication." In *Post-Nationalist American Studies*, edited by John Carlos Rowe, 110–28. Berkeley: University of California Press, 2000.

Maltby, William S. *The Black Legend in England: The Development of Anti-Spanish Sentiment, 1558–1660.* Durham, NC: Duke University Press, 1971.

Marshall, Paule. *The Chosen Place, the Timeless People.* New York: Harcourt, Brace and World, 1960.

Martí, José. *The America of José Martí: Selected Writings.* Translated by Juan de Onís. New York: Funk and Wagnalls, 1954.

Martin, Judith N., Robert L. Krizek, Thomas K. Nakayama, and Lisa Bradford. "What Do White People Want to Be Called? A Study of Self-Labels for White Americas." In *Whiteness: The Communication of Social Identity,* edited by Thomas K. Nakayama and Judith N. Martin, 27–50. London: SAGE, 1999.

Martínez, Manuel Luís. "Telling the Difference between the Border and the Borderlands: Materiality and Theoretical Practice." In *Globalization on the Line: Culture, Capital, and Citizenship at U.S. Borders,* edited by Claudia Sadowski-Smith, 53–68. New York: Palgrave, 2002.

Martínez, Oscar. *Border People.* Tucson: University of Arizona Press, 1994.

———. *U.S.-Mexico Borderlands.* Wilmington: Jaguar Books, 1996.

Mason, Peter. *Deconstructing America: Representations of the Other.* New York: Routledge, 1990.

McGuirk, Rod. Associated Press. "Iraqi Exiles around World Vote in Election." *ABC News,* January 30, 2005, http://abcnews.go.com/International/print?id=455018. Accessed May 5, 2005.

McKenna, Teresa. *Migrant Song.* Austin: University of Texas Press, 1997.

Michaelsen, Scott, and David E. Johnson, eds. *Border Theory: The Limits of Cultural Politics.* Minneapolis: University of Minnesota Press, 1997.

Minh-ha, Trinh T. "Other than Myself/My Other Self." In *Travellers' Tales: Narratives of Home and Displacement,* edited by George Robertson, 9–26. New York: Routledge, 1994.

Moctezuma, Eduardo Matos. "Aztec History and Cosmovision." In *Moctezuma's Mexico: Visions of the Aztec World,* edited by Davíd Carrasco and Eduardo Matos Moctezuma, 3–97. Niwot: University Press of Colorado, 1992.

Montaigne, Michel Eyquem de. *The Essays of Montaigne.* Translated by E. J. Trechmann. 1927; repr., London: Oxford University Press, 1946.

Moore, David L. "Silko's Blood Sacrifice: The Circulating Witness in *Almanac of the Dead.*" In *Leslie Marmon Silko: A Collection of Critical Essays,* edited by Louise K. Barnett and James L. Thorson, 149–83. Albuquerque: University of New Mexico Press, 2001.

Morrison, Toni. *Playing in the Dark: Whiteness and the Literary Imagination.* Cambridge, MA: Harvard University Press, 1992.

Nafisi, Azar. *Reading Lolita in Tehran: A Memoir in Books.* New York: Random House, 2003.

National Commission on Terrorist Attacks upon the United States. *The 9/11 Commission Report.* New York: W. W. Norton, 2004.

Navarro, Sharon Ann, and Armando Xavier Mejia, eds. *Latino Americans and Political Participation.* Santa Barbara, CA: ABC-CLIO, 2004.

Niemi, Robert. *Russell Banks.* New York: Twayne, 1997.

Nobles, Gregory H. *American Frontiers: Cultural Encounters and Continental Conquest.* New York: Hill and Wang, 1997.

O'Gorman, Edmundo. *The Invention of America.* Bloomington: Indiana University Press, 1961.

Padilla, Genaro. *My History, Not Yours: The Formation of Mexican American Autobiography.* Madison: University of Wisconsin Press, 1993.

Pastor Bodmer, Beatriz. *The Armature of Conquest: Spanish Accounts of the Discovery of America, 1492–1589.* Translated by Lydia Longstreth Hunt. Stanford: Stanford University Press, 1992.

Paz, Octavio. *The Labyrinth of Solitude: Life and Thought in Mexico.* New York: Grove Press, 1961.

Pease, Donald. "New Americanists: Revisionist Interventions into the Canon." *Boundary 2* 17, no. 1 (1990): 1–37.

Pérez-Torres, Rafael. "Refiguring Aztlán." In *Postcolonial Theory and the United States: Race, Ethnicity, and Literature,* edited by Amritjit Singh and Peter Schmidt, 103–21. Jackson: University Press of Mississippi, 2000.

Perrigo, Lynn I. *The American Southwest: Its People and Cultures.* Albuquerque: University of New Mexico Press, 1971.

Pesquera, Beatriz M., and Denise A. Segura. "With Quill and Torch: A Chicana Perspective on the American Women's Movement and Feminist Theories." In *Chicanas/Chicanos at the Crossroads,* edited by David R. Maciel and Isidro D. Ortiz, 231–47. Tucson: University of Arizona Press, 1996.

Phillips, Caryl. "Unmarooned." Review of *Texaco. New Republic* 216, no. 17 (1997): 1–7.

Peterfield, William, John Erskine, Stuart P. Sherman, and Carl Van Doren, eds. *The Cambridge History of American Literature.* New York: Macmillan, 1917.

Porter, Carolyn. "What We Know That We Don't Know: Remapping American Literary Studies." *American Literary History* 3 (1994): 467–526.

Pratt, Mary Louise. *Imperial Eyes: Travel Writing and Transculturation.* London: Routledge, 1992.

Prescott, William H. *History of the Conquest of Mexico and History of the Conquest of Peru.* New York: Random House, 1936.

Price, Richard, and Sally Price. "'Shadowboxing in the Mangrove': The Politics of Identity in Postcolonial Martinique." In *Caribbean Romances: The Politics of Regional Representation,* edited by Belinda J. Edmondson, 123–62. Charlottesville: University of Virginia Press, 1999.

Puri, Shalini. "Canonized Hybridities, Resistant Hybridities: Chutney Soca, Carnival, and the Politics of Nationalism." In *Caribbean Romances,* edited by Belinda J. Edmondson, 12–38. Charlottesville: University of Virginia Press, 1999.

Rabasa, José. "Allegory and Ethnography in Cabeza de Vaca's *Naufragios* and *Commentarios.*" In *Violence, Resistance, and Survival in the Americas,* edited by William B. Taylor and Franklin Pease G.-Y., 40–66. Washington: Smithsonian Institution Press, 1994.

———. *Writing Violence on the Northern Frontier: The Historiography of Sixteenth-Century New Mexico and Florida and the Legacy of Conquest.* Durham, NC: Duke University Press, 2000.

Radway, Jan. "What's in a Name?" In *The Futures of American Studies,* edited by Donald E. Pease and Robyn Wiegman, 45–75. Durham, NC: Duke University Press, 2002.

Rebolledo, Tey Diana. *Women Singing in the Snow: A Cultural Analysis of Chicana Literature.* Tucson: University of Arizona Press, 1995.

Regier, Ami M. "Material Meeting Points of Self and Other: Fetish Discourses and Leslie Marmon Silko's Evolving Conception of Cross-Cultural Narrative." In *Leslie Marmon Silko: A Collection of Critical Essays,* edited by Louise K. Barnett and James L. Thorson, 185–206. Albuquerque: University of New Mexico Press, 2001.

Retamar, Roberto Fernández. *Caliban and Other Essays.* Minneapolis: University of Minnesota Press, 1989.

Reyes, Alfonso. *The Position of America and Other Essays.* Translated by Harriet de Onís. New York: Books for Libraries Press, 1971.

Ribeiro, Darcy. *The Americas and Civilization.* Translated by Linton Loma Barrett and Marie McDavid Barrett. New York: E. P. Dutton, 1972.

Richard, Nelly. "Postmodernism and Periphery." In *Postmodernism,* edited by Thomas Docherty, 464–70. New York: Columbia University Press, 1993.

Richardson, Bonham C. *The Caribbean in the Wider World, 1492–1992: A Regional Geography.* Cambridge: Cambridge University Press, 1992.

Richardson, Charles F. *American Literature (1607–1885): The Development of American Thought.* New York: G. P. Putnam's Sons, 1887.

Robinson, Cecil. *No Short Journeys.* Tucson: University of Arizona Press, 1991.

Rodriguez, Richard. *Hunger of Memory.* New York: Bantam Books, 1982.

Roediger, David R. *The Wages of Whiteness: Race and the Making of the American Working Class.* New York: Verso, 1991.

Rowe, John Carlos. *Literary Culture and U.S. Imperialism: From the Revolution to World War II.* New York: Oxford University Press, 2001.

———. "Post-Nationalism, Globalism, and the New American Studies." *Cultural Critique* 40 (1998): 11–28.

Sadowski-Smith, Claudia, ed. *Globalization on the Line: Culture, Capital, and Citizenship at the U.S Borders.* New York: Palgrave, 2002.

———. "The U.S.-Mexico Borderlands Write Back: Cross-Cultural Transnationalism in Contemporary U.S. Women of Color Fiction." *Arizona Quarterly* 57, no. 1 (2001): 91–112.

Sáenz, Benjamin Alire. "In the Borderlands of Chicano Identity, There Are Only Fragments." In *Border Theory: The Limits of Culture Politics,* edited by Scott Michaelsen and David E. Johnson, 68–96. Minneapolis: University of Minnesota Press, 1997.

Sahagún, Bernardino de. *Conquest of New Spain: 1585 Revision.* Edited by S. L. Cline. Translated by Howard F. Cline. Salt Lake City: University of Utah Press, 1989.

Said, Edward. *The World, the Text, and the Critic.* Cambridge, MA: Harvard University Press, 1983.

Saldívar, José David. *Border Matters.* Los Angeles: University of California Press, 1997.

———. *The Dialectics of Our America.* Durham, NC: Duke University Press, 1991.

Saldívar, Ramón. *Chicano Narrative: The Dialectics of Difference.* Madison: University of Wisconsin Press, 1990.

Saldívar-Hull, Sonia. "Feminism on the Border: From Gender Politics to Geopolitics." In *Criticism in the Borderlands: Studies in Chicano Literatures, Culture, Ideology,* edited by Héctor Calderón and José David Saldívar, 203–20. Durham, NC: Duke University Press, 1991.

Salyer, Gregory. *Leslie Marmon Silko.* New York: Twayne, 1997.

Sartore, Richard. *Humans Eating Humans.* Notre Dame, IN: Cross Cultural Publications, 1994.

Scheuer, Michael. *Imperial Hubris: Why the West Is Losing the War on Terror.* Washington, DC: Brassey's, 2004.

Schueller, Malini Johar, and Edward Watts, eds. *Messy Beginnings: Postcoloniality and Early American Studies.* New Brunswick, NJ: Rutgers University Press, 2003.

Séjourné, Laurette. *Burning Water: Thought and Religion in Ancient Mexico.* New York: Grove Press, 1960.

Seshadri-Crooks, Kalpana. *Desiring Whiteness: A Lacanian Analysis of Race.* New York: Routledge, 2000.

Shakespeare, William. *The Tempest.* Edited by Stephen Orgel. Oxford: Clarendon Press, 1987.

Shell, Marc, and Werner Sollors, eds. *The Multilingual Anthology of American Literature.* New York: New York University Press, 2000.

Sheridan, Thomas E. *Los Tucsonenses: The Mexican Community in Tucson, 1854–1941.* Tucson: University of Arizona Press, 1986.

Shome, Raka. "Whiteness and the Politics of Location." In *Whiteness: The Communication of Social Identity,* edited by Thomas K Nakayama and Judith N. Martin, 107–28. London: SAGE, 1999.

Silenieks, Juris. Review of *Texaco,* by Patrick Chamoiseau. *World Literature Today* 67, no. 4 (1993): 1–2.

Silko, Leslie Marmon. *Almanac of the Dead.* New York: Simon and Schuster, 1991.

———. "A Geronimo Story." In *Come to Power: Eleven Contemporary American Indian Poets*, edited by Dick Lourie, 81–94. New York: Crossing Press, 1974.

———. Interview. In *Winged Words*, edited by Laura Coltelli. Lincoln: University of Nebraska Press, 1990.

Simpson, Lesley Byrd, ed. and trans. Introduction to *Cortés: The Life of the Conquerer*, by Francisco López de Gómara, xv–xxvi. Berkeley: University of California Press, 1964.

Singh, Amritjit, and Peter Schmidt, eds. *Postcolonial Theory and the United States*. Jackson: University Press of Mississippi, 2000.

Slater, Mariam K. *The Caribbean Family: Legitimacy in Martinique*. New York: St. Martin's Press, 1977.

Soja, Edward W. *Postmodern Geographies: The Reassertion of Space in Critical Social Theory*. New York: Verso, 1989.

Sollors, Werner. Introduction to *The Multilingual Anthology of American Literature*, edited by Marc Shell and Werner Sollors, 1–11. New York: New York University Press, 2000.

Soman, Alfred, ed. Preface to *The Massacre of St. Bartholomew: Reappraisals and Documents*, edited by Alfred Soman, vii–xi. The Hague: Martinus Nijhoff, 1974.

Spicer, Edward H. *The Yaquis: A Cultural History*. Tucson: University of Arizona Press, 1980.

Spiller, Robert E. *The Cycle of American Literature*. New York: Free Press, 1955.

Spivak, Gayatri Chakravorty. *The Post-colonial Critic: Interviews, Strategies, Dialogues*. Edited by Sarah Harasym. New York: Routledge, 1990.

———. "The Rani of Sirmur." In *Europe and Its Others*, vol. 1, edited by Francis Barker, Peter Hulme, Margaret Iversen, and Diana Loxley, 128–51. Colchester: University of Essex Press, 1985.

Sprouse, Keith Alan. "Chaos and Rhizome: Introduction to Caribbean Poetics." In *A History of Literature in the Caribbean*, vol. 3, edited by A. James Arnold, 79–86. Philadelphia: John Benjamins, 1997.

St. Clair, Janet. "Death of Love/Love of Death: Leslie Marmon Silko's *Almanac of the Dead*." *MELUS* 21, no. 2 (1996): 141–56.

Stage, Christina W. "We Celebrate 100 Years: An 'Indigenous' Analysis of the Metaphors That Shape the Cultural Identity of Small Town

U.S.A." In *Whiteness: The Communication of Social Identity,* edited by Thomas K Nakayama and Judith N. Martin, 69–96. London: SAGE, 1999.

Stanford, Ann Folwell. "'Human Debris': Border Politics, Body Parts, and the Reclamation of the Americas in Leslie Marmon Silko's *Almanac of the Dead.*" *Literature and Medicine* 16, no. 1 (1997): 23–42.

Starr, Larry. *A Union of Diversities: Style in the Music of Charles Ives.* New York: Schirmer, 1992.

Sundeep, Sahay, Brian Nicholson, and S. Krishna. *Global IT Outsourcing: Software Development across the Borders.* Cambridge: Cambridge University Press, 2003.

Takaki, Ronald. *A Different Mirror: A History of Multicultural America.* Boston: Little, Brown, 1993.

Teale, Tamara. "The Silko Road from Chiapas, or Why Native Americans Cannot Be Marxists." *MELUS* 23, no. 4 (1998): 157–66.

Thomas, David Hurst, ed. *Columbian Consequences.* Vol. 3. Washington: Smithsonian Institution Press, 1991.

Thomas, Hugh. *Conquest: Moctezuma, Cortés, and the Fall of Old Mexico.* New York: Simon and Schuster, 1993.

Todorov, Tzvetan. *The Conquest of America: The Question of the Other.* Translated by Richard Howard. New York: Harper and Row, 1984.

Torres-Saillant, Silvio. "The Cross-Cultural Unity of Caribbean Literature: Toward a Centripetal Vision." In *A History of Literature in the Caribbean,* vol. 3, edited by A. James Arnold, 57–75. Philadelphia: John Benjamins, 1997.

Trent, William Peterfield, John Erskine, Stuart P. Sherman, and Carl Van Doren, eds. *The Cambridge History of American Literature.* New York: Macmillan, 1917.

Trinkaus, Charles. "Renaissance and Discovery." In *First Images of America,* edited by Fredi Chiappelli, 3–9. Berkeley: University of California Press, 1976.

Trotter, Robert T., and Juan A. Chavira. *Curanderismo.* Athens: University of Georgia Press, 1981.

Turner, Frederick Jackson. *The Frontier in American History.* New York: Henry Holt, 1920.

———. "Sections and Nation." In *Frontier and Section: Selected Essays of Frederick Jackson Turner,* 136–53. Englewood Cliffs, NJ: Prentice Hall, 1961.

Turner, Frederick W., III. Introduction to *Geronimo: His Own Story*, edited by S. M. Barrett. New York: E. P. Dutton, 1970.

Vaca, Nicolás C. *The Presumed Alliance: The Unspoken Conflict between Latinos and Blacks and What It Means for America*. New York: HarperCollins, 2004.

Vega, Garcilaso de la. *Royal Commentaries of the Incas*. Translated by Harold V. Livermore. Austin: University of Texas Press, 1966.

Vila, Pablo. "The Competing Meanings of the Label 'Chicano' in El Paso." In *The U.S.-Mexico Border: Transcending Division, Contesting Identities*, edited by David Spener and Kathleen Staudt, 185–214. Boulder: Lynne Rienner, 1988.

U.S. Census Bureau. "Hispanic and Asian Americans Increasing Faster than Overall Population." Press release, June 14, 2004. http:// www.census.gov/Press-Release/www/releases/archives/race/001839 .html. Accessed May 5, 2005.

———. PHC-T-1, table 3, April 2, 2001. http://www.census.gov/ population/cen2000/phct1/tab03.pdf. Accessed May 5, 2005.

Wander, Philip C., Judith N. Martin, and Thomas K. Nakayama. "Whiteness and Beyond: Sociohistorical Foundations of Whiteness and Contemporary Challenges." In *Whiteness: The Communication of Social Identity*, edited by Thomas K. Nakayama and Judith N. Martin, 13–26. London: SAGE, 1999.

Ward, Geoff. *The Writing of America: Literature and Cultural Identity from the Puritans to the Present*. Cambridge: Polity Press, 2002.

Ware, Vron, and Les Back. *Out of Whiteness: Color, Politics, and Culture*. Chicago: University of Chicago Press, 2002.

Weber, David. "The Idea of the Spanish Borderlands." In *Columbian Consequences*, vol. 3, edited by David Hurst Thomas, 3–17. Washington: Smithsonian Institution Press, 1991.

Whatley, Janet. "Impression and Initiation: Jean de Léry's Brazil Voyage." *Modern Language Studies* 19 (1989): 15–25.

———. Introduction to *History of a Voyage to the Land of Brazil, Otherwise Called America*, by Jean de Léry, translated by Janet Whatley, xv–xxxviii. Berkeley: University of California Press, 1990.

Wiegman, Robyn. "Introduction: The Futures of American Studies." *Cultural Critique* 40 (1998): 5–9.

————. "Whiteness Studies and the Paradox of Particularity." *Boundary 2* 26, no. 3 (1999): 115–50.

Wildman, Stephanie M. "Reflections on Whiteness: The Case of Latinos(as)." In *Critical White Studies: Looking Behind the Mirror,* edited by Richard Delgado and Jean Stefancic, 323–26. Philadelphia: Temple University Press, 1997.

Williams, Paul L. *Al Qaeda: Brotherhood of Terror.* Parsippany, NJ: Alpha, 2002.

Wilson, Rob. *Reimagining the American Pacific.* Durham, NC: Duke University Press, 2000.

Zamora, Lois Parkinson. *The Usable Past.* Cambridge: Cambridge University Press, 1997.

INDEX

Endnotes are indicated by the letter *n* following the page number(s). The number following the *n* is the note number.